Jazz Changes

JAZZ
CHANGES

MARTIN WILLIAMS

New York   Oxford
OXFORD UNIVERSITY PRESS
1992

Oxford University Press

Oxford   New York   Toronto
Delhi   Bombay   Calcutta   Madras   Karachi
Petaling Jaya   Singapore   Hong Kong   Tokyo
Nairobi   Dar es Salaam   Cape Town
Melbourne   Auckland

and associated companies in
Berlin   Ibadan

Published by Oxford University Press, Inc.
200 Madison Avenue, New York, New York 10016

Oxford is a registered trademark of Oxford University Press

Library of Congress Cataloging-in-Publication Data
Williams, Martin T.
Jazz changes / Martin Williams.
p.   cm.   Includes index.
ISBN 0-19-505847-X
1. Jazz—History and criticism.   2. Jazz musicians.   I. Title.
ML3507.W525 1991
781.65'09—dc20   91-9116   CIP   MN

1 2 3 4 5 6 7 8 9

Printed in the United States of America
on acid-free paper

For *VR, MLM, DK, PB,*
JΛ, LW, MC, MO, MLP,
JW, IC, PK, and *HK*

Preface

A book like this one may not need a prefatory note. A glance at the titles on the contents pages should tell a reader a great deal about what it contains and what it hopes to be. But I would like to give it at least a brief word of introduction.

Jazz Changes begins informally with jazz musicians themselves in brief appreciation-profiles; musicians observed in recording studios at rehearsals, and in clubs; musicians consenting to be interviewed about their lives and their music; musicians in give-and-take conversations.

Musical analysis and opinion come in the other sections of *Jazz Changes*. Some of the latter go back to my earliest days as a record and concert reviewer. Perhaps the reader will agree that they still have substance and interest these thirty years later. I have also included some parodies and other pieces I intended to be humorous, and if the reader recognizes for himself which of them I so intended, my hopes for them have at least partly succeeded.

The writings that follow originally appeared in a variety of places. I am particularly grateful to Dick Hadlock, *Down Beat, Saturday Review, International Musician,* ASCAP *Today,* Fantasy Records, Atlantic Records, Impulse, E M I, Gunther Schuller, Hank O'Neal, and Robert Asen for making possible their inclusion here.

Alexandria, Virginia   Martin Williams
August 1991

Contents

Part III

PROGRAM NOTES

Part IV

REVIEWS AND OBSERVATIONS

I

MOSTLY
MUSICIANS

≈

≈

≈

≈
Earl Hines:
In Appreciation

On a Friday evening in the winter of 1964, pianist Earl Hines stepped casually onto the stage of the Little Theatre, a small house in the Broadway area of New York, for the first of a series of informal concerts. "I am going to pretend that you are guests in my living room," he told his audience, "and I am going to play some for you. Let's all relax."

The occasion proved to be a critical triumph for Hines, and the beginning of probably the most remarkable comeback in jazz history. From that evening, Hines went on to other nightclub and concert engagements. He enjoyed renewed recording activity. He was the subject of an influential *New Yorker* profile by Whitney Balliett. He began to win the popularity polls. He was selected to represent American culture by a State Department arranged tour of Soviet Russia. He was elected, in 1965, to *Down Beat's* jazz "Hall of Fame," joining such musicians as Louis Armstrong, Coleman Hawkins, Count Basie, Duke Ellington, and Charlie Parker.

The renewed career was not a matter of simple nostalgia on the part of Hines' audiences. Earl Hines could still play piano with the vitality, improvisational dexterity and, on the right numbers, the totally disarming charm of his youth. I watched him a couple of years ago record and re-record the opening for a television show, for take after take, while the video taping was plagued with one accident or directorial dissatisfaction after another. Hines,

3

working at fairly fast tempo, didn't repeat himself, and, although he kept good naturedly protesting that one more run-through was sure to be his last, he never really seemed to tire.

Certainly the "Hall of Fame" honor for Hines was deeply deserved. It should be eminently clear by now that the impetus for "swing" music, the style which listeners and musicians found so enthralling during the 1930s, was the innovative work of Louis Armstrong, as it was translated by other instrumental soloists and by big band arrangers for fourteen-piece ensembles. One of Armstrong's early associates, and probably the first man to grasp his style and translate its implications to the keyboard, was Earl Hines. Indeed, Hines contributed directly to Armstrong's own evolving style. The pianist himself says that he had hit upon his general approach before he and Louis met, and in fact Hines had played some cornet as a young man. Speaking of their association in Chicago in the 1920s, he told Balliett, "Louis Armstrong and I first worked together in the Carroll Dickerson orchestra at the Sunset. Louis was the first trumpet player I heard who played what *I* had wanted to play on cornet. I'd steal ideas from him and he'd steal them from me. He'd bend over after a solo and say way down deep in that rumble, 'Thank you, man.'" The news of this Hines-Armstrong musical discourse spread across the country on classic jazz recordings like *West End Blues, Skip the Gutter,* and *Weather Bird.*

Hines maintained his position as the most advanced jazz pianist in a subsequent association with the New Orleans clarinetist Jimmie Noone. They were members of a little band at the Apex Club in Chicago and musicians from Armstrong through Maurice Ravel came to marvel. Armstrong had remarked, "A lot of after-hour spots were real groovy, too. There was the Apex, where Jimmie Noone and that great piano man, Hines, started all this fine stuff. . . . They made history right there in the Apex. The tune *Sweet Lorraine* used to gas everybody there nightly. I was one of the everybodies."

It became perfectly obvious that a man of Hines' talents and leadership would soon be working on his own. An early opportunity came when he was called to New York in 1928 to do some solo recordings (*Blues in Thirds, A Monday Date*). The second came on the heels of the first, when he was offered the leadership of a big band at a new Chicago nightclub to be called the Grand Terrace.

The Hines orchestra played for shows and for dancing, hence played a variety of styles for a variety of reasons. Hines told Russ Wilson, "It never was a typed organization because I didn't want it to become such. That's why I used a variety of arrangers from all over the country—so there'd be no certain style. And I'd exchange arrangements with Fred Waring, Tommy Dorsey, and Jimmy Dorsey. The only time the listeners knew it was my band was when they heard my piano.

"We got a lot of different sounds, but we needed them for the shows we played. Why, the first section of the shows was an hour and a half long, so you know how much music we had to play."

Nevertheless, the style of the Hines band in the early 1930s was through the talents of the leader, soloists like trumpeters George Dixon and Walter Fuller, trombonist Trummy Young, and clarinetist Omer Simeon, and arrangers like Jimmy Mundy and Cecil Irwin—one of the most interestingly executed big band jazz styles to emerge before 1935. Indeed, it should be no surprise that Benny Goodman lured Jimmy Mundy away from Hines for pieces like *Madhouse* and *Swingtime in the Rockies.* (It is an interesting footnote that a version of the latter piece was performed by Hines as *Take It Easy* three years before the Goodman fans had heard it.)

Hines, meanwhile, had himself a radio wire out of the Grand Terrace, had himself an intriguing theme in *Deep Forest,* had been nicknamed "Fatha" by a radio announcer who was indulging in a little ad lib kidding on the air, and had himself a hit as well as a durable standard in *Rosetta.* Tenor saxophonist and arranger Budd Johnson, soon to become a Hines associate, told Frank Driggs of his first encounter with the band. "Earl Hines had a great band, one of his greatest. Teddy Wilson was starting to write some arrangements for the band then and they sounded great. They were at the Grand Terrace, and I'd always pictured what they looked like. So, being real ambitious at the time, I went down there and asked if I could sit in. At the time, Earl played with the band, and continued playing by himself right through intermission. I got a chance to play with him during intermission. . . ."

Hines continued to acquire soon-to-be illustrious sidemen. There was singer Herb Jeffries, singer-trumpeter-violinist Ray Nance, and, a couple of years later, a talented young Chicagoan named Billy Eckstine.

It was during the next few years that certain of the "young Turks" of the jazz world began to appear in the Hines band, musicians like trumpeters Freddy Webster and Benny Harris, for examples, and, by the mid-40s, the Earl Hines orchestra was a haven for the soon-to-be outstanding modernists of jazz. It had Dizzy Gillespie in its trumpet section, Benny Green among its trombonists, Charlie Parker on tenor saxophone (switching from alto so that room could be made for him), and Sarah Vaughan as a second pianist as well as singer.

In 1948, Hines rejoined Louis Armstrong, as a member of the six-piece Armstrong "All Stars," which included clarinetist Barney Bigard, trombonist Jack Teagarden, and drummer Sidney Catlett, and which was, individually, one of the best ensembles that Armstrong had ever led. When Hines left the trumpeter in 1951—the departure was not exactly amicable, but that is another story—he moved to the West Coast, where he lived and worked quietly and where, by the mid-50s, he was leading a small Dixieland ensemble which featured cornetist Muggsy Spanier at a San Francisco club called the Hangover.

Listeners in Great Britain knew that Hines was still playing brilliantly; he proved it in a brief tour during 1957 with Jack Teagarden. But in this country the fact was somehow kept relatively secret until the Little Theater concert. Indeed, at the time that concert was offered him, Hines had almost decided to retire from music and open up a little shop on the West Coast.

Hines was and is, however, an incurable optimist. "I try never to worry," he explains. "And why should I be unhappy and pull down my face and drag my feet and make everybody around me feel that way too?" The words are probably a key to his music as well as his personality.

Today Hines generally tours with his trio—piano plus bass and drums—and with the tenacious Budd Johnson, who is regularly brought out in a feature spot for a couple of numbers per set in his timeless tenor saxophone style. With this ensemble, Hines appears annually in clubs in major cities in the United States and Canada.

He is also about to acquire a new and permanent home on the West Coast. The old Del Monte cannery in San Francisco is currently being remodeled into an entertainment complex of five or six rooms, including bars and cabarets and shops, and Hines is to have a guaranteed five to ten months a year contract on his own, plus a voice in selecting and booking the other talent. And as this is written, there is another European tour of three weeks of concerts in the offing for the fall of 1968, and, for this, Hines plans to add three more horns.

The man who led big bands for so many years probably wishes he could carry a larger group. "I think all of us who had big bands have that feeling," he once told Russ Wilson, "because there's more to work with; the sound is bigger, and it's more enjoyable. . . .

"So I like the big bands, and I want a big band, but if conditions won't allow it, I just can't have it, that's all."

On the other hand, it was Earl Hines the solo pianist who changed the course of jazz history. And it was Hines the pianist who, in 1964, showed them at the Little Theater how much he still had to say. He'll do all right. (1968)

≈

≈

≈

≈

Winnowed Ways:
A Conversation
with Bob Wilber

The 1966 concert of the Duke Ellington Jazz Society at New York's Barbizon Plaza Theater was well attended and well received. It presented some rarely discussed or revived examples of Ellingtonia, the small-band pieces recorded during the 1930s and early '40s under the nominal leadership of some of the orchestra's star soloists, among them alto saxophonist and some-time soprano saxophonist Johnny Hodges.

The music director of the concert, who also conceived it and transcribed and scored the music, was saxophonist-clarinetist Bob Wilber. On his newly acquired, 30-year-old, curved soprano saxophone, Wilber also took Hodges' part on some pieces, and that was perhaps more than justified. An occasional instructor and main influence on Johnny Hodges was soprano saxophonist Sidney Bechet, and Wilber first came to prominence when he was a pupil of Bechet's.

Wilber grew up in Scarsdale, N.Y. By his early teens he had not only heard all the popular swing bands of the 1930s but also had explored the jazz of earlier years. It has been said that to learn the music properly, a young jazzman not only should study the past but live through it in his own work. Wilber has done that, as revealed in our conversation.

Williams: A lot of people speak as though you were under a kind of curse as a result of studying with Bechet and liking his music. Did you feel you had to make a deliberate effort to break away?

Wilber: Yes, definitely. In the late '40s, it got to the point where people wanted to exploit me commercially merely from the fact that I played like Sidney. "Gee, he sounds just like Sidney," they'd say. At that time, Sidney's popularity was growing in this country.

At first it was flattering, and I didn't mind it, but then I got a little tired of it. People wanted to hear me play Sidney's choruses note for note. And yet there was an ambivalence because I really loved the way he played, and I felt it was helping me to find my own way to absorb him. But it got to the point where I finally gave up the soprano saxophone because I was determined to get away from Sidney's way of playing. I didn't take it up again until less than a year ago.

Williams: You're back with it. Why—because it might help get more jobs or because you want to be?

Wilber: Because I want to be. I've gone through a lot of musical scenes since giving it up, and a lot of different influences, and now I can't play it like Sidney even if I want to. It doesn't come out that way.

Williams: What did you do first to break away?

Wilber: Well, pretty much listening to a lot of other kinds of music and exposing myself to a lot of other influences besides Sidney. I studied with Lennie Tristano and Lee Konitz for a while in 1950. And in the '50s I spent about five years studying legitimate clarinet, which I hadn't done since high school—I had dropped it for many years when I was strictly interested in jazz.

Williams: What about the study with Tristano?

Wilber: I was fascinated by those early records he made, and the group that he had with Warne Marsh and Lee Konitz. I wanted to find out what the heck they were doing. Because I'd been listening to Bird and Diz when they were first on 52nd Street in the '40s, and I thought that for others to use the way they phrased and the harmonic context of the music was like a strait jacket. To me, it didn't have the freedom that the earlier music did. It seemed that Tristano was trying to break out of this into something new, and I wanted to find out what it was.

Williams: Do you still hold that opinion?

Wilber: No, I don't think the thing worked out. Essentially I think the movement as a movement can't be considered a success.

Williams: Do you still hold your former opinion about Bird and Dizzy?

Wilber: Yes, and I feel that a lot of the avant-garde music today is a reaction to the bebop form, which the players found more and more constricting. Now they're breaking out into a kind of freedom which existed in earlier jazz.

I sometimes felt that the constriction was in me and not in the style, but during the '50s I had a chance to play with a lot of different players, younger players, who were playing in the bop idiom. When I played with such musicians, I always felt there was a kind of subtle power that made everybody play the same notes, same figures, same phrases, no matter what instrument. Everybody was playing Bird. There was less freedom of expression and less individuality.

Williams: Did you have such a feeling about Louis Armstrong's earlier influence?

Wilber: No. With Louis it was an expansive, open thing.

Williams: Do you think, say, Milt Jackson was playing Bird?

Wilber: Yes, in a sense, I think.

Williams: When did you get particularly interested in Lester Young?

Wilber: Ever since hearing Basie records when I was a kid. Lester represented complete freedom of expression to me. He never blew changes, up one change, down another—up and down changes. With him, it was a different thing from bop. And all the players who came along in the '40s who based their playing on Lester Young, they weren't doing the same thing that Lester was, I don't think.

Williams: They were using his phrases.

Wilber: But they were using them in a strictly harmony-oriented music, and Lester's wasn't. It was more melodically and rhythmically oriented—harmony was definitely the third element. This is the part of what I always felt was the tyranny of bop, that the music was too tied to the harmony, harmonic thinking, that there was no individuality of melodic expression.

Williams: Except for the inventors?

Wilber: I feel that the inventors were as much victimized by the strait-jacket of the bop form as the less creative players. I feel that Parker, as talented as he was, felt obligated to play within a framework of constantly changing, very definite harmonies— minor-seventh chord to dominant-seventh, chromatic minor-seventh. . . . All these patterns that everybody had to play in those days. This was the hip thing. I feel Parker was as much a victim of this type of thinking as anybody.

Earlier players, and Lester Young particularly, would have four bars of basically one chord, and whatever passing chords a soloist wanted to put into his playing were implied in his melodic line. It was up to him to make the choice. There was nobody laying down any this-is-the-way-it's-got-to-go behind him.

Williams: But the soloist was still playing four-bar phrases, which is another kind of a strait jacket perhaps.

Wilber: And yet I felt that the bebop rhythm section with everybody playing variations on the accents at the same time— except the bass player, who was the only one laying down a 4/4 time—left less freedom for the soloist than the earlier swing-style rhythm section. There, everyone was laying down a carpet of time, and the soloist had this freedom to move around above it.

I felt there was a confusion about swinging, and I think it still holds in jazz. If you play eighth notes accurately against a 4/4 beat, you can create a certain type of rhythmic excitement due to the constant repetition of the eighth notes. But that isn't swing, I don't think. And a lot of the rhythmic excitement of bop comes from the constant repetition of eighth notes.

Williams: We sometimes think that it's the audience who is interested only in what is currently fashionable, but many musicians are too. Yet if a musician hears someone whose style he already knows well, why should he listen too carefully?

Wilber: To get some inspiration and hear what other people are doing. I know when I started going to those Sunday afternoon sessions that were held at Jimmy Ryans [52nd Street Club] in the '40s, they weren't cutting sessions. The idea was "let's get together and play—let's find some common ground." There was enough common ground in those days, even though it was the beginning of what you might say was this big split between traditional and modern jazz.

I remember a session with Pete Brown and Bunk Johnson on the same stand. They figured out something together, got something going. I don't really know what made that tremendous split between the traditional and modern jazz in the late '40s and '50s, but it didn't help the music, and it hurt everybody, I felt.

Williams: You were in the Army in the early '50s, right?

Wilber: Two years. I went in in '52.

Williams: What did you do afterwards?

Wilber: I looked around to find out what my old buddies from Scarsdale and Westchester, whom I had played with, were doing. They weren't doing too much so I said let's get something going of our own. None of us at that point knew quite what we wanted to play. We felt we'd like to get a group together and experiment, to find out what we could play and what hit us. We called ourselves the Six.

At this point there were traditional-jazz fans, modern-jazz fans, traditional-jazz night clubs, modern-jazz clubs, you know—never the twain shall meet. Our first job was at Ryans, and we'd play *Royal Garden Blues,* and then we'd turn around and play some original by myself or John Glasel or Tommy Goodman. The fans were very confused.

Williams: You didn't play *Royal Garden Blues* in an old way, however. Did they know that?

Wilber: Yes. Someone would request *Royal Garden Blues,* and we'd say sure, fine. He'd come up after and say, "Where's *Royal Garden Blues?*" "We just played it." And he'd say, "Yeah? But it didn't sound like *Royal Garden Blues.*"

Then later on, with some changes in personnel, we played down at the Cafe Bohemia in the Village, *the* modern place at the time. A lot of the colored patrons resented the fact that there were no colored players in the group. So we got cold stares right from the beginning. Then we'd play *Royal Garden Blues* down there, and the customers didn't want to hear that old-time jive.

We couldn't convince anybody, but we knew we were right. What we were driving at was that there's a oneness about jazz, and there's a rightness about it, and that there should be a common ground on which all jazz musicians meet and create musically together, without any loss of individuality.

You know, I came to realize that an awful lot of people who follow jazz really hear style rather than content. Style is all, and content they don't seem to comprehend too much. A lot of people who like Dixieland have got to hear that sound of that trombone, clarinet, trumpet. If they hear that, they're happy. It can be Phil Napoleon and his Memphis Five or it can be Louis Armstrong and His Hot Five. It all sounds just about the same to them. I think it's also true with so-called modern-jazz fans. There's a certain sound of the saxophone and trumpet playing a line in octaves. That sound is what they want to hear.

Williams: How long was the Six together?

Wilber: For about a year in 1955 we worked sporadically. We did the Newport Jazz Festival, and we made a record for Norman Granz. Soon there seemed no more work forthcoming so we more or less split up. Then, after another year, we said let's give it another try. This time the personnel was a little different. Johnny Glasel was still on trumpet, with Eddie Phyfe on drums, Sonny Truitt on trombone, Bob Hammer on piano. We managed to get more work, but the band was getting away from the original idea more than I really wanted it to, getting to sound more like the stock modern groups of the time, but that was where the work was.

One of the things people said about the Six was that it could play both traditional and modern. But that wasn't what we were doing at all. We wanted to show that there was one way for our band to play jazz, and this way was such a way that we could use traditional material and modern material and new material. That there was no basic conflict between the old and the new—the new was a continuity of the old.

Williams: When did you join the Bobby Hackett group? That's the next event in your career that most people know about.

Wilber: I worked at Condon's downtown place for two years, '56–'57, with Wild Bill Davison and Cutty Cutshall before joining Bobby.

Williams: Were you playing just clarinet then?

Wilber: Just clarinet. I was working on tenor on the side, but I wasn't playing it in the club. At this time there was a kind of pressure against the saxophone in traditional jazz. These people that came there, they didn't want to hear a saxophone.

Williams: Some of the earliest New Orleans records have saxophones on them.

Wilber: I never could understand it, but there it was—fact of life. I was there for two years, and then we did an English tour with Eddie's band. It was a very successful tour. The people liked the band. It went over very well. They didn't understand Eddie too well, but to some extent that was their fault. If they had really observed Eddie, they would not have expected any more than they got—a witty, erratic guy, with a certain charm to him. In some places they kept yelling for a guitar solo. They expected to hear some great performance on the guitar.

The Hackett band was playing at the Henry Hudson Hotel in New York. I was replacing Tom Gwaltney, who played clarinet but who was primarily a vibraphone player in the group. When Hackett called me about the job, he said, "I want you to join the band—you got to play a few vibraphone parts." I said, "I don't play any vibraphone." He said, "Oh, there's nothing to it—very simple little thing."

Well, most of the arrangements had been written by Dick Carey, and they weren't that simple. So I took a few vibraphone lessons . . . and I got enough vibraphone so I could play chords and things behind Bobby on the ballads—the main reason that he wanted it anyway. It was a very interesting band. It had been at the hotel for quite a while before I joined in the winter of 1957 for about four or five months. The place really didn't do any business except on weekends—Friday and Saturday nights were jammed with people dancing.

Williams: How would you compare the musical intentions of the group—and I take it they were largely Dick Carey's—with those of the Six?

Wilber: To some extent, similar. Dick has a feeling for tradition in jazz, and he knows it. But at the same time he was studying with Stefan Wolpe and was very wrapped up in 12-tone, serial music and the most modern, far-out things. He was trying to incorporate this into the jazz idiom. But we had a fantastic repertoire that encompassed everything in jazz.

Williams: What do you think of the record the group made for Capitol, by the way?

Wilber: I wasn't with the band at the time, but the record was not representative. It showed only the conservative side of the band's work. Apparently the producer of the record listened to a lot of the things that the group was playing and said, "We just can't record that—that's much too cool for the front office. That's not what the company expects from Bobby Hackett at all."

But it was Bobby's band. He was doing what he wanted to do, and he was having a ball—stretching out himself and getting some new ideas from playing in an idiom which was sometimes a little strange to him too. He got Benny Golson to write some of his things for the group. We did *Whisper Not* and a couple of other things that Benny wrote. We did some Monk tunes.

Williams: You have studied in the past with Bechet and Tristano. Are you studying at present?

Wilber: Yes, and on a different instrument. I'm studying piano with Sanford Gold and spending a great deal of time on it. Originally, I started because I'm doing some song writing and I wanted to be able to demonstrate my pieces better. But I find it is also helping me in arranging and in soloing too. An improvised solo is a spontaneous composition, after all. I learn more about composition through studying piano, and, therefore, I learn more about soloing.

Then I've been doing some things that are not strictly for esthetic kicks, but I think they're important. I had a single out on

Columbia, which was definitely in the pop vein and, we hoped, for the pop market. It was an instrumental version of *Everyone's Gone to the Moon,* which was a big hit in '65 for Jonathan King, an English singer.

Williams: What did you play on it?

Wilber: I play soprano. There was an engineering gimmick—I recorded the melody, oh, four or five times, and each time it was placed a little off center, so it sounds like an echo of itself. It got a kind of a crazy, ethereal sound. . . . It was very commercial, and it was an effort to get into the record market where things are happening. You see, I have a feeling about jazz, that it's got to be part of the pop music scene to survive and be healthy. I feel there are some exciting things going on in the market place in music, more than in the rather introverted jazz scene, with the cults and the hip business, and all that. I really feel that jazz was in healthier shape in the days when it was out there—in the dance bands in the '40s. They were playing jazz, but they were playing for people.

Williams: Do you get much regular studio work?

Wilber: Not as much as a lot of players, but I really haven't concentrated on it. I would like to if it could be combined with creative work. But I think that can be kind of a dead end. A lot of players get buried in that kind of work. If you get successful at it, you don't have any time for anything creative. It's a difficult scene in New York today, to know what to do. So much of the record work is sitting down and playing those notes on that paper, you know. That can get pretty deadly. And the TV studio scene is not the secure thing it used to be because more and more they are getting to the place where everything's on a freelance basis, or else it's 13 weeks at a time. . . .

Williams: Are you ever afraid of the idea of freelancing forever?

Wilber: Well, there is a certain lack of security in it, a lack of knowing what's going to happen, but that is compensated for by the variety of experiences you're always having, always in a new situation, dealing with different people. You never get into a rut. So I think you take the advantages along with the disadvantages.

It's sure better than punching a clock. I can't imagine myself doing that—like the Radio City Music Hall Orchestra for 20 years, playing six shows a day. And I've never gotten into the Broadway pit-band scene. That can be a fairly secure thing. Once you get on the circuit, you can just go from one show to another. But I'd still like to be in an area where I feel that I have a certain say about the final product. Where I'm not just a saxophone player who could be replaced by a hundred other guys—where I'm just supposed to play the notes right and keep quiet.

That's why I say that in the pop field of music there's a certain excitement. There's a creativity in putting out what you would call a market record. Knowing that you have to please your audience but at the same time trying to get in it as much of what you think of as quality as possible. It's walking a tightrope, you know. But some of the greatest jazzmen have been doing it for years. Louis and Duke and everybody. They have to stay in that marketplace and produce something that people want.

Williams: For them it isn't something that they're burdened with and would like to get rid of. Somebody asks Duke Ellington to play *Alice Blue Gown,* and he'll play an arrangement of that that will lay you out.

Wilber: To me the *Hello, Dolly!*s are great for jazz when they come along. You listen to *Hello, Dolly!,* and Louis is in there swinging and playing great; it's got a good feel and it's fine musically. *Hello, Dolly!* in 1965 is the same thing *Heebie Jeebies* was on a much smaller scale in 1926. *Heebie Jeebies* still sounds great. And *Hello, Dolly!* will sound great 20 years from now. (1966)

≈

≈

≈

≈

Billie Holiday:
Anatomy of a Tragedy

The following profile-appreciation was written for a frankly
Playboy-style men's magazine called *Swank*. I had written
about Billie Holiday before—more than once—but it seems
to me that writing this kind of piece, for *Swank's* kind of
readership, made me speak of her with an understanding
that I had not brought to her life and art before. I hope the
reader will agree.

Billie Holiday came out on the stage, sang her songs, took a brief
polite bow, and left. There was little showmanship and little that
was affected about her. She didn't sit on top of the piano or shed
big tears for the people. She didn't reach heavenward or frame
her face with her fingers or sit on the edge of the stage. She didn't
get herself up to look like a pathetic waif.

Yet, in her most successful days, in the 1930s and 1940s, she
had something of the same well-heeled supper club audience that
had attended Helen Morgan, the "torch singer" of an earlier
decade, and was to attend Edith Piaf, the small French gamin, or
to adore Judy Garland. That is because, like them, Billie Holiday
was a superb singing actress—better than them, to many of her
followers, more genuine, more real, less self-indulgent.

But whatever Billie Holiday had to say, she said musically. Her
musicianship was not an aspect of her act, it was her essence.
And that musicianship gained her a recognition and respect of

musicians of all sorts, all styles, all schools, the world over—
something Helen Morgan or Judy Garland or Edith Piaf could not
have. When Billie Holiday sang *The Man I Love* or *I Cried for You*
or *Yesterdays* or *Them There Eyes,* the songs became hers—hers,
sometimes, in ways that their original composers might not
approve of.

"Mom and Pop were just a couple of kids when they got
married," she said. "He was eighteen, she was sixteen, and I was
three." The marriage didn't last long either. Her father was a
musician, a guitarist, Clarence Holiday, who rose as far as the
influential Fletcher Henderson orchestra at one point in his
career. Her mother was Sadie Fagan. And Billie was born
Eleanora Fagan in 1915 in Baltimore.

Her stage name, Billie, came from a youthful admiration for
the silent film star Billie Dove. And the Fagan, where did it come
from? Billie knew. She was entitled to it. Her great-grandmother
had a special little house out back on the Fagan plantation. Mr.
Charles Fagan had his white wife and children in the big house,
and his black slave mistress and sixteen mulatto children out
back.

Billie had a special rapport with her great-grandmother, and
she was with her when she died. The child had lain down with
her, fallen asleep, and wakened to find great-grandmother's arm
around her neck, tightly now in death. Only the little girl's
screams brought help.

By the time she was six, Billie had begun to do cleaning jobs for
the white ladies of Baltimore. And the change she made had to go
into the family money, not her own pocket. Always, she sang as
she worked; she sang whatever she had heard.

Then she heard something that was very special to her. Alice
Dean kept a whorehouse on the corner of the block. A whorehouse could afford a phonograph and some records. So, to hear
Louis Armstrong and Bessie Smith, Eleanora Fagan began to run
errands for Alice Dean and her girls. "If I'd heard Pops and
Bessie wailing through the window of some minister's front
parlor," she pointed out, "I'd have been running errands for
him."

Her mother went to New York, worked as a maid, saved 900 dollars, came back to Baltimore and set herself up keeping a rooming house. One of the roomers took Billie, age ten, to another building and tried to rape her. A very bad scene followed and they were both arrested. He got five years. She got eleven. The judge simply refused to believe her age, for one thing. She was sent to a Catholic institution, but her mother, with the help of a white employer, got her out some months later.

Billie and Mom went to New York. No more Baltimore justice. But no domestic work for her either, Billie decided. So, she took the other available route. She became a prostitute, a call girl (she was pretty enough to be in that class). She was caught, arrested, and sent to a jail where the rats were almost as big as cats. To her dying day, she was convinced that she landed in that jail because she refused to accommodate a well-known (but unnamed) Harlem politician. Willful Billie simply hadn't *wanted* to accommodate him, call girl or no call girl.

Music was to save her. She decided she wasn't going to be a hooker any more. Her mother was sick and couldn't work. The rent was due. "We were so hungry we could barely breathe." Billie set out on a very cold evening and walked down Seventh Avenue from 145th Street to 133rd Street. She covered every bar, club, cabaret, joint, after hours place, and at that time there might be a dozen to a block. She asked for work, *any* kind of honest work.

Former customers approached the reformed hooker but she turned them down. She went into Pod's and Jerry's Log Cabin Club. She ordered a drink, the first she had ever had, without a dime in her pocket. She told Jerry Preston she wanted to try out as a dancer. He said to go ahead. Dick Wilson, the house pianist, struck up something and she did her two steps. It was pitiful. Then Wilson said, "Girl, can you sing?"

"Sure I can sing. What good is that?" But she asked him to play Earl Hines's sadly optimistic *Travelin' All Alone* to prove she could.

It was like something out of a 1930s musical. People stopped talking. They stopped laughing. They stopped drinking. Their jaws dropped. Some began to cry. Wilson led her into *Body and Soul*. Everyone in the room was with her. And when she finished, no one applauded. There was a dead, stunned silence. Then it was broken by a rain of coins showering onto the dance floor where she stood.

She picked up 38 dollars, and gave half to Wilson. Preston came over and said, "Kid, you win."

"First thing I did was get a sandwich," Billie later remembered. "I gulped it down . . . I ran out the door. Bought a whole chicken. Ran up Seventh Avenue to my home. Mother and I ate that night . . ."

At fifteen, Billie Holiday was a professional singer.

Among musicians, her reputation spread, but with the public her rise took a bit longer. It was not until three years later, in 1933 that she made her first record, singing with a Benny Goodman group, and she was terrified at the experience. Then Goodman sideman, pianist Teddy Wilson of the Goodman Trio and Quartet, got his own recording contract, and Billie Holiday became his regular recording singer. Before long she was cutting sides on her own as "Billie Holiday and Her Orchestra" as well.

It's interesting to know how these remarkable "pick up session" records were made. In those Depression years, they were produced, not so much for sale to citizens as for use in juke boxes in black neighborhoods, chiefly urban. A small group of the best musicians available would gather in the studios—men from the Fletcher Henderson, Duke Ellington, Count Basie, or Benny Goodman bands, say. They'd be given simplified "lead sheets" (a melody line, some simple chords, and the words) to the latest would-be hits. Or they might do an occasional established standard song. They quickly worked up little arrangements, largely featuring solo variations on the music and Billie's singing, and they made records.

What they achieved is truly remarkable. An absurd song like *A Sailboat in the Moonlight (and You)* becomes a classic. A good song like *More Than You Know* is given a definitive performance.

Outside the studios, Billie Holiday's successes, occasional

failures, and foredoomed indignities continued. She sang at the Harlem Apollo Theater and was so frightened at her opening that someone literally had to shove her onto the stage to get her started. She became band singer with the rising Count Basie Orchestra. In Detroit, the management decided she was "too high yellow" to sing with that black band, and demanded that she put on dark make up.

She became Artie Shaw's band singer—a white band—and Shaw somehow immediately took her on a Southern tour. Nevertheless, he fought (and won) some battles for her in the South. But when they got to New York's Hotel Lincoln, in the Blue Room, the pressure got worse. The management demanded that she come in by the service entrance. She resigned.

She became "Lady Day," so named by her friend Lester Young, the great Count Basie tenor saxophonist. She got the kind of job that determined her future audiences at a club called the Café Society Downtown, where a white supper club clientele discovered her and made her a star. And she married. A spoiled, self-indulgent man named Jimmy Monroe, who introduced her to heroin. "It wasn't long before I was one of the highest paid slaves around," she ironically remarked. They brought her white gowns, white gardenias, and white junk every night.

She wasn't bothered by anyone—police or Treasury Agents or F.B.I.—until she tried to get off her habit. She borrowed some money and had herself committed to an expensive sanitorium. They promised her that her presence, the reasons for it and her treatment would be kept an absolute secret. But from the moment of her discharge, she was followed and hounded by police of all kinds. She didn't stay off drugs, and her life became a continuous hell-on-earth.

In 1946, she was invited to Hollywood to appear in a movie called *New Orleans* with Louis Armstrong. She went with high hopes, but when she got there, it turned out she was to play a maid.

In 1947, she was sentenced to the Federal Women's Reformatory at Alderson, West Virginia, for possession of dangerous drugs, under circumstances which many people saw as a travesty of due process of law. She did not sing one note while she was there. She could not.

But when she sang solo at Carnegie Hall on her discharge, the occasion was a sell-out and a triumph. Her vocal intimacy filled that huge hall and reached every customer. But there was one thing about the occasion that shamed her so much that she could admit it only toward the end of her life: she had gone back on heroin before the concert. And when she pinned the famous gardenias in her hair before she went out on stage, she jabbed herself in the scalp. She finished the performance with blood running down her face.

The problems of a complex human being like Billie Holiday do not all come about because of what life hands her, however. "As far as I'm concerned," said singer Carmen McRae, "she is her worst enemy. She has temperament. I guess she was born with it—I mean, I don't think it's because she's a star. She's been unhappy for a long time . . . Singing is the only place she can express herself the way she'd like to be all the time. Only way she's happy is through a song."

And yet, as her long-time accompanist, Bobby Tucker, put it, "She has the *most* terrible inferiority complex. She actually doesn't believe she can sing."

Remember her fright at her first record date and her first appearance at the Apollo—the experience came to her many, many times again, before large audiences and small.

Everyone else knew she could sing. Musicians of all sorts knew she could. What gained her such respect, respect of a sort that so many other singers could not have? She did not have much range, after all, nor much volume. Her voice did not have much body either. Yet it had an absolute, irresolute strength to it, even toward the end. The quality and sound of that voice can be shocking when one first hears it, yet, one quickly realizes, it was intrinsically a part of every gradation of sadness and joy that her songs conveyed.

She could make the fastest tempos or the slowest dirge without rhythmic faltering. Musicians didn't "back" her nor she "lead" them. She had a built-in sense of time which she could vary with delays, anticipations, and other tantalizing devices, but which never failed her.

But most of all, there was what she herself indicated when she said, "I hate straight singing. I have to change a tune to my own way of doing it. That's all I know."

Billie Holiday had a superb intuitive taste and talent for melody. But not the kind of taste that would make her refuse to do inferior songs or reject middling songs. From Louis Armstrong, she learned to embrace any song and transform it.

She could spot the weaknesses in a popular ditty, get rid of them and sing something of her own in their place. She could make very special melodies out of very banal material.

She even had a way with good melodies. She opens *The Man I Love* by raising one note, adding an extra accent, delaying one phrase slightly, and she re-composes it thereby. She changes one note in the opening to *More Than You Know,* and bends another, and gives us a rich new song. She also knew when to leave a superior song alone. Hear her on *Lover Man* or her own song, *God Bless the Child.*

Perhaps the best example of all comes with *These Foolish Things,* which might become a mawkishly self-pitying thing, and which was virtually designed for the chic, tea-dance styling of a musician like Eddie Duchin or even Lawrence Welk.

Billie Holiday recorded it twice, once in 1936, early in her career, and again in 1952. On the first version, one can sense that she spotted certain weaknesses in the melody, but she seems not completely sure what to do about them—she bends some notes and avoids others. In the 1952 reading, she is completely in charge of the piece, and proceeds to re-write it out of her own intuitive talent into an unforgettable melody. In *These Foolish Things,* Billie Holiday took something that was merely superficially pretty, and turned it into something lastingly beautiful.

Her voice had changed by then. Deteriorated some said. Gone, others said. They were wrong. She did more sing-speak than singing, true. But the frayed edge of that sound came not from the changes in her voice, but from a supressed sob, a sob so deep that if she ever let it go, it would bring pain more wracking and tears more lasting than any human could stand.

Billie Holiday was found lying in a corridor bed of a New York municipal hospital in July of 1959. She had lain there, thin and wasted, for days without anyone's knowing who she was. She died some days later in a private room, under arrest and under guard for possession of narcotics. Some well-meaning friend had brought the dying Lady a last snort of heroin, and a nurse had found it in a tissue box.

When singer Edith Piaf died in Paris, French journalists turned immediately to one of the country's leading intellectuals, the late Jean Cocteau, for a statement. Cocteau spoke feelingly of her talents and of France's loss at her death, but it was not the first time that he had praised her. Nor was Cocteau the only Frenchman of arts and letters who had spoken of her talents and thereby added to her stature in the eyes of her countrymen and the world.

I confess I thought immediately of the sad and harassed death of Billie Holiday.

But who spoke for Billie Holiday? (1972)

≈
≈
≈
≈

Brookmeyer, Mulligan, and the Concert Jazz Band

Gerry Mulligan's Concert Jazz Band, founded in 1961, has become an intermittent, frequently revived institution in the years since. In the meanwhile, it had been the immediate progenitor of the Thad Jones–Mel Lewis orchestra and its successor, the Mel Lewis Orchestra. Mulligan's "movie work," referred to in the brief encounter recorded below, would include his fine vignette as a shy, inept suitor in the film version of *Bells Are Ringing,* an appearance (as himself) in an episode of the Ben Gazzara TV series, "Run for Your Life," etc.

Bob Brookmeyer's puzzlement at the fact that I was interviewing him rather than the leader on the founding of the Concert Jazz Band continued after the piece appeared in *Metronome.* There were no protests voiced by Gerry Mulligan, however.

When the word first spread that Gerry Mulligan was forming a "concert jazz band," a lot of rumors spread with it. One of the first was that Bob Brookmeyer would be a member, the first soloist and first arranger after Mulligan, and that his enthusiasm was running very high. He was not, I learned, official "musical director," but he was rehearsing the band on occasion and very much wrapped up in its progress. Nevertheless, here was Bob

Brookmeyer, after all these years, back in a chair in a brass section, reading a part—a sideman again.

I decided to talk to him rather than to Mulligan in order to get some feelings about the band that might prove to be as interesting as the leader's. Accordingly, I warned Brookmeyer to expect me one evening at the *Village Vanguard*.

I had to be fast in getting from a front table to the back door to catch Brookmeyer on the way out after the first set—and I thoroughly confused the headwaiter in the maneuver. Anyway, I overtook Brookmeyer in the street and after I reminded him that I had a pencil and intended to take notes, the conversation went something like this:

"Sure, I'll talk about the band. I love to. But I can't say anything official or about policy. Why don't you talk to Gerry?"

"Everybody talks to Gerry. I wanted to ask you. And from what I have heard this band has meant a lot to you."

"It certainly has. And not just me. But you'll have to check this with Gerry."

"I will. But, look, why don't we tell people how a thing like this starts? I mean, for example, it takes money. Where did the money come from?"

"From Gerry's movie work. He didn't want to borrow it, and he didn't want this band to have an angel. The first estimate was that it would take $30,000 to get it started and maintain it until we could see whether it would go. Arrangements, for example; the fellows who have contributed can't afford to write on hope or speculation as they could when they were younger. They have to have commissions."

"That's another thing, I said. When a band like this starts, where do the arrangements come from? You don't begin with old ones for something like this, do you?"

"No. The book had to be new—scored or re-scored just for this band. That was part of the idea. We began with twenty-seven things, from Al Cohn, Phil Sunkel, Johnny Mandel, Gerry, Bill Holman, me . . . We didn't want to borrow or trade with other bands, either, the way some groups do. Except Duke. Gerry asked Duke for some things, but he hasn't sent them yet.

Otherwise, we don't want things other people have played. *Young Blood* is rescored for us from the way Gerry did it for Kenton. A couple of things are rescorings of arrangements from Gerry's Tentette album on Capitol. And Johnny Carisi rewrote *Israel* for us the way you heard it in the last set . . . Look, Gerry doesn't need any refractor when he talks. Why don't you ask him?"

"Well, partly because, as I said, I know this band means a lot to you . . ."

"To me, yes. But Mel Lewis left his wife and family behind in California, and the security of studio work, to come here and squeeze his way onto the bandstand at the *Village Vanguard* with us. And Nick Travis left a dependable job on the Jack Paar show, Buddy Clark originally came with Mel, Don Ferrara, and . . . but talk to Gerry. What he says goes."

"What was all of that stuff about there being only one soloist after you and Gerry, or whatever it was?"

"Well, you heard. We have at least seven soloists now—Gene Quill, Jim Reider, Don Ferrara, Nick Travis. We had Conti Condoli—Clark Terry replaced him—Willie Dennis—besides Gerry and me. Zoot Sims was with us for the Monterey festival. And we will have more. There are no duds in the band now, because all of us are enthusiastic, and we all know this is something we have to do. We believe in it. It is the chance we all still have to play jazz.

"We had a five-week lay-off last fall before we went back to the *Vanguard* in the middle of September. It was during that time that the changes in personnel were made and the enthusiasts joined.

"When we first opened the band at *Basin Street East*, last year, the band sounded bad in several ways. A lot of people put it down, or said it was loud, or other things. But some others were so glad to find a fresh attitude, a fresh big band sound, and musicians who were also fresh. Those people saw the possibilities in what we were trying to do and were patient; some of those people were musicians who wanted to join and help. Now we know. This band plays two kinds of sets: very good or very bad. Stay and listen. When you hear a good one, you will know what we know.

"I really was beginning to feel that jazz was passing me by. The newest things I have heard in person—I go to listen to Ornette or George Russell's group and I love them. But playing like that is not possible for me. I feel the way I think Buck Clayton may have felt around 1947.

"I put on a Joe Turner record and it gives me a starting point, but the newer things make me feel I am finished, and I'll have to wait out the rest of my life making soft-drink jingles for television. This band puts me in jazz, making jazz music I can love and respect.

"But talk to Gerry. He is the best spokesman for what we're trying to do."

"Are you doing any more writing for the band?"

"I haven't got the time while we are into it and working. I wish I did. Neither does Gerry. But we both did some writing during our winter layoff."

"By the way, this is some sort of precedent, isn't it? A big band with no piano—except for occasional piano things from you and Gerry."

"I suppose so. But you don't need it. What do you hear of a piano in a big band anyway?

"But I can't speak about policy. Gerry and I have even disagreed about a couple of little things. I'm just trying to help. Check all this with him before you print it, will you?"

When I went back into the *Vanguard*, I was sure I had the headwaiter thoroughly confused. Gerry, on the other hand, said it was all all right with him. (1961)

≈

≈

≈

≈ Outspoken Trumpeter

In 1955 Ruby Braff was a new star trumpeter in the *Down Beat* International Jazz Critics Poll, with a style that was a phenomenon for a musician of Braff's age, 28 at the time. His style reflected his basic love of Louis Armstrong and of Billie Holiday, Lester Young, and other jazz artists of the 1930s, with a glance or two, chiefly in phrasing, at subsequent players.

Yet, many felt, he was not (like some of the New Orleans revivalists, for example) merely coasting on the achievements of others; he was not just having an easy time of it in a style in which most of the artistic battles had already been won by others—he had found a personal challenge in the idiom of his choosing.

Braff's subsequent associations have been mainstream, but like most of the older players of that period, men with whom he is inevitably associated, he finds himself playing the Dixieland repertory as well and, in his case, enjoying it.

We spoke in Braff's Riverdale apartment north of Manhattan, a retreat he discovered several years ago after living for some time in the stone, concrete, and asphalt atmosphere of Greenwich Village. From his windows, one can see real trees, some real grass, and open sunshine.

The conversation revealed Braff's feelings and observations on music as of now. His tone and constant chuckles also revealed his abiding sense of humor and sly irony.

Williams: How did you get interested in jazz?

Braff: Well, I don't know. I just started playing in 1935. Nobody I knew thought of it as jazz at first. We just played, you know, played tunes.

Williams: When did you start thinking about it as jazz?

Braff: Well, they were talking about it on the radio. Stations would play 15 minutes of everybody, Guy Lombardo, Louis Armstrong, Duke Ellington, everybody. And the announcers would say "this is a jazz record" about Louis or Duke—the ones with the feeling I liked.

Williams: How old were you?

Braff: Oh, about 7 or 8.

Williams: You mean you were playing trumpet at that age?

Braff: It's true. I worked professionally in little groups a few years after that, at 9 or 10 or 11 years old. At 12 I used to sub for the cats in the Silver Dollar Grill in Boston.

Williams: Was your family musical?

Braff: Nobody in my immediate family played music. As a matter of fact, they opposed it. When they thought of musicians in those days—well, if you weren't a symphony man, you were a bum. No one thought that jazz would ever become so sophisticated that people played it in concerts. And they just wanted it to be a little hobby for me. Some of my distant relatives were musicians, on my father's side of the family, and nobody liked them too much.

Williams: Were you playing by ear then?

Braff: Yeah. I knew all the tunes that they played, all the standards and the pop tunes of the day.

Williams: Somebody told me it was only fairly recently that you took up reading.

Braff: Yeah. When I was a kid, no teacher could explain about syncopation. Even if they could read syncopation, they couldn't explain why you didn't play it exactly the way it was written. It just became confusing to me, and I just never paid any more mind to it, you know. And I met this wonderful guy a few years ago, Ward Silloway, the trombone player. He was playing with us at Jack Dempsey's. George Wettling had the job. It could have been the greatest. We worked from about 11 to 2 in the morning. Can you believe it? That's the way it was. Ward was playing. Pee Wee Russell. And Wettling.

Ward always was afraid to play jazz. In all the bands he had played in—Bob Crosby, Benny Goodman—there was always some star trombonist there before him who would play all the solos. He became very inward about it. I used to encourage him, because he plays good. One night he heard me say that I couldn't read, and he said, "Are you serious? I can read anything—I'm very good, really. Why don't you let me show you something about it?" And he took me on, to meet him every Wednesday in the Fred Waring Building, where he had a few pupils.

I didn't know but most of the time he was going there, he was there just for me, however, and paying for the room. He would never let me know things like that. He'd say, "What's the matter? You play much more than that when you play jazz—why are you tired here? Could it be that you get so busy reading that you're doing everything wrong? Pressing and pinching that thing against your mouth too hard because you're so busy?"

He knew how to apply things to my home ground. He'd say, "That's not hard, that little thing there. You play it a thousand times a day, but you don't know it. Look."

And I'd say, "Yeah, gee."

What a patient, wonderful, wonderful person. So I'd go home and try to write out little things based on what he'd shown me. Count reading, for instance. I didn't know what that means, if you have an upbeat and a downbeat—you know, like, one *and* two *and*. In school, the teachers never showed me, but he did. He'd say, "Look, just do everything ridiculously slow." And he would write it on the exercises: "ridiculously slow."

He started me off on one of the hardest advanced trumpet books; I don't know if guys in the studio could sit down and sight read and play those things. The first page is in about six flats, and it goes into different tempos and different changes.

I said, "I can't. . . ."

And he said, "You learn it measure by measure—we'll start out right now, right like that."

And you know, after some weeks, I got to play most of the

things in that book due to his beautiful patience and his beautiful outlook on things. . . . Gee, I don't believe it.

Williams: What happened to jazz at Jack Dempsey's?

Braff: After a couple of weeks they decided against it. It's too bad, because I've always loved that place, and I think it could be a great jazz room in the middle of town.

Williams: People are apt to think of you and some of the groups you play with as kind of revivalists, revivalists of swing music.

Braff: Well, people are prone to label things, and it's easy to put labels on things instead of looking for music. Why don't they learn to find out what the truths are in music instead of labeling things? Would they know what to call it when Charlie Parker played with Vic Dickenson—when they would play the *Muskrat Ramble* together at Storyville in Boston? And Erroll Garner would be on piano at the same time, with Pee Wee Russell too? I never knew any great musicians who couldn't get together and produce lovely music if they all knew the tune and agreed to play it. To me that's the test. After all, there are certain laws. No matter what style you play, you have to adhere to certain rules. And if you don't have a beat, you don't have a beat.

Williams: A few years back, it seemed that there was a new Ruby Braff LP almost every month.

Braff: No, it was never like that. For a couple of years I made albums once in a while but certainly not as often as many other people do. I haven't made my own album now in about two years. I have recorded, at the Newport festival and things like that.

This whole record industry has gone mad! Its sense of values has gone completely nutty. Companies have become greedy. And they're hurting themselves and hurting music in the long run. All they're looking for is whatever fad will sell a million records tomorrow. It's okay to record the kind of people who will sell. But you should record those people so that you can afford to record good things and be building something for the future.

Imagine the position now of men like John Hammond, a pioneer, you know, a pioneer in jazz recording, and guys like George Avakian—people who have been very daring and done many wonderful things that it took a lot of guts to do. These men are under this terrible pressure from record companies that they must produce records that will sell. When I talk to some of those guys about an album, if I have an idea for one, they might say, "Can it sell 60 or 70 thousand?" I get the idea that what they are really saying is that they don't want to record me. Because I know they record many people that don't sell 60,000 records!

On the other hand, it's indicative of the position that they've allowed the heads of companies to put them in. That's shameful. John Hammond wanted to record me for Columbia last spring, he said, and for about four months kept me on the hook talking. Finally one day, he called me up and said, "I just can't—you know how these companies are." What did he mean "how these companies are"? He's supposed to be something in that company. They respect him. He has turned out many albums for them. Certainly a company like that has money for sleepers—you know, for things that are going to sell maybe over a long time. Segovia or somebody—I don't care who it is.

Some a&r men have become lunatics; you can't even talk to them. They start to believe in the bad things that they record. They themselves, who know better, have better taste, are walking around saying, "Yes, isn't that wonderful." I look at a man like that, and I *know* that everything he's stood from in his life is dead set against this junk that he's recording, and he's trying to talk me and himself into it. That's really terrible.

Williams: Do you want to identify John Hammond specifically in what you said before? Or shall I leave the name out?

Braff: In this instance you might just use it, because I think it's important. This is not a knock against him. I just feel this is part of a social sickness that all these people are getting involved in with record companies. Where is the daring? And where is their sense of quality?

Some a&r men I have noticed wear musicians like neckties. I mean if you thought somebody was very good yesterday, certainly he ought to be very good today, unless he has changed radically. I don't know, it might be part of that record thing again, of these guys higher up exerting this pressure on these people and driving them so they lose faith in their own instincts and taste.

John Hammond has done wonderful things. That's why I'm harder on him than on someone else. He can well afford to stand up on his two feet and speak out. Instead of being a drag to a musician, let him be a drag to the man he has to answer to, higher up in the company. Or look at George Avakian. That guy was so daring. And he used to let me make any kind of thing I wanted. I was never a hit seller, but he let me. Wonderful. All of a sudden, when he was going to work for Victor, he said, "I'll tell you what we're going to do. I'm thinking of recording you with Frankie Carle." I was so shocked that I probably said something terrible to him that I didn't mean. Is this what I have come to, that I have to make a record with Frankie Carle? What has his way of playing got to do with my way of playing?*

Williams: There are a couple of jazz record companies that are in trouble right now.

Braff: They're in trouble? And why do you think they're in trouble?

Williams: Well, this is your interview, not mine. But I think it's probably because modern jazz as a style has become almost commonplace, and all the companies that grew up chiefly to popularize it have now done their jobs. Some companies, now that the soul jazz thing has burned out, well, they haven't got any place to go right now—or they think they haven't.

Braff: That's what happens when you deal with gimmicks instead of dealing with the truths, with honesty in music. I always feel that great artists who are really dedicated to what they believe are truths are the people who will survive—musically and artistically. Those are the only people in the world I take seriously.

Williams: Well, that reminds me that you used to write record reviews for the *Saturday Review.*

Braff: That was John Hammond's idea, as a matter of fact. It helped get me in a lot of trouble.

Williams: What do you mean?

Braff: Well, a lot of people resented any comment on their

---

*George Avakian, in a subsequent letter-to-the-editor of *Down Beat* remembered Braff's reaction quite differently: "He said yes," Avakian reported.

records from a musician. They'd rather have had Lawrence Welk or Adolf Hitler or someone say something about their records—as long as he said something good—than someone who had something that might be constructive. Also, I didn't have much space, and my copy was cut, shortened. I worked hard. I spent all night listening to the LPs and breaking my head—I'd lean over a little backwards and then try it again tomorrow. It started to really get to me. I started worrying about it. It's hard.

Williams: Yes, it is. And it doesn't pay too good either, does it?

Braff: No. It doesn't pay good at all. But I got a lot of free records out of it. Some of them are good, you know.

Williams: As of this moment, what do you think would be your own ideal record date?

Braff: Well, there're so many things. I would like to do an album with another trumpeter and with two rhythm sections, his and mine. His would never play when mine is playing; when he comes in, his rhythm section comes in. It would be wonderful to do that one with Clark Terry. I like his playing, and I know we could have a good time playing together. I would like to make a kind of a date with just me and Al Haig. And no other instruments. No drums, no bass. Like I did with Ellis Larkins once. Al Haig made that sound on those Stan Getz records that I love. His beautiful, tasty comping. Like the Count himself, he's got a thing that's beautiful. And his solos are beautiful. He's a great musician. And I would like to do a date with a big band, and have a lot of singing and playing—lots of comedy participation by the musicians on the date.

Williams: Your singing?

Braff: Yes. I'd like to get some of those things going of that kind and make the musicians do things like that. But it's out of the question unless I can really get away with that every night: improvised jazz theater. Bring out all the character in about 16 guys, and have them improvise verbally and musically every night.

Williams: You mean a kind of jazz cabaret sort of like the Second City or The Premise?

Braff: Yeah, something like that. Only I think it would be more interesting because by the very nature of its setup, it would allow me to have guests coming in and out all night long. And we carry on, see, on the stage. We'd have to have movable sets that could be changed very quickly, on rollers, very light, so that immediately people could move into positions to do things, without its being noticed. You'd need a regular backing. But I can pull off similar things on a small scale on a record that would be very revealing. An improvised musical theater.

Williams: I heard you had a funny job last summer.

Braff: Yes, with the Newport festival guys, out at the Bay State race track near Boston. Bud Freeman, Zoot Sims, Dick Wellstood, Benny Morton.

Williams: I wish I had heard Zoot Sims and Bud Freeman together.

Braff: Well, the longest set we'd play was the first one of the night, about 20 minutes. From then on we'd play about two minutes at a time, between races. But we had a lot of fun watching the horses. You know, I'm beginning to believe I don't like to think in terms of jazz anymore. I'm full circle back where I was when I was a kid and hadn't even heard the word *jazz.* I'm a musicmaker. I *know* who should play a chorus and when. I know how long a number should take. I know when it's dragging. I know when it should start. I know when one chorus is enough of somebody—or a half.

Williams: Well, I know you have some pretty strong thoughts about *that.*

Braff: Yes, I sure do. But you have to have. I suppose most people who've been doing something for a long time have their own feelings about it. But after all, I was brought up listening to three-minute records, where men have become immortal on four bars. They didn't need to ramble on and play exercises to let somebody know that they were there. Four well-placed bars by Pres would be enough for me, and I would be proud if any one of those four bars belonged to me. It seemed people took great pride in what they played. If they soloed at all, it was important. So they made sure that those few little things were good—like champions, they didn't waste punches.

That's what we have to learn, all our lives. To discipline ourselves, control ourselves, and be more discriminating. Not what they're saying today: "Be more free!" That word *freedom* that they use is a cop-out to get away with murder. That isn't what I call freedom. Freedom is the freedom to have control over your emotions and of music, the knowledge and wisdom to use them in a controlled and wonderful way to mean something, not to get away with choruses of exercises on the stand. That's disastrous. That would make anyone run from a joint if they had any feeling for music.

Look at how lovely Gerry Mulligan and Bob Brookmeyer play together. They get up there with their little quartet, and how much music they get out of it! Look, if you play the wrong chord, it's the wrong chord. It doesn't matter how free you think you are—that is the wrong chord. The composer did not write that chord. he stayed up all night figuring that out, and he knows much more about it than you do with the little "heads" you're writing. Those people just don't understand what goes into putting a piece of work together.

Williams: Who are "those people"?

Braff: I'll tell you who "those people" are. Those people are people who have been influenced by music from about 1950 on. It is unfortunate they came into an age of no individuality. They never heard different treatments and renditions of one piece. They have no way of comparing. Guys like us heard all kinds of styles of music, all kinds of ways to play a single song. We heard a million people do the same piece.

Furthermore, those people are people who don't recognize that jazz is only one corner, and a tiny one, and not a very popular one, of the world of entertainment in general. Without being able to recognize and enjoy and love many of the other corners of entertainment, which are just as engrossing as our own things, it's very, very hard for anyone to have a good healthy picture of music and American life, and play. And that goes for musicals, in the theater, and other great performers. I mean people like Judy Garland, who are just as thrilling to hear as an Ellington performance to me.

But all right, forgetting about other musical performers. In jazz itself, not to have heard the Frankie Newtons, the Bobby Hacketts, all such people. To have heard only this sewing-machine, eighth-note music—it makes it impossible for you ever to produce four bars of music that I want to hear. Music that will make me come away saying, "Oh! Did you hear that chorus he played! Did you hear that gorgeous four bars or that wonderful chorus he played?" I seldom come away from any joint feeling like that. I feel, "Ugh. Gee, I got to get home and turn on my Lady Day records or somebody like that, until I get back feeling normal again."

I hear nothing but a kind of stiff hatred in that music. Where's the romance? Where's the love, the caressing, of melody? Where's the caring? Where is it? Where did it go? The older cats—whatever guys are still alive, if they're in shape mentally and physically today—are playing better than they ever played before. Ben Webster sounds tremendous. He's marvelous. Another is Johnny Hodges. And Bird! Oh, if Charlie Parker had had another 15 to 20 years to play! Lester Young—luckily you heard him in all his mellow and mature things before he passed away. And Billie Holiday.

But these people now—some of them will never get a chance to mellow and mature into anything. Because the vehicle they have chosen musically, artistically, and philosophically, will never give them one minute of peace of mind. They'll never find one note of truth. They'll have to go back and find out what it's all about in the first place.

Jazz isn't just a young man's thing as some people think. It takes years to play anything good. (1964)

≈

≈

≈

≈ # Dial Days:
A Conversation
with Ross Russell

In the mid-1940s, Ross Russell found himself back from duty with the wartime merchant marine. He opened the Tempo Music Shop in Hollywood, Calif., a store specializing in jazz records.

In late 1945, Dizzy Gillespie arrived for a turbulent booking at Billy Berg's club, bringing with him a sextet that included Charlie Parker, Milt Jackson, and Al Haig, a group which set off the strongest of controversies among jazz fans. Tempo had become the hangout for the young Los Angeles musicians, and soon Russell was running a label called Dial, devoted to recording the then new and highly controversial music of Gillespie, Parker, and their associates.

He made his first date in early February, 1946, with Gillespie, and he made the second date that Parker recorded under his own name. Thereafter, Russell did several more with Parker and other pioneer modernists as well, in Los Angeles and later in New York. Russell also did some of the earliest and most substantial critical writing on modern jazz.

He came to such activities almost by contradiction. He had grown up on the jazz of the mid-'30s, but, like many of his generation who took the music seriously, he also had explored its past. He loved Jelly Roll Morton and Louis Armstrong, and he wrote an often-republished essay on James P. Johnson.

Russell has previously reminisced about Parker, and the results are in Bob Reisner's compilation *Bird: The Legend of Charlie Parker*. His relationship with Parker also unquestionably formed the basis for the fictionalized story of an early modern jazzman in Russell's novel *The Sound,* a book that received strong reactions from reviewers—rather strong pro and very strong con.

One incident in the Parker-Russell relationship should be raised here. The story is still current in jazz circles that Russell agreed to help Charlie Parker get discharged from Camarillo State Hospital—where the altoist was admitted after suffering a breakdown in Los Angeles—only if Parker agreed to re-sign with Dial records. Russell's side of that story is reported in the Reisner book:

"I might say that the Dial contract had reached an option point while he was in Camarillo. Before he came out, I discussed this with him, and I told him that I thought in view of the fact we only made one record date that produced four sides that were considered very good, that he ought to renew the contract for a year. He agreed to this, and that's the way that went. Some people have kinda put me down on this, I guess, and Bird had another version of it later on, but that's the way it was."

Since Russell has dealt elsewhere with his relationship to Parker at some length, an attempt was made in this interview to steer the talk toward other aspects of Russell's work in the '40s:

What it was like to work with some of the other musicians. What it was like to record modern jazz when it was scorned by many and bought by only a few. What it was like to find himself, quite unexpectedly, with a couple of potential hit records on his hands. What happens to an artistically valuable catalog like Dial's when its founder is forced to sell it for financial reasons. How he views it all now after almost 20 years. Inevitably, though, the subject of Parker also came up.

What follows is a slightly edited version of a conversation which had taken place two years earlier in the WBAI studios in New York, as broadcast on "The Scope of Jazz."

Williams: You recorded some other people besides Charlie Parker for Dial. Erroll Garner, Dizzy Gillespie. . . .

Russell: Fats Navarro, Howard McGhee, Dexter Gordon, Wardell Gray. . . .

Williams: Your first date was supposed to have been Bird and Dizzy but ended up being Dizzy, Lucky Thompson, Milt Jackson, and the rest, without Bird. I was in and out of Los Angeles at the time, with the Navy, and often in the Tempo Music Shop. I remember your coming in the morning after that first date, and there were a lot of young musicians there waiting to hear all about it. You had some acetates of the date under your arm, and you were saying that Dizzy kept complaining that the ceiling was so low he couldn't turn his horn up.

Russell: I don't remember saying that but I must have. The Glendale studio did have a rather low ceiling so that's probably correct. We recorded in different studios after that date. The second date, for instance, which featured Bird and produced *Ornithology* and *A Night in Tunisia,* we did at Radio Recorders. For the third date we found another studio with an extremely high ceiling. You know, there is another dimension which attaches to a specific recording and which is due to not only the engineering but the characteristics of the room.

Williams: You once said that the men on that second date, except for Parker, had a lot of trouble with *A Night in Tunisia.*

Russell: They had an awful time with it. And Dodo Marmarosa, who was the pianist, was a man that could play practically everything.

Williams: Isn't it strange to think about it? That piece, now it's commonplace; everyone plays it, and some are bored with it, I'm sure.

Russell: And the record that year, the Boyd Raeburn version on Guild of *A Night in Tunisia,* or *Interlude* as it was also called, was a kind of a must for every hip collector.

Williams: I suppose it is, as you have said, a matter of learning to phrase in a very different way—from a different rhythmic base than anybody had done in jazz before. You can hear Lucky Thompson on that record phrasing more or less in the Ben

Webster or Don Byas manner. Not that there is anything wrong about that—just that it is a different and simpler way of making melodic-rhythms from what Bird is doing. I remember hearing several musicians say that harmonically this music—although the texture of it was thicker, the changes came more rapidly— that they had heard people like Charlie Shavers and Roy Eldridge use many of these things before. But the point is that rhythmically the phrasing was very different from anything they'd heard.

Russell: Incidentally, that's why when I hear people put someone like Ornette Coleman down, I'm suspicious again. Maybe you could criticize some things about Ornette Coleman, but rhythmically he's extremely strong, and I'm sure that he's bringing back a lot of new interest in rhythmic elements and new life to the jazz language. As you know, this is a thing you just can't buy, a thing you can't learn in school.

Williams: Another thing, you notice that some musicians who will last from one period of jazz into the other as respected players, although they will be playing in a new idiom harmonically, rhythmically they stay pretty much where they were. For example, Coleman Hawkins.

Russell: Yes, I was just thinking of the record Coleman Hawkins made for Riverside with Thelonious Monk. Very interesting for that reason. Both styles very valid, of course. And very interesting contrast between Monk and Coleman Hawkins.

Williams: You usually managed to record modern jazz as it was actually heard in clubs at the time. There were limitations, of course. One was that most of your recording was done on 78-rpm records and had the limitation of time, of about three minutes.

Russell: The practical limit might have been $3\frac{1}{2}$ minutes. And some Dial records, the ones we felt had no interest at all for jukebox consumption, were $3\frac{1}{2}$ minutes. But the jukebox people and the distributors, kept saying, well, keep under $2\frac{1}{2}$ minutes. You know, the nickels (now it's dimes) went faster that way. And even though we weren't making a jukebox product, we still had to be governed by the general demands of the industry.

Williams: In those days, you couldn't have made a record that was any longer than about 5½ minutes, and that would have been a 12-inch record, which would have been more difficult to produce. . . .

Russell: And distribute, and highly breakable, and so on.

Williams: What I started out to say was that you were recording the music the way it was played in clubs. You hired the sidemen that the leaders wanted. . . . You didn't bring your own ideas of music to bear and act as a musical director of your record dates—something that sometimes happened to Charlie Parker later.

Russell: You might compare producing a record date to casting a play. The minute you start changing actors around, you get something entirely different. For instance, I'm sure that a play like Ionesco's *Rhinoceros* was very different in New York with Zero Mostel than it was in Paris with another actor.

Williams: But who put Zero Mostel in *Rhinoceros?* Not the author. However, it's the author, the leader, who puts the musicians in his own group. It's Charlie Parker who picked his rhythm section.

Russell: That's right. My basic feeling about making records is the one you imply: the musician is the man who is going to produce the music, and if he's good enough for you to take in the studio, he knows what he's doing, and he knows the people he will work with best.

I must have been fortunate, because then I had no technical musical background; my approach was only that of a dilettante, a person who appreciated the music. I felt I couldn't tell anybody in the studio what they should do, how many bars they should play, what a coda should be like, or that they should read something off a paper. So I tried to pick the right leader. I felt that Charlie Parker was the dominant musician and that he would pick his sidemen.

I think the only time I made any suggestions different from the leader's was for the date we did with Bird, Erroll Garner, Red Callender, and Harold (Doc) West, which produced some interesting results.

However, the really pure records on Dial I think were the last three dates we made, the ones in New York with Max Roach, Duke Jordan, Tommy Potter, Miles Davis, and Bird. That was Bird's working band of the time.

Williams: As long as we are talking about Charlie Parker, there are a couple of questions I would like to ask you, for the record, about his collapse. As I understand it, he was in very bad shape at the legendary *Lover Man* date. Then, later that night he was arrested; he had set a fire in the lobby of a downtown hotel.

Russell: My partner, Marvin Freeman, and I finally located him, some five days after his arrest. He was handcuffed to an iron cot in the psychopathic ward of the Los Angeles County jail. We managed to have his sanity hearing transferred from the scheduled court to that of Stanley Mosk. Mosk is an enlightened and liberal man, who was then sitting on the municipal bench in Los Angeles. He is now attorney general of California. Howard McGhee and I appeared on Bird's behalf and succeeded in our suggestion that Mosk commit him to Camarillo State Hospital. There was hope at Camarillo. Bird might well have been behind closed doors for years otherwise.

Williams: He was released.

Russell: After a stay of some six or seven months. It was because I, a supposedly respectable businessman, proprietor of a retail store, and operator of a recording firm—you know how these things seem on paper—was willing to sign papers assuming responsibility for him as long as he might remain in California. At the time of his release, a group of people—Maynard Sloate, Eddie Laguna of Sunset records, the late Charlie Emge (then *Down Beat*'s man in Hollywood), and I—put on a benefit concert with the AFM's approval and raised a sum of money to help Bird with his rehabilitation problems at release.

Williams: To go back to the business of studios, the engineer on the New York dates was named Doug Hawkins, right? Was he a musician, incidentally?

Russell: Doug Hawkins is a Juilliard graduate.

Williams: I'm sure that it helps.

Russell: Yes, it sure does. I later did classical dates for Dial, kind of far-out things like 12-tone music, and used Hawkins. He could read a score, and, believe me, it did help.

Williams: You were one of the earliest to record modern classical music on LP. Dial records had a multifaceted career.

Russell: We did have the first jazz LP. It didn't sell very well. It was *Bird Blows the Blues,* Charlie Parker on all blues selections.

That was 1949, and the LP had not been accepted by the jazz record distributors and buyers at all. Then when the LP was accepted, only the 10-inch LP was accepted. Later, of course, it was all 12-inch, and everybody had to change over. But that's the record business.

Williams: I'd like to get even more specific about your procedures at dates. There was one record of yours which seemed to me very successful in that it caught musicians at a peak of performance, the like of which is seldom caught in a recording studio. This was *The Chase* with Wardell Gray and Dexter Gordon. It was one of those rare records that not only went beyond the studio but had an excitement that's even rare in a club. It was 6½ minutes long, released on two sides of a 78.

Russell: Yes, they played a performance uninterrupted, and we divided it between two sides of a record. We had a series of saxophone choruses, and we could easily find a place to stop.

Williams: Why did you record it? Had you heard these guys play together?

Russell: Dexter and Wardell were playing around Los Angeles, conducting this musical chase almost every evening, and it was creating a great deal of comment. It seemed like a good idea to get them into the studio and record it.

Williams: This was about as close to a hit record as you had, wasn't it?

Russell: This was our most successful instrumental record. The biggest seller on Dial was the Earl Coleman vocal on *This Is Always,* but that was a real jukebox record, and it appealed to people who were not particularly interested in jazz. Actually, we lost a lot of sales on both records because we weren't expecting them to hit, and we couldn't get copies pressed up quickly enough. We weren't geared for it. By the time we had caught on to the fact that we had a couple of good sellers, the peak had passed, and it was too late.

Williams: How did *The Chase* date go?

Russell: Very well. There were no problems because they did what they'd been doing probably the night before—and many nights before that. And there was a great deal of enthusiasm for it. I remember we took pictures—ridiculous pictures—in the studio of both of these guys—Dexter, a very big man, Wardell, rather slender and smaller—chasing each other and holding their saxophones. But the date did have a great deal of warmth and enthusiasm. It was one of those dates that made itself.

Williams: Incidentally, what about the status of Dial records, an invaluable catalog musically. . . . Where did they go?

Russell: A pretty good question. I sold Dial in the mid '50s to the men who operated the Concert Hall label and who, in turn, started a mail-order record club called Jazztone. Some time later—perhaps a couple of years—I understand that they sold their entire catalog, including Dial, to Crowell-Collier Co. . . . Some of the Dial records came out on Jazztone.

Williams: Then, a few of them, badly edited, and incidentally the same masters that appeared on Jazztone, appeared on a label called Baronet. There were about four—by Dizzy, Bird, Garner—from Dial masters.

Russell: Who was behind Baronet?

Williams: I don't know. However, more recently the Charlie Parker Record Co. issued one LP from Dial material. Then they issued that date with Red Norvo, Bird, Dizzy, Teddy Wilson, etc., which was recorded for Comet but which you bought for Dial. However, the Parker company now seems to be inactive, unfortunately.

As you mentioned before, you recorded Erroll Garner for Dial in 1946. Later you also released some things by him that were made informally, extended performances that were made at somebody's house.

Russell: Those were made by Timmie Rosenkrantz in New York in about 1944. I was the first to bring out some of them, but later others came out on Blue Note. However, we did two Dial studio dates with Erroll, of course. One was the Charlie Parker date that produced *This Is Always* and *Cool Blues*. In addition, I did a trio date with Erroll. I don't know exactly how it came about except that, for one thing, he liked the studio in which we made *Cool Blues*. He liked the piano, he liked the engineer. We were able to get a very wonderful sound. Curiously, it was a tremendously large room—it looked like a warehouse. But for some reason the acoustical properties of the room produced a marvelous piano sound.

Anyway, Erroll and I got together to do a date. We were going to do four sides, but the date went so well and so rapidly that we ended up by doing eight, if my memory is correct. He was delighted with it, and it was the sort of date where the a&r man just sits and listens to the artist. He played exactly what he wanted to and even improvised a couple of things in the studio or played things he hadn't played for some time.

Williams: I know that later Garner was supposed to do everything in about one or two takes at the most and play through a great repertory at great speed, rejecting some of the things but accepting most of them.

Russell: That's just the way this date went. I think we may have done three takes on one tune and two on a couple of others, but a lot of them were one-take things. He would finish and say over the microphone, "That's it. Set up another acetate and we'll do. . . ." He's that kind of a musician. He's a man who has to feel right to play, and when he does feel right, which fortunately is most of the time, the music just flows.

Why don't you ask me about the things we *didn't* do on Dial, some of the regrets. You know there was one musician around after Dial moved to New York who was not tied up to a contract that I sincerely regret not having recorded, and that is Thelonious Monk.

Williams: Why didn't you?

Russell: I just don't know. And I think that today Thelonious Monk is probably the most original, vital, traditional force in jazz.

Williams: I know of another group you might have recorded, according to your wife, before you threw in the towel and dissolved the company. In fact it might have saved the day to record them: Milt Jackson, John Lewis, Kenny Clarke, Percy Heath—the Modern Jazz Quartet, although they weren't quite using that name then.

Russell: That's right. John Lewis offered it more or less as a friendly gesture, and I said no, I'm going out of the record business.

Williams: Just at the moment that you had begun to record modern jazz in 1945, it was barely past its beginning and still a controversial music. Then, at the moment when even the best of it was beginning to be acceptable to a large public, you left it.

Russell: Actually I didn't make any jazz records after about 1948. We went into a classical program—avant-garde classical music. Later on we did some folk music, calypso, Caribbean music, and that kind of thing. And we issued some Earl Hines and Roy Eldridge records that were exchange items from European labels who issued Dial stuff over there.

Williams: There was another Dial record—a curious record. . . . It was a take of *Ornithology,* clearly by the Charlie Parker group with the same sequence of solos except for one. Charlie Parker doesn't solo on it, and in his spot, Dodo Marmarosa does play a solo. What happened?

Russell: It was an early take of *Ornithology.* When we issued it, it was not put out as a Charlie Parker record, as you know. It was used much later when we were trying to make up a Dodo Marmarosa LP.

Williams: But what happened in the studio: Charlie Parker didn't solo, so why did they even finish the piece?

Russell: I don't really know. Bird kind of turned his back and walked away or something. Everybody else went on, and Dodo just played the 32 bars where Bird would have played.

Williams: Ornithology reminds me that there is another Charlie Parker story currently afloat. Some people say he never would take a standard chord sequence and put his own title on a new line that he wrote to it. Of course, *Ornithology* is actually Benny Harris' version of one of Bird's old Jay McShann solo licks, expanded over the chords of *How High the Moon*. But the story has it that when Bird did this sort of thing, he would call the result by its original name, and it was only record companies that changed titles because they didn't want to pay high royalty rates for standard tunes. In other words, he would have called this piece, according to the current story, *How High the Moon*. Is that so?

Russell: I don't know what he'd do otherwise, but when that record was made, it was all set—it was *Ornithology*. He said, "We're going to cut *Ornithology* now," and this was it. There was no question at all about where it originated. He did say that it was a co-composer credit, Benny Harris and himself. But in many cases he came up with titles. *Klacktoveedsedsteen* is a very good one. I understand that a lot of the things might be, oh, 16 bars from one piece and eight bars from another.

Williams: To go back to Dodo Marmarosa, you did some Dodo Marmarosa trio records.

Russell: Yes. I always thought that Dodo was a marvelous pianist. I always liked him. I thought that he was a musician who brought a lot of the technique of the classical piano to jazz and yet had become almost entirely part of the jazz scene—he wasn't a hybrid pianist; he was a real jazz pianist.

Another thing about Dodo—he had a marvelous sense of time, and he was able to play up tempos with great facility. I used to go over to his house, and he would play Bach two-part inventions by the hour. I suppose this gave him a great deal of digital facility, but he had a wonderful jazz feeling. I remember that, instead of going to bed at 3 or 4 o'clock—which would be normal for a musician in California, where the bars closed at 2—he often used to stay up until a rather unearthly hour, until dawn. And the reason was so he could go out and stand in the front yard on the lawn and listen to the birds. He was quite serious about this. And if he were walking down the street and he heard certain noises, like church bells or something, he would just have to stop—he would be transfixed. It was rather clear to me that Dodo lived in a world of sounds—and pretty high-quality sounds too.

Another interesting thing about him was that he felt he was

limited by the size of his hands. I remember on one date we made with a group, Dodo was the pianist, and he was playing terribly well, but otherwise the date wasn't going so well. I wanted to stop recording him with the band and make some Dodo Marmarosa solos with a rhythm section right away. He was almost on the verge of tears. He said, "Man, I don't have the hands for it." He held his hands up and said, "Look at these tiny little hands. They're just too small. I can't do anything with them." Of course, the records he's made give the lie to that.

Williams: I've often thought, in this current Crow Jim tendency among certain New York musicians, that, after Bud Powell, there were few pianists who played with the modern guys in the early '40s except white players. And some of their names, of course, were Al Haig, perhaps the best of all; George Wallington; Dodo Marmarosa—even George Handy at times.

Russell: Joe Albany is another might-have-then-been-great that had this same approach. Actually, both Joe Albany and Dodo came from similar homes—middle-class American homes with parents who were born on the other side, from southern European countries, and who brought a great love of music with them, with a great deal of respect for classical music. Both Dodo and Joe Albany have excellent piano training, and it certainly shows in their playing. This is a tremendously interesting thing to me— the cultural things that are handed down. It is fascinating how our particular society and cultural attitudes try to suppress these things. For instance, the last thing that the average second-generation Italian-American wants to be is an Italian-American. He wants to submerge himself into American culture, whatever that might be—jukebox sounds and so on. And yet if you go through the list, look at all the singers and musicians who came from this particular background, where there is a great love of music, not in an intellectual way but in a really democratic way.

Williams: I think it was a sociologist who did some kind of tabulation about the ethnic and national backgrounds of jazz musicians. Of course Negroes were first. And I think next were Jews, next Italians—which, of course, are not two exclusive categories. . . . After that, things came down to such a sparsity that it didn't mean much, as I remember. . . .

Russell: It's interesting what's happening today in the jukeboxes. I've been working on my second novel, which will be about the record business and the involvement of a one-man corporation, particularly with a girl singer—who incidentally will probably be from an Italian-American background.

I have been forced to listen to a great many of jukebox favorites, and the conclusive thing that strikes me is that we're starting to level off on a lot of things—that prejudice is much, much weaker, it seems to me, than it was 20 years ago. Now the kids, the average middle-class white kids who are putting dimes and quarters into a jukebox, are listening without prejudice, without reservation, to singers who come from all kinds of backgrounds. For instance, Paul Anka I understand is of Syrian background. Ray Charles now speaks to everybody, not just the urban Negro.

Williams: I'm not so sure all around. If a Negro girl singer made a record a few years ago and a white girl covers the record for another label and follows it pretty closely (this has happened, as you know), the white girl's record will probably be the bigger hit. However, I *don't* think that necessarily we should look at that as prejudice.

I remember talking once to a couple of white truck drivers who were my age and who had grown up during the swing period. They were about as unprejudiced, I think, as any people can be; I could detect nothing of malice or superiority in their feelings. They told me that they had listened to all the swing bands the way I did. And they said they didn't like Duke Ellington. I got very specific with them. I picked one of the white bands that was very influenced by Ellington. I said, "Do you like Charlie Barnet?" They said they liked him better than Ellington. I don't think color meant a thing to them as such. I think that the way of playing was different for them and that Charlie Barnet's way of playing appealed to them more. And I'm sure there *was* a difference in attack, in emotion, between the two bands, even on the same piece. I think that sort of thing happens still.

Russell: I think that was more true ten years ago than it is now.

Williams: I think you're probably right. . . . I heard a white musician the other day speaking frankly about this. He said he had worked with a group—the leader was a Negro and most of the guys in it were Negroes. The trumpeter, however, was a very young white player. And my friend said . . . that in this trumpeter, for the first time in his life, he could not have told—could never have told—that he was a white musician, even after weeks of hearing him night after night. And he said, "If I'm going to be frank about this, I think I could always tell before. I talked to the trumpeter, and he . . . said, 'Oh, all the guys my age are that way. You can't tell anymore.'" However, my point is that even if there were [a difference], a difference isn't necessarily a sign of something wrong.

Russell: Yes—quite the contrary. I think we need differences. . . . The essential point is that there are cultural differences, and that's important because every group has something to contribute to the total culture. And such contributions can make American culture very important, rich, varied, and democratic.

Williams: Let's go back to Gillespie for a moment. He was a major innovator. . . . On your first records, he led a small group through several examples of theme-solos-theme. What does he do now if you go to hear him? Often he will tell jokes and sing songs and be very funny. . . . What is his solution to the problem of standing up and playing for people night after night?

Russell: As a musician he has to keep playing and working in order to live. That is the big problem. And you just can't be at your best every night. As it happens, I heard Dizzy recently, and he played very well but not sensationally. I had heard him six months before, and I'd never heard him play better. I think Dizzy is probably the best musician playing today—certainly on his good nights. His articulation on a trumpet is just marvelous. He knows exactly what he's doing. . . . He's a very vital force and a very well-adjusted person, I think.

Williams: Remarkably so. But, again, you've got this kind of a conflict. What does Dizzy Gillespie do? Well, he plays the trumpet. . . . Of course, he sings and clowns—and the clowning is perfectly natural to him. . . . But, like the majority of jazz performers, he's an instrumentalist. . . . a brilliant trumpet player. What do you do when you're just that?

Russell: Well, there's always tomorrow, you always have to make a living as well as live with yourself, and if you're a musician, you have to keep blowing. I have heard Coleman Hawkins in places which I don't think are the best settings for him. But that is his profession; he has to keep playing. Or take Jess Stacy. The last time I spoke to him he was working regularly on the coast as a piano player in a better-type restaurant-bar, where he may have to play a lot of requests. Music becomes a trade. And once your vogue is over, your creative period has disappeared, as it does for many people, then you're a craftsman at best. . . .

Williams: There is little or no tradition for a jazz musician to work within. We know a lot about what a novelist will be likely to be able to do when he's 60, although it may just be repeating himself well.

Russell: Or an attorney may get more valuable as he gets older. But jazz is probably a younger man's music. And the other big problem that we all know about is that the jazz musician is a creative artist working within a commercial framework. To many a nightclub owner, he's just a trumpet player, say. It doesn't matter whether it's Al Hirt or Dizzy Gillespie or somebody else, really—he's a trumpet player, some kind of attraction that he buys at a price. But the jazz musician is trying to be creative within this framework, and that's where the conflict arises.

Williams: Well, maybe the solution that many men follow is the best one. You're really creative maybe one night out of six— that night you really are out to prove to yourself that you can still do it. The rest of the time you entertain people the best way you can without killing yourself at it. . . .

Russell: A novelist—or any creative man—in America has many of the same problems. He writes a successful book and then he may be expected to—or may be tempted to—go to writing what the publisher and the public wants. He has to earn his living. One way or another, many other people share the jazz musician's basic problem. (1964)

≈

≈

≈

≈

John Lewis:
Spontaneous Restraint

"I write pretty well on demand. I can do better under pressure than just waiting for something to come."

The speaker is composer-pianist John Lewis. His most immediate reference is to his score for the United States Information Service short documentary *De l'eau et de l'espoir* (*Of Water and Hope*) concerning American assistance in water conservation in Morocco. Lewis, who completed his score in less than six days, provided two main themes for the film—*Blue Necklace* (an intriguing combination of the American blues and North African sounds, in which the composer plays a wood chime) and *The Jasmin Tree*. They are played on the soundtrack by the Modern Jazz Quartet.

Lewis is of course best known for his work with the Modern Jazz Quartet, as pianist, composer, and musical director. And the Modern Jazz Quartet, in its approximate twenty-year history, has established itself as perhaps the most illustrious, most highly praised, and certainly most durable small ensemble in jazz history—indeed the most durable ensemble of any size aside from the Duke Ellington orchestra.

I have given the quartet's approximate age only because it is difficult to date its beginning exactly. Its first membership was a bit different from its current personnel, but it may be said to have started when vibraphonist Milt Jackson, pianist Lewis, bassist Ray Brown, and drummer Kenny Clarke were all members of trumpeter Dizzy Gillespie's 1947–48 orchestra. Indeed, as such, and with the great bongo player, Chino Pozo, the ensemble made its first recordings.

Lewis once described the quartet's genesis to Francis Thorne. "We had played together for two years with Dizzy's band. . . . The trumpet players' music was particularly difficult in that band and they needed a lot of rest. The rhythm section played quite a lot of relief, and it also gave Milt a chance to play."

And in the beginning, the quartet, as such, was recording under Milt Jackson's leadership. "From that time, we knew how nice the music felt, and how easy it was to play together."

Each member of the ensemble was by this time working more or less regularly as someone else's sideman. So, in order to stay together for future recordings, and eventually as an established ensemble, "we hit on the idea of making the group coopera-tive. . . . This condition still exists, and though it is not perfect, it has worked quite well for a long time." One of its imperfections, it soon became apparent, was that a true and absolute democracy would not work, so Lewis was made musical director.

More recordings were made, the jazz public discovered the quartet, the word spread to a wider listenership, and soon the M.J.Q.—now with Percy Heath as its bassist and Connie Kay as its drummer—was able to take engagements on its own, to fill night clubs and concert halls, and eventually gain the recognition and respect of musicians and listeners of all sorts and persuasions the world over.

John Aaron Lewis was born in 1920 in La Grange, Illinois, but raised in Albuquerque. His forebears included Louisiana Colored Creoles and American Indians. With such a mixture of black, red and white blood lines, Lewis unhesitatingly said (a few years ago when such terminology was more in vogue), "I am an American Negro." His family was musical. His mother studied singing with the daughter of Mme. Schumann-Heink, and Lewis himself was introduced to the piano keyboard at age seven.

Lewis was playing locally for dances by the time he was in his teens, and he knew most of the celebrated figures in jazz not only from recordings and radio broadcasts, but also from in-person tours. Indeed, one of the most vivid memories of his boyhood was of knowing Lester Young, later the great innovative tenor saxophonist of the Count Basie orchestra, who spent some time in Albuquerque and performed with local musicians.

When Lewis entered the University of New Mexico, he not only continued his music studies, he also undertook a second major in anthropology. His interest in the latter subject, he explains quite frankly, was that he wanted to know whether the generalizations, and the slurs he had heard, and experienced, that were based on race had any real or scientific basis.

John Lewis' experience in the Army in 1942 to 1945 was a turning point in his life, for there he met the great jazz drummer, Kenny Clarke, and it was largely through Clarke's encouragement that he entered music upon his discharge.

While he was a member of the Gillespie orchestra, and was contributing such pieces as *Two Bass Hit, Stay on It,* and the more ambitious *Toccata for Trumpet and Orchestra* to its book, Lewis continued his music studies at the Manhattan School of Music, from which institution he took two degrees. He also spent a few months in Paris. That experience, which was, one might say, the beginning of a love affair, was reflected in such later Lewis titles as *Vendome, Concorde, An Afternoon in Paris,* and in the fact that he now owns a home on the French Riviera, where he spends several months of the year.

After he left Gillespie, and while attending the Manhattan School, Lewis worked with Illinois Jacquet, Charlie Parker, Lester Young, Coleman Hawkins, Ella Fitzgerald, and many other leading lights, and he repeatedly proved himself a superb accompanist who could not only anticipate on improvisers' direction, bolster him or her and the musical texture, but subtly and unobtrusively protect the player or singer in stressful moments.

With the increasing recognition awarded the Modern Jazz Quartet, Lewis remained active in other areas of music. He composed *Three Little Feelings,* which was originally a part of a 1956 Town Hall concert by a "Music for Brass" ensemble.

Indeed, to some observers, *Three Little Feelings* is, aside from some of Duke Ellington's longer pieces, one of the better "extended" works written by a jazz musician. (Ellington is, not so incidentally, Lewis' most admired jazz composer.) It is also a fine introduction to his writing and an example of the way that John Lewis can take the most apparently simple, even traditional ideas and put them to the most delightfully personal, even ingenious use—a capacity which is probably his greatest compositional virtue.

He performed with members of the Stuttgart Symphony, leading them in his own works, and remarking that with such conducting he had now made practical use of all he had learned at the Manhattan School.

Lewis got his first opportunity to score a movie when he worked on the French film, *Sait-On Jamais,* called *No Sun in Venice* in its American release. In that film, he worked with the quartet, and added *The Golden Striker* to its repertory. His next movie assignment was more elaborate. He wrote the score for the Robert Wise–Harry Belafonte picture, *Odds Against Tomorrow,* employing a brass and reed ensemble, and featuring improvising jazzmen in key positions—Milt Jackson, pianist Bill Evans, guitarist Jim Hall, and others. Gunther Schuller commented in *The Jazz Review* that the score "utilizes jazz music as a purely dramatic music to underline a variety of situations not specifically related to jazz. . . . It can serve its purpose in the film but it can also stand as absolute music, apart from the original dramatic situation."

Subsequent Lewis film work has included the Italian film *A Milanese Story* (which added *In a Crowd* to the M.J.Q. repertory), and *De l'eau et de l'espoir.*

Perhaps it was this ability to reassess and revitalize the traditional that led Lew Christensen of the San Francisco Ballet Company to commission Lewis to provide a score for an Adam and Eve ballet, *Original Sin,* in 1961. And perhaps it was the same turn of mind that led Lewis himself to write his suite *The Comedy,* dedicated to the analogous improvisational nature of traditional *commedia dell'arte* and jazz. And he participated as both writer and performer, along with composer Gunther Schuller, the Beaux Arts String Quartet, and the Modern Jazz Quartet, in a pioneering "third stream" concert that combined classical forms played by the Beaux Arts and jazz improvisation by the Modern Jazz Quartet.

On that latter occasion, the Beaux Arts String Quartet and the Modern Jazz Quartet each performed separately, and then jointly on Lewis' *Sketch* and Schuller's *Conversations.*

Such activities inevitably led Lewis and the other members of the quartet to a special arrangement, some eight years ago, whereby the ensemble would work together for six to eight months of the year, and its leading members—Lewis as composer and Milt Jackson as performer and leader of his own ensemble in clubs and concerts—would go their separate ways for the remainder of the year. He composes away from the piano keyboard, "in another room. Or on the road, in a hotel room. If I were at the piano, I would just sit there and play."

Pressed for his own favorite among his works, Lewis names *Midsommer,* his celebration of the Swedish summer festival, originally performed in his Stuttgart collaboration.

Others might name his *Django,* his cortège dedicated to the great Belgian-French gypsy jazz guitarist, Django Reinhardt. That work was one of the earliest of the Modern Jazz Quartet's pieces. It has been played and scored by Lewis and many others (including everyone from Gil Evans to Michel Legrand) for ensembles of various sizes and instrumentations. Yet it remains in the quartet's repertory as a vehicle for fresh improvisation at each performance. And that fact is surely good evidence of its composer's conviction, indicated above, that his heritage as a jazz man guides everything he does as a musician. (1972)

≈
≈
≈
≈

Recording with Bags

Even with its daily wrap-around line of attending tourists, New York's Radio City Music Hall does not look much like a movie palace. It looks even less like a recording studio, but if you go through the stage entrance, take an elevator to the seventh floor, climb up a flight of stairs, and pass through a couple of unmarked green doors, you will find yourself at Plaza Sound, a large recording studio, well equipped and well cared for (there is a good piano, and it is kept in tune), that is usually used by, among others, Riverside records.

Riverside booked Plaza's facilities on a day last spring to record one of its more illustrious contractees, vibraharpist Milt Jackson.

Jackson is perhaps known as the most immediately compelling player in the Modern Jazz Quartet. But he has been successfully making records on his own for years, with groups small and large. On this occasion, Jackson was to record with a brass orchestra of four trumpets, three trombones, tuba, three French horns, and a rhythm section. To do the scoring, there was Melba Liston, a brass player herself, a trombonist, as well as arranger (she has worked with the bands of Dizzy Gillespie, Count Basie, and Quincy Jones), and perhaps the only woman to make her way successfully in the strange subculture of modern-jazz record dates and public performances—for that matter, she is one of the few women instrumentalists and composers to make her way successfully in any kind of jazz.

The date was called for 1 p.m., but several of the players had arrived early, among them pianist Hank Jones, drummer Charlie

Persip, and trombonists Jimmy Cleveland and Quentin Jackson. Also present was trumpeter Clark Terry, who had, in the parlance of the American Federation of Musicians, "contracted" the date; that is, he had assembled the specific players to fit Liston's instrumentation.

Terry is also in effect a constantly alert concertmaster—he holds run-throughs of difficult parts and helps to revise scoring as needed. On this occasion, he was to act as a responsible and humorous buffer between a quiet-spoken Liston and a sometimes talkative group of players.

Milt Jackson himself already was setting up his vibraharp, with the help of an assistant, and picking out his mallets. Jackson is a small, thin man, and he is usually cheerfully quiet—indeed, it is as if Jackson usually says something only if he absolutely has to. But today as he worked, he was chatting freely and constantly with Jones and Terry. Perhaps the introverted Milt Jackson was becoming as extroverted as his music.

By 12:50 p.m., the studio was abustle with greetings. In a corner two trumpeters were in a serious discussion of the relative merits of mouthpieces.

At 12:55 p.m., a door at the far end of the studio swung open and in walked Melba, to be greeted enthusiastically. Liston, a pleasant, handsome woman of medium height, was dressed in a dark skirt and a salmon-leather jacket. She carried two evidences of her dual position in life: a handbag and a briefcase containing her scores.

Almost on her heels, entered Orrin Keepnews, a&r man for Riverside and producer of the date. Sporting a recently reshaped Van Dyke beard and a Meerschaum pipe, Keepnews wended his way across the studio, nodding briefly to the small group of visitors and wives near the door. He shook hands with Hank Jones, spoke to some of the musicians, and then entered the studio booth to take his place beside Riverside's engineer Ray Fowler.

By this time, all the players had arrived save one, trumpeter Thad Jones; he had been mistaken about the hour of the date but was now on his way. The room was a lively buzz of talk, and everyone seemed eager to go to work. It was decided to get in some rehearsal of the arrangements until Thad arrived. The brass was seated on a raised platform facing Liston, and to her left Jackson and the rhythm formed a kind of semicircle. Milt crossed to Melba, picked up his part, glanced at it, looked up at her, said with an enigmatic half-smile, "Hard! I knew that," and crossed back over to his instrument.

An almost uncanny aspect of any jazz record date is the ability of the players to accomplish several things at once—some casual, some trivial, some genial, some noisy, some exacting, some serious. And now, as Terry helped Liston distribute the parts among the players, Jackson and Hank Jones held a conversation on the various types of address books they had used, Jackson discussed his coming tour with the Modern Jazz Quartet, Jones sounded an A for the brass to tune up to, and both managed to gain an idea of what music they would be playing for the next four hours by glancing casually at Liston's scores.

In deference to the nominal leader and star of the date, Melba said to Milt, "Shall we run down the blues?"

And the star, not so much in deference to his arranger as in the statement of a man who is usually ready to play anything any time, as long as he is playing, said, "I don't care."

So the arranger said to the orchestra, "Get out the minor blues." As they did, she instructed, above their muffled but continuing conversation, "This is a very soft, light thing," all the time snapping her fingers quietly and slowly to indicate the tempo.

"Ready, horns?" But they weren't. There was still some sporadic tuning up, so she held up a bit longer. Then she started them in a slow, muted transmutation of Jackson's basic blues theme, known in its classic version as *Bags' Groove*. (Bags, Jackson's nickname, supposedly derived from his appearance after several sleepless Detroit nights spent in celebration of his Army discharge in the mid-'40s—but anyone who has seen him without his glasses knows that the nickname might have been appointed any time, for his eyes nearly always look bagged.)

After one chorus of *Bags' Minor Blues,* several players made the collective mistake of slipping into major. Unexpectedly, it was Jackson who stopped them with, "Well, is this minor or not?"

A spontaneous, "Hey, Bags!" came from somewhere in the middle of the group. This interjection might have implied, "Well, so *you're* taking charge. . . . That's sort of new. Before, you might have looked surprised at a thing like this but let somebody else do the correcting. You're right—we goofed. But we like you in this new role. . . ."

This had all sunk in immediately, and Jackson had moved over by Hank Jones and was showing him an apparently hilarious mistake that the music copyist had made on his part. That part, it should be noted, like most jazz soloists' parts, consisted of a few written ensemble figures and long stretches of chord symbols, within which harmonic framework the player is to improvise.

On a second try, they finished the piece, and its opening gentleness proved to be contrasted, about halfway through, in a sudden shout of brass encouragement. On that shout, Jackson— arms flying even in a run-through—rode to a further ad lib variation. Then the opening delicacy was restored by horns and vibes at the balanced ending of the piece.

Jackson: "Is that what I'm supposed to play at the end?"

Liston: "Whatever you like."

The French horns, meanwhile, were running over a short section among themselves.

Jackson: "When they have those eight bars forte, what am I supposed to do? Go on playing right through? Yeah, I am?"

He seemed shyly surprised and delighted at the idea.

Liston turned to the group and said, "Right there break it on the third beat. Do-do-lit-do-*wah!*"

As they ran the piece through again, she did no time-keeping but conducted only the dynamics and the feeling she wanted by an expressive pantomine: closing her eyes, moving her hands delicately in the air, swaying slightly, and tilting and turning her head to the sound of the music.

At the end Terry said, "We can make that rot now."

"Rot now?" countered Jackson as they both laughed.

But as if to correct himself, Terry turned to the trumpeters and indicated a section of the score with, "Let's try that part at letter E again."

Then they worked on something called *Bossa Bags*. Jackson joked that he was sure that the bossa nova had to be on the way out by now, and Terry countered that it couldn't be just yet because he had only recently made one. But even a slight indication on Jackson's part that he might be concerned with what could make a hit record seemed a new concern for him to be voicing.

Thad Jones arrived, took some kidding about the reasons for his tardiness, and quickly participated in a second run-through of *Bossa Bags*. The score wasn't easy, and at one point Hank Jones succeeded in smoothing a minor disagreement between two of the horn men by amusingly underlining their verbal exchange with threatening silent-movie tremolos.

"I'm gonna scratch the intro and let the rhythm take it," Melba announced to an unresponsive din. Then louder: "Scratch the intro!"

"Then what about a drum solo?" Persip asked quietly. But he was already joining piano and bass in working out a new beginning. They worked it up quickly, but as Keepnews called through the studio loud-speaker for them to try recording a first take of the piece, Terry and Liston had their heads together, revising the ending according to an idea Terry had.

The group memorized the new conclusion quickly, and in a few minutes engineer Fowler was reading "Session No. 156, Reel 1, Take 1" onto the rolling recording tape, and after one brief false start the first take had begun.

During the performance, everyone looked deadly serious and strictly business until Jackson's eyes bobbed up at the end of his solo. He was smiling, as usual. He always seems pleasantly surprised when an improvisation comes off well.

The take was played back—chiefly to check matters of recording balance—and the conversation gradually buzzed up in the studio. It was, after all, only the first take, and first takes are usually technical things.

The new Milt Jackson entered the engineer's booth briefly to tell Keepnews that he had decided the minor blues did not have the sort of commercial potential for a release on a 45-rpm single. So they might as well expand the arrangement with improvised choruses by some of the trumpeters.

Then the old Milt Jackson played a fine solo as they tried another take of *Bossa Bags*.

Immediately, Terry requested "one more take right away," sensing that the psychological moment for a really good version of the piece was imminent.

As they played, Hank Jones' feet danced away under the piano, Jackson leaned attentively over his instrument, and, at the finish, the brass men smiled.

As the reverberations drifted off, Liston called out to the booth, "Let's hear that one!"

She seemed casually confident as the playback began to fill the studio, even joining drummer Persip in a brief dance. She was listening carefully, though, and toward the end stopped abruptly, having heard one wrong note from the 11 instruments. From the middle of the orchestra the culprit, one of the French horn players, immediately confessed.

"We'll put it in the liner notes that he played a wrong note," Jackson cracked.

The rest of the take, however, had been good, and they could briefly lift the passage in question from a previous take and splice it in. So much for *Bossa Bags*.

It was time for a slow ballad, the sort of piece that Jackson's natural earthiness can transform so brilliantly. As Terry and Liston passed out the copies of *Flamingo*, Jackson and Hank Jones were already kidding the introduction with a few overripe trills, as if to clear the piece of any latent sentimentality.

The run-through suggested that Liston had done some of her writing in Jackson's style, but simpler, so as to underline the kind of thing he would improvise. It worked effectively. The run-through also revealed a great deal of muted work for the trumpeters and a need for supplementary tympani. This meant that Fowler had to move some of his mikes in closer to the horns and that Persip had to assemble and tune up some new equipment. Jackson, meanwhile, was obviously eager to play again. And Terry, as usual, was running down a few rough spots with the horns.

"Let's go from the top," said Melba.

"Matter of fact, we could try one if you like," said Terry.

"Okay, let's see how it sounds."

But the opening proved to be tough, and they decided that as soon as they got a good version, they could hold it and splice it on to a good performance of the rest of the piece. (Ah, the joys of tape!)

The tempo was especially slow, creating a mood hard to sustain if everyone isn't playing well. Jackson's solo moved from wild, double-time embellishments of the theme to simply bluesy melodies—and back again, contrast upon contrast. With eyebrows raised, he faced his vibraharp fiercely and then bent over it abruptly, his arms and hands always moving above and around its keyboard. It was as if he had to coerce warmth and melody out of so cold and metallic an instrument. Many vibists take an easy way out by settling for a simple, appealing percussiveness, but Jackson is always a passionate melodist. Still, he is never without his humor, and at one point when he apparently felt the trumpets were playing with a bit too much schmaltz, he tossed them back such obvious musical schmaltz that they came off it immediately.

"Did the copyist make some mistakes in there—are there any wrong notes?" suggested someone over a loudspeaker from the booth.

"No," said Melba, "that's part of the sound I want."

"See," said Jackson, smiling an aside to Fowler, who was in the studio untangling some of the wires, "she wrote that in."

Meanwhile, the arranger had moved into the control booth to give her full attention to a playback of the last take. She was retreating not only from the usual conversation in the studio, but also from the fact that it had been increased by the arrival of a messenger from a nearby delicatessen carrying a heavy load of coffee and doughnuts.

She stood with her back to the loudspeakers and her eyes shut, taking in the music. Sometimes she sang quietly along with the brass, sometimes she only swayed with it. The expression on her face was a kaleidoscope of passion, pain, release, and finally, peace. During the solos she waited politely attentive; during the closing ensemble passages she closed her eyes again, raised her hands in delicate movement, and, at the end, smiled without comment. Then, still moved, she turned to Keepnews and said something that sounded like "t-tttt-th-th-t."

"Sure," he said, understandingly, "we can fade out the ending gradually."

A wise leader saves a 12-bar blues for the moment in the record date when spirits begin to flag, for playing the blues can lift them. And now Melba suggested they record *Bags' Minor Blues*, expanded with solo choruses by the trumpets.

"You'll see why I got A to play his solo before B," Keepnews was saying in the booth. "If I didn't, B might just coast through some of his clichés."

It worked apparently, for B played a very good chorus.

A couple more takes were done, and Jackson came into the booth, asking Keepnews if the last one was okay. Keepnews agreed it was and when Jackson had left, remarked, "A year ago he would have just left it up to me or Melba and said nothing. I wish I had the first date I did with him to do all over again, now that his shyness is gone."

Back in the studio, someone had distributed W-2 forms, the income-tax withholding slips, and the musicians were filling them in, a sign that the date was over.

In a few minutes they were into the final number, a superior but little-known ballad by Buddy Johnson called *Save Your Love for Me*. They made it on the third try. Persip's brushes made a faintly broken whisper across his snare drums. Jimmy Cleveland chewed gum at a wildly fast tempo between his slowly delivered trombone phrases. In the middle, Jackson abruptly bent over his instrument for a ringing cascade of notes and smiled broadly at the cleanly executed shaking brass crescendo that answered him. He began his delicate solo section in double-time, and the bass, piano, and drums went with him immediately by a kind of collective intuition.

Melba was almost swirling with the tempo. Then she raised her arms to signal a return to the lyric quietude with which the piece had begun, and the last notes rang out.

At the end, "*Magnifique!*" Terry exclaimed.

"Play it back, and then we'll go home," Keepnews said to Fowler in the booth in complete agreement. (1963)

≈

≈

≈

≈

Steve Kuhn, Piano

In the 1940s there was published a book of casual humor, anecdote and interview by H. Allen Smith called *Low Man on a Totem Pole*. Such a volume may seem an unlikely place for an historian of American music to be doing research, but there is a chapter in it about a small child, the son of an avid jazz fan with a sizable collection of swing-era recordings. The infant boy, barely able to talk, was very fond of the records and able to tell one group from another. He is described at one point as pointing to the phonograph and gleefully identifying "Benny Gooman, Benny Gooman!"

That listening prodigy was Steve Kuhn, and he remained something of a prodigy for years thereafter. While still a teenager and a high school student in Boston, he was working with the likes of Coleman Hawkins, Vic Dickenson, Chet Baker, and Serge Chaloff. Out of the prodigy class, he subsequently worked in New York with John Coltrane, Kenny Dorham, Stan Getz, Art Farmer, and Charles Lloyd.

Steve Kuhn was born in Brooklyn, and as indicated, he began his acquaintance with jazz at a tender age. As soon as he was physically able, he was putting the records on the turntable and playing them for himself. And by the time he was five, he knew that he wanted to be a musician. On the advice of his father, who had been taught violin in his own youth, he undertook piano as the best place to start, a place from which he could move on to other instruments if he wanted to. He has never wanted to.

As Kuhn remembers it, he found it very difficult to play the

69

classics that were an inevitable part of his instruction without doing some tampering. "Apparently I could improvise some even then, and it was hard for me not to when playing the little Bach and Mozart pieces I was assigned. My teacher knew about my interest in jazz, so as a reward for a good lesson, he would bring in some of the Pine Top Smith and Meade Lux Lewis boogie woogie transcriptions that had been published and let me play them."

In 1947, the elder Kuhn's business took him to Chicago for three years, and then to Boston in 1950. It was in Boston that Kuhn began working as a sideman accompanist to the aforementioned visiting stars, or with local men like Ruby Braff, as a kind of house-pianist at Storyville and its downstairs branch, Mahogany Hall. He also became an irregular regular at the Stable with Herb Pomeroy's sextet.

Kuhn also continued his studies, now with Margaret Chaloff, the renowned classical piano teacher who loves jazz and has been a friend to jazzmen—Charlie Parker used to refer to her as "Mama" and she is very proud of that fact. Her son was of course Serge Chaloff, the baritone saxophonist. Chaloff became a major influence on the young Kuhn and gave him ideas about comping and how to play behind a soloist, ideas about soloing, and a general approach to the problems involved in getting up in front of people and making music.

"We took all kinds of jobs in little clubs around Boston for about eight or nine dollars a night. And often Serge would be yelling out to me the changes he wanted to hear in the piece we were playing, but I never felt he was doing it insultingly. I would come off the stand drenched in perspiration time after time, but I really felt as if I'd done something up there. It was hard work too, because we usually had to work without a bass player," Kuhn recalls.

Another influence on Kuhn was Dick Twardzik, the Boston pianist who died in France in 1955 while touring with the Chet Baker group. "I admired Twardzik very much, particularly harmonically. He listened to all the modern European composers and was quite advanced.

"He would play relief piano at the Stable, and he was supposed to be on for about twenty minutes. But he would get so involved that he might play on and on, usually working on the same piece. Finally, Herb Pomeroy gave him an alarm clock, and when the bell would go off, Dick would stop exactly where he was, pick up the clock and leave the stand.

"He once paid me a compliment on my playing—I was still very young then—and of course I've never forgotten it."

By this time, Kuhn's modern jazz influences were beginning to emerge. He still loved Fats Waller, for one, but he had begun to admire Erroll Garner, Horace Silver—particularly for his feeling—Lennie Tristano, Tommy Flanagan, and above all, Bud Powell. It was only after he had begun to learn from Powell's work, by the way, that Kuhn began to appreciate Art Tatum.

It was not until some time later, during his last year in college, that Kuhn began to appreciate Bill Evans, a player to whom he is sometimes compared. "When he got it together, to me, it was as though he had done something that most of the good jazz pianists had been contributing to, and reaching for, for several years," Kuhn says.

Meanwhile, still in high school, Kuhn had begun to work around Boston on his own in a trio with drummer Arnie Wise, and, at first, bassist John Neves, later Chuck Israels.

In the summer of 1955, incidentally, Kuhn was scheduled to perform a Prokofiev piano concerto with the Boston Pops Orchestra, and he and Margaret Chaloff worked on it for a year. But it turned out the orchestra didn't know the piece and couldn't take the time to rehearse it.

The following fall, Kuhn was at Harvard as a music major, and work with the trio continued. In 1957, he, Israels, and Wise made a trio recording for United Artists, but the session came at a time when UA was losing interest in jazz and it was never released.

In the summer of 1959, Kuhn was a scholarship student at the School of Jazz in Lenox, Mass. It was an important session for that school in several ways, and one of these was the presence of two other students named Ornette Coleman and Don Cherry. "I was put into the same group with Ornette, and we were playing his music. It was the best group, and I was flattered to be in it. At the same time, I was confused about what to do. Max Roach was the faculty instructor of the group, and John Lewis was also around a lot of the time. I asked John how he thought I could best fit into the music. I knew what Ornette was doing. I have absolute pitch and I could hear the quarter tones and micro-tones of his music."

Kuhn did find a way to fit in, and in the final school concert he played a relatively simple melodic solo on Coleman's *The Sphinx*. Many another pianist with Kuhn's technical equipment, but with less discretion and taste, would surely have thrown caution to the winds and been all over the keyboard showing off his prowess.

Schooling done, Kuhn headed for New York to seek a career as a jazz musician. In the fall of 1959, he became a member of Kenny Dorham's quintet—Dorham had also been a faculty member at the School of Jazz—along with baritone saxophonist Charles Davis and bassist Butch Warren. They worked in Brooklyn, did jobs in Washington, Montreal and elsewhere, and had a stay at the Five Spot in New York.

"Then I heard that Coltrane was leaving Miles Davis and looking for a band. I called him up, saying that I didn't know if he knew who I was, but could we get together and just play a bit. I knew it sounded funny and that it wasn't the usual way of doing things, and I said so. He said he'd let me know. He called me back—I suppose he must have been asking around about me in the meantime—and said we'd rent a studio and play some. We played for about two or three hours. Then we went out and had dinner. He was kind of quiet about things, as he always was about everything. We drove back to his house on Long Island and played some more, about four or five hours this time. Afterward, he and his wife rode me back to Manhattan, and when they let me off, he said he'd call. Two days later he did call. He simply named a salary and asked me if it would be all right. We opened at the Jazz Gallery with bassist Steve Davis and drummer Pete LaRoca.

"He was all music—everything was music for him. I had never met anyone in jazz so completely intense and dedicated about the music before Coltrane," the pianist said.

"As for my work with him, I figured I could do *anything*. But with the freedom I was allowed, I ran too much of the spectrum, and the result wasn't really together. Finally, he gave me notice, saying that he had to and couldn't really tell me why. To tell you the truth, I was just about to give *him* notice, because I knew it wasn't working musically. But the event was still hard for me to swallow. I simply hadn't found myself stylistically. I was not supporting him, really. In a sense I was competing. He wanted McCoy Tyner, and when I heard them together, I knew McCoy was supporting him.

"I would see Coltrane afterwards, of course. I remember once I ran into him on the street, and he said to me quite seriously, 'Steve, show me something new.' Imagine! Me show *him* something new. He never stopped searching. His total dedication never let up."

Asked whom he would name as the epitome of swing, incidentally, Steve Kuhn unhesitatingly answers, "Coltrane."

Early in 1961, Kuhn joined Stan Getz through the intervention of the late bassist Scott LaFaro. Kuhn greatly admires Getz's technique, facility, and harmonic imagination. "He is a marvelous player, and his ballads are masterful."

When he left Getz, Kuhn felt that perhaps now he could really get together his own trio. To that end, he rented a studio and made a record of his own, hoping to place it with an established company. He didn't succeed.

Before long, Kuhn was working with Art Farmer's quartet, after the departure of guitarist Jim Hall and at the suggestion of bassist Steve Swallow. But during that time there was a trio album for a small label, Contact.

For the past two and a half years, Steve Kuhn has also been a part-time piano teacher. His students have represented all levels, from beginners through amateurs to professionals. "I was against doing it at first, but now I feel that as my own playing schedule permits, I want to maintain as many students as I can for the rest of my life. I learn a lot from it."

Otherwise, Kuhn has held out for the past two years for work as a leader of his own trio, taking on an occasional gig, perhaps, but no regular jobs. He has also made a very well-received album for Impulse, *The October Suite*, a collaboration between Kuhn and composer Gary McFarland, another fellow-student from the 1959 session of the School of Jazz. Kuhn feels that the music on this album, although it involves a string quartet on some selections and a woodwind group on others, is also representative of the kind of music his trio makes. "I think that in the last ten years, I have learned all that I'm going to learn from the jazz tradition. My influences are assimilated and my own style has taken shape. I listen to a great deal of classical music, including Chopin and Liszt, but especially from Debussy to the present. But in my own playing, I think jazz is where my feeling is. If my music represents a kind of converging of two idioms, all right, but for me there is no question that the jazz feeling is the strongest.

"We play selected standards, a couple of originals by Carla Bley, and, more and more, my own originals. We need some point of departure, some frame of reference, and so does the audience, but we treat the pieces without preconceptions as to tempo or chord changes. We may pick a standard—a new one, say, like one of Burt Bacharach's pieces—but we might use only parts of its melody, its opening phrase or opening couple of phrases, as a basis for what we improvise."

Kuhn feels strongly that communication with an audience is the crux of the matter for a musician, and he believes that the concert stage presents the best future milieu for his group. Not just the big halls in the large cities, but the hundreds or thousands of smaller halls throughout the country, particularly those on college campuses.

"The auditoriums are there, and so are the potential audiences—appreciative audiences, I think, for jazz of all kinds. Someone has got to get it together, set up the circuit and start the booking. We'll play clubs too. There's one advantage to playing in clubs, you know. You don't often come away feeling the evening has been too short." (1968)

≈

≈

≈

≈ # Rehearsing with
the Jimmy Giuffre 3

Jimmy Giuffre's current music involves the sort of improvisation that is called by that graceless and ambiguous name, the "new thing." And like many musicians working on such free and spontaneous playing, Giuffre rehearses often. It is partly a matter of keeping himself and his music well practiced, of course, and of trying out new pieces. But it is also a matter of personal pleasure and of aesthetic adventure, for Giuffre and his associates are discovering a new musical idiom. Each rehearsal will probably fulfill new possibilities for the music, rejecting some approaches and affirming or suggesting others.

Giuffre's rehearsals take place informally in his apartment. They are also somewhat flexible as to personnel. The Giuffre 3 currently includes Steve Swallow, bass, and Don Friedman, piano. However, several players have provided the piano and bass parts at rehearsals, particularly since pianist Paul Bley, who had worked a great deal with Giuffre, joined Sonny Rollins about a year ago and since Swallow began working with the Art Farmer Quartet last fall.

It is gratifying to discover how many young players can contribute to a free and challenging idiom like Giuffre's, a music which does away with traditional melody forms and traditional harmonic and rhythmic guideposts and makes heavy demands for unpremeditated invention on the player. But from the first time that pianist Friedman made a session, both he and Giuffre knew that Friedman's response to the idiom was exceptional, and Friedman soon cast his lot with Giuffre for all the group's appearances.

Several bass players have made Giuffre rehearsals for the pleasure and challenge of the music, but when Swallow is away and when Gary Peacock is not working with Bill Evans, Peacock will probably be the man playing with Giuffre.

Jimmy and Juanita Giuffre's apartment is on the Upper East Side of New York City. It is the kind New Yorkers call a "railroad flat," meaning that the five small neat rooms are strung out one after the other, that there is no hallway, and one room leads directly into the next. The front room has a Steinway grand and is the music room. Two rooms to the rear is Jimmy's study, with a tape recorder that usually figures as an important part of rehearsing.

Wednesday afternoons are usually rehearsal times, and on a recent Wednesday Giuffre, Friedman, and Peacock gathered to try a new extended piece called *Trio in Flux*.

The first to arrive out of the cold, slushy New York streets is Peacock. He is not carrying his own bass but plans to use an instrument Swallow leaves at the Giuffre place. In a few minutes Friedman arrives, and soon the trio is sitting around the Giuffre kitchen table variously sipping coffee, tea, or (for Friedman) a glass of water. After a quota of news and small talk, someone says, "Well, let's play," and without another word the three men move to the living room.

Giuffre begins to comment on *Trio in Flux*. It is a piece in five parts, each introduced by a written section, and lasting, in performance, roughly 15 minutes. The opening and closing parts are for the full trio; the second part is a duo for bass and piano; the third is a duo for clarinet and bass; the fourth for clarinet and piano.

Thus all the combinations and textures for the trio are explored. The score is marked "no tempo (moderate)," and no steady tempo should be set up in performance—the player tries to let each of his musical phrases find its own best tempo.

As with most of the Giuffre 3's current pieces, the themes don't set up chord structures on which to improvise and don't necessarily establish keys or modes for the players to improvise in. The written part suggests musical ideas—and moods, if you will—upon which the players build their melodies. Furthermore, although one player may predominate for a given moment, all three are equal melodic participants, and the music is a collective melodic effort as it unfolds.

However, *Trio in Flux* itself has a further aspect: even in the written parts, the players take the phrases one at a time, each man playing off each of his lines as he feels it. Each man should listen to the others, and make his part fit in properly, and no player should get too far ahead or behind. Thus the written parts of the piece will also sound different in each performance.

"It is like three actors, three comedians," Giuffre explains. "Each man knows his own lines and his own movements. But each time they work, each man has to hear the others and allow for their lines and movements, and each allows for the special timing of the others. For instance, in playing my one phrase here [he points to the score] I allow the piano part to come off before I go into my next phrase here. But one time Don may not play this as fast or slow as the next time or give the notes exactly the same kind of accents, so my pause and response will be different each time too. Stretch or condense as you want to.

"First, let's work on the written parts, and we'll improvise later."

The musicians begin. As they play the first section, three interdependent lines seem to be moving in an enormous musical space. The movements of the lines are personal, but each responds to the other.

At the end, Giuffre, who has been standing in the curve of the piano, turns to Friedman.

"Just to pick on you a little about the last part," he says and moves toward the keyboard and Friedman's music sheet, "I think it would be better if you break these phrases up with more space in between them."

Friedman nods.

They play the opening section again. It is familiar, yet different.

"That was perfect," says Giuffre. "I would say, let that last note lay there for a long time. Now let's go to the next part."

It is for Friedman and Peacock and is like a discourse, with Friedman asserting high notes and Peacock replying with "yes, but . . ." notes from below. Then the argument reverses, with Peacock moving upward, Friedman downward. At the end, Peacock's instrument reverberates.

"This has to be very strong," says Giuffre, pointing to Peacock's part. "That G-flat has to ring with everything you've got."

The duo starts again as Giuffre moves into the next room to catch the balance of the two instruments.

"What do you have in the third bar?" Friedman asks the bassist, apparently puzzled by what he has heard.

The two men play the section again. As its last notes hang in the air, they seem to plea for the improvisation that would normally extend and finally resolve the written section.

Next, the duo for clarinet and bass.

"Keep the drive up without going into a steady tempo," says Giuffre after the first try. And again, "Good, but can you do it just a little slower, because my part needs stretching out. No, wait—that sounds in tempo. It sounds like quarter notes."

They try it again, and Giuffre pronounces it good: "Once more and we've got it."

The next section is for piano and clarinet, and after they have run it through once, Giuffre says, "It's working out well, but you were just a bar ahead of me. The good thing is that we were working together so that the audience could hear everything each of us does. There's no part being wasted."

Friedman's bass notes are moving upward now. Giuffre re-enters high. At the end, he lowers his clarinet, smiling, "I beat you out that time. But that doesn't matter, of course."

Peacock looks at Giuffre, saying, "The idea is to get each part to have its own movement."

"Yes, I don't want it to be symmetrical horizontally. Okay,

Letter E. This part here"—he holds up his part to the others—"is very complex, so we will stretch it out."

About a third of the way in, Peacock plays a wrong note, emits a heavy groan, and follows it by a Bronx cheer. Laughter by the three then assents to a new start.

"The pace you play at is your own, plus what the other guys are doing—I just think of giving it movement," Giuffre says to the room in general, gesturing with a sweep of his right arm. Then he turns to Friedman and continues, "Gary's got the most busy part in this." Peacock solicits Friedman's help in tuning up the slightly seamy bass, after which he begins working on his part.

Soon Friedman says, "Let's try Letter E again."

Giuffre agrees with "Take some time on these cadenzas." They begin, Giuffre playing with loose fingering and loose embouchure to get the sound he wants. Suddenly he stops in midphrase.

"Hey! My horn fell out of my mouth," he says with a laugh. "You know that happened to me onstage once."

They begin once more. "No, wait!" It is Giuffre, laughing again. "I was trying to play your part." He is looking up at Peacock.

The ending is played with such unity that Friedman's smiling notes seem to echo inside Peacock's bass, and Peacock's broad sound inside the piano's sounding board.

"Now," says Giuffre. "I think we've got that, so let's try it all the way with the, ahem. . . ." He pauses, coughs officiously, and then says very carefully, smiling, "Im-prov-i-ZA-tion."

As Peacock scat-sings a fragment of his part to try it rhythmically, Giuffre heads toward the tape recorder. He has a second thought, however, and returns, saying, "I remember this now—during the duets, the other fellow could add some color, from the theme material maybe, while the other two are improvising. But not if it sounds contrived. A figure maybe."

There is some discussion of the idea, and Peacock suggests, "Maybe I should play something pianistic or clarinetish."

"No. Maybe just a phrase if it fits, but your own. Well, let's do a version of it on the tape, and see what happens."

Giuffre moves back to the recorder to switch it on. Then he announces, for the benefit of the microphone, *"Trio in Flux"*—and then laughs: "Trio influx—too many trios."

The opening is sharp and strong. Giuffre hits a long note, making it more than one by loosening his embouchure and sounding its overtones. (He has written it in the score: "overtones, loosen embouchure.") In the improvising, Friedman takes off in a humorous flutter of notes, and Giuffre scurries behind him in imitation. Then they are both into strong melodies in the middle register. Next Giuffre darts high, then low. And at one point Friedman augments a strong chord with the additional sound of the clap of the piano top as he slams it back into place.

Friedman not only lets each piano phrase move with its own rhythm and momentum, separate from the next, and without benefit of a steady tempo, but he can let each phrase swing with real jazz rhythm. That capacity and his open wit fit this music excellently.

Giuffre gradually diminishes a note into silence, and they all know the section is over. A pause. Then Peacock leads into the next section for piano and bass. Here the busy improvisation takes on an intermittent third part, shared equally by Peacock's occasional percussive sounds thumped on the side of his bass and Friedman's discreet manipulation of his piano top. A little bit of overdoing, and these effects might become grim or even ridiculous, of course, but the two handle them with musical taste and feeling. Then the bassist is using his bow, and Friedman occasionally strums the piano strings with his fingers and fingernails as new sounds and textures emerge.

Suddenly there is a disruptive, flapping sound as the tape runs off in the next room. Giuffre rushes in, turns off the machine, and is back for the last notes of the duo.

They are into the last session, with all three men participating. All the lines are still clear and independent but interrelated. Peacock's sustained final note and Friedman's reverberations finish it.

"Everybody ready to hear that?" the leader asks, moving toward the tape recorder in the next room.

"Yeah, I'd like to hear that," says Peacock. Friedman nods in agreement.

The tape is rolling on the playback. The three musicians listen. A crescendo followed by a pause finds Giuffre with his arms raised, shaking both his hands and thrusting out his right foot, smiling broadly. The music ends jarringly at the point where the tape had run out.

"You sure learn a lot from hearing yourself back right away," Giuffre says to mutual nods.

Giuffre returns from the kitchen with three small glasses of beer, and the musicians unwind with small talk. "Hey, do you realize we are a West Coast trio?"

At a pause, Peacock begins to speak seriously and almost formally on the music: "You know, I have the feeling that the volume of this music creates a weight, regardless of which register you're playing in. Ordinarily, the lower parts of the piano, say, are heavy, and the upper notes are light. But in this music I don't feel that at all. Here, loud in any register, high or low, is heavy. Quiet, high or low, is lightweight. Of course, I don't have the range of dynamics on bass that the other instruments have."

"Well," Giuffre contributes, "the bass in this music is definitely called upon to play three or four times as loud as in any other, and it usually takes a player a while to realize that."

"There was a very good thing that happened in our duo," Friedman says to Peacock. "When I played down, you went up high; when I played high, you went low; when I went slow, you moved faster. . . ."

"Fine," Giuffre says, "as long as it doesn't get monotonous or seem mechanical. Or as long as one man doesn't take over and dominate the music."

Peacock is back to Friedman's thought, saying:

"The point I wanted to bring out is that I can get presence—I can get the audience to hear me clearly—by playing low when you're high, high when you're low, by leaving holes, and so forth. But that in itself has nothing to do with the music necessarily. Then, I can play something that does fit musically but doesn't have presence and isn't heard. It's essentially my problem, I know, and not yours." He gestures toward Giuffre and Friedman.

"Also you are usually microphoned," says Friedman, "and here you're not. . . ."

"No, not in this music," Giuffre says, emphatically.

"I don't know whether *we're* playing too loud," he adds, pointing to himself and Friedman.

"No," Peacock decides, "the bass player has to hear how he is situated within the musical context and play accordingly.

The room holds a pause for a couple of beats, after which Giuffre speaks for the three of them: "Let's do some more." Peacock wiggles his eyebrows in assent. Friedman moves to the piano.

Giuffre is in the rear again to start the tape recorder. Friedman, a gleam in both eyes, slyly starts blocking out some chords. Peacock starts to walk along behind him. After about 30 seconds of this conventionality, the pianist is complaining, "I'm tired already."

Giuffre re-enters, saying, "Look, before we do the piece again, want to try playing something, just the two of you for a little bit? Want me to listen?"

Peacock turns to Friedman and says, "Let's play the duet." Immediately they go into the second part of *Trio in Flux*. Each of Friedman's crisp phrases swings its own way. And Peacock's musical logic carries its momentum in complement.

"I didn't notice any lack of presence that time," the bassist says at the end.

"I think you're right," Giuffre agrees. "But the piano has so many overtones in this room that they blotted you out sometimes. It was partly the room, partly the material, and partly the instrument. Now, after all this talk, let's do another tape."

They are into the piece. This time Giuffre has moved from the piano's curve and stands behind Friedman's keyboard, in the midst of the group and its suspended sounds.

When each section of *Trio in Flux* is over, each player knows it almost intuitively, and all three turn to the next written part together. And there is never any doubt for a listener either when the group's free exploration of a section is over emotionally or musically.

The piece is finished, and Friedman says quietly, "That was sure a lot different from the first time."

Giuffre takes a step toward the recorder in the next room, commenting, "I think we did all the things we talked about doing." (1964)

≈
≈
≈
≈

Giuffre/Brookmeyer Reunion

The Jimmy Giuffre-Bob Brookmeyer Five proved to be a short-lived undertaking, and of course both men have gone on to many activities since, but the attitudes and ideals of each man revealed in this joint interview seem to me to have remained central to each man's career.

"I wanted to play music. I wanted to be where I had been happiest in the past. And that sort of thinking led me to Jimmy Giuffre."

The speaker was Bob Brookmeyer, who has spent the biggest part of his time the last few years recording jingles, accompanying an assortment of pop singers, and doing the other various tasks involved in "studio work." Some musicians—including some first-rate jazz musicians—can work the studios contentedly. But Brookmeyer was a bit less than contented, it would seem.

Giuffre's response to the proposition that he and Brookmeyer form a group was positive. "We've been on the same wave length for years. Actually, I suggested a couple of years ago that we get together and play a gig or two. Bob was involved in too many things then," he said.

Now Giuffre, playing tenor saxophone and clarinet, and Bob Brookmeyer, playing valve trombone, are involved in the new Bob Brookmeyer–Jimmy Giuffre Quintet.

The group has been in rehearsal, usually at Giuffre's studio, for several months, and it appeared in public for the first time last November, at one of the Jazz Interactions Sunday afternoon sessions. Also participating is Giuffre's associate of several years, pianist Don Friedman. The bassist is Chuck Israels and the drummer Steve Schaeffer.

The quintet does not unite Brookmeyer and Giuffre for the first time. However, their memories of their very first meeting differ slightly, and run more or less this way:

Brookmeyer: "I first met Jimmy when I was playing with Stan Getz in California in 1953. We were at Zardi's in Los Angeles, and Giuffre would come in and play with us on Mondays. He was playing a lot of baritone in those days, as I remember."

Giuffre: "But wasn't it at Harry Babasin's that we met the first time?"

Brookmeyer: "That's right. It was at Harry Babasin's. Or was it?"

Giuffre: "I came up with the score to my *Fugue,* my atonal fugue."

Brookmeyer (emphatically): "And I was very impressed with it. Have you ever heard it? You should hear it. I was also impressed with Jimmy's intensity, particularly during those Monday nights at Zardi's."

Brookmeyer had joined Stan Getz soon after leaving Woody Herman. He stayed with Getz for a year before joining Gerry Mulligan, with whom he was associated until the spring of 1957.

Giuffre was, of course, a Herman alumnus, too, having provided the clarinetist-leader with (most notably) *Four Brothers.* Giuffre's best-known subsequent position was as a member of Shorty Rogers' Giants. But when he left Rogers' group in early 1956, it was, eventually, to form the Jimmy Giuffre 3, the ensemble that played *The Train and the River.* The 3 is perhaps the most respected, and certainly the most fondly remembered, of all the groups Giuffre has led.

The Giuffre 3 began with the leader tripling on clarinet and tenor and baritone, Jim Hall on guitar, and Ralph Pena on bass. No drums. No piano. An unusual enough instrumentation and personnel to begin with, perhaps. But the makeup of the 3 was to become even more unusual, and the presence of Brookmeyer was to make it so.

The group had found a semipermanent home at the Village Vanguard in New York, but Pena decided he wanted to resettle in California. Giuffre's permanent solution to the loss of a bass player was to go after a valve trombonist—but a particular valve trombonist named Bob Brookmeyer.

Brookmeyer had been a fan of the 3 since its first arrival in New York. He lived near the Village Vanguard and dropped in regularly. In late 1957, before a Sunday matinee, Giuffre gave Brookmeyer a phone call.

"Want to go to dinner this evening?" he asked. Brookmeyer answered that he was busy with some writing and couldn't. Giuffre's response was to call him again during the matinee and repeat the invitation. Receiving another no, he tried again after the performance. When that didn't work, Giuffre presented himself at Brookmeyer's door, asking with assumed innocence, "Hey, want to go out to dinner?"

At dinner, Giuffre invited Brookmeyer to become a member of the 3, but *not* a fourth member.

"I would tell my friends," Brookmeyer said, "'I'm joining Jimmy Giuffre.' They'd say, 'Oh, he's adding a trombone?' And I'd answer no. And then they'd say, 'You mean no bass?' They said a lot of other things too."

Whatever they said, the Jimmy Giuffre 3 featuring Bob Brookmeyer lasted more than a year; a unique jazz ensemble with no bass, no drums, and Brookmeyer as occasional pianist.

At the end of that year, Brookmeyer did not permanently disappear into the studios. In 1960–1961 there was the Gerry Mulligan 16-piece Concert Jazz Band, for which the trombonist was soloist, composer, and sometime unofficial music director during rehearsals.

He also has been a mainstay in the Thad Jones-Mel Lewis Orchestra since its formation, and co-leader, with Clark Terry, of a delightful and much admired quintet. The latter two projects, however, have been for kicks and psychic income on a part-time basis, while Brookmeyer recorded the cola jingles and the bank-loan commercials and reported nightly to the Mort Lindsay Band on the Merv Griffin show, along with other jazzmen Jim Hall, Art Davis, Bill Berry, and Richie Kamuca.

There is evidence of the former Giuffre-Brookmeyer association in the book of the new quintet. Brookmeyer requested that Giuffre redo *The Train and the River* for the group, and he has also made it known he would like them to play Giuffre's *Gotta Dance*. But in those pieces, there will be little effort to re-create the past directly.

As Giuffre put it, "One thing you come to realize, starting fresh and from the ground, is that it's a slow process. It takes about five or six months to jell. Bob's *Spring* is the core of where we are now. We play that, we dive into it, and there's our little lake of sound. We work from that. We don't expect to be as stylized as we were with the 3, with no drummer. We're making a new music, however, newly written for this group and the men we are working with."

Brookmeyer added, "I pushed him into the two older pieces because they were good pieces. But otherwise it's sort of like writing a play in public. It may change, alter in character, as we go along."

Among the contributing playwrights so far are pianist Friedman, who has added *Contrasts* and a scoring of his *Circle Waltz* to the book, and bassist Israels, who has contributed *Saraband*. Giuffre's new pieces include an *Old-Fashioned Stomp,* which he wrote after watching the *Bell Telephone Hour's* television documentary on Duke Ellington and rehearing some of the very early Ellington works, like *Black and Tan Fantasy.*

The new group's basic style might be described as ensemble-oriented mainstream-modern, and it therefore represents something of a stylistic retrenchment for Giuffre, who has been

involved with "free" or, as he prefers to call it, abstract music
during the last few years; music without preconceptions as to
tempo, key, or structure.

But a stylistic retrenchment is not the same as an artistic
compromise. Giuffre wants to play music, and if managers,
bookers, a&r men, and clubowners tend to shy away from Giuffre
the abstractionist, then there is another and perfectly legitimate
way for Giuffre to make music that satisfies him, gets past the
management, and reaches the audiences.

"My own temperament has swung back to a need for more
definition and strength in my playing, and using a centered-ness,
a core of 'givens,' helps me to gain that," he said.

Giuffre feels there is an army of people who want to hear
melody, by which he does not mean just ensemble parts, of
course. Improvised melody is still melody. "But we enjoy playing
ensemble," he says, "and we know we *should* enjoy it."

As always, Giuffre is aware of group textures. "One thing we
try to do in the blowing sections," he explained, "is retain the
character of the piece, with backgrounds and other things, so
that it's not just the old, pat formula of 'head,' solos, 'head.' It
broadens the palette also. We don't want just one sound, *one*
sound and stick with it—although that's supposed to be the
commercial way, they tell me."

A remark like that brings up the subject of business, and the
business of music is something that both men face up to with a
degree of realism. There are obvious advantages. Both, after all,
are jazzmen with well-known names, with a certain built-in
reputation and a certain built-in following. Further, the quintet
combines their names.

"We both know we're going to have to travel and put up with a
lot of things—and we both know what those things are," Brookmeyer said. "It is not a rehearse-today-get-immortal-tomorrow
proposition, and we know that. But we want to make music—our
music. And we know what we have to go through to do that."

Giuffre said: "We know what we can do and what we can't do
musically. Each of us has been playing long enough to be straight

about that. And between us there is no static, either personal or musical."

"You can't mind anyone else's business," Brookmeyer added.

Returning to the question of studio work, Brookmeyer speaks almost incredulously of the accomplished young jazz-oriented musicians who frequently approach him for the keys to the jingle factories and the TV studios. "It wasn't like that with me," he said. "I wanted to play trombone in order to play music. The real thrill is hearing it—standing out in front of the Basie band or the Jay McShann Band when you're young and hearing and knowing, I want to do *that!*

"Not to grow up with a love of what you do—that's really very difficult, and for some of us, impossible."

"It's pretty hard for him to function in a fake atmosphere," adds his partner quietly. (1968)

≈
≈
≈
≈

A Night at
the Five Spot

The Five Spot Cafe in New York City sits at the corner of Cooper Square and St. Mark's Place. The address may sound a bit elegant unless one knows that St. Mark's Place is an extension of Eighth Street into the East Side and that Cooper Square is the name given a couple of blocks along Third Avenue at the point where Third Avenue ceases to be called the Bowery. All of which means that the Five Spot Cafe is at the upper reaches of New York's now dwindling skid-row area.

It was once a pretty sordid stretch of sidewalk, this Bowery, but since the city removed the Third Avenue elevated train tracks and let the sunshine in a few years ago, the street has been given something of a face-lift, or at least a wash-up, and the number of alcoholics who stagger along, panhandle in, or recline on its sidewalks has declined constantly.

This current paucity of winos along the Bowery is only one indication of fundamental changes taking place in the general area of the East Side below 14th Street. There are, for example, about six prospering off-Broadway theaters there. And some of the old pawn shops and secondhand clothing stores have disappeared, to be replaced by collectors' book shops, paperback-book stores, and even a music store.

Right across the street from the Five Spot, an old greasy-spoon lunch room has been transformed into one of those chi-chi hamburger palaces, the kind where the counter is made of unfinished wood and the menu reads "beefburgers, seventy cents."

The area was once the upper end of New York's Lower East Side. But now it is being called the East Village. And that nominal aspect of its transformation is coming about because a little more than ten years ago, the artists and writers and painters moved there from across town to escape the spiraling rents and the increasingly middle-brow atmosphere of Greenwich Village on the West Side. The Five Spot owes its existence as a jazz club to these transplanted artists and the cultural interests they brought with them.

The current Five Spot Cafe is a fairly large room as New York jazz clubs go. One enters it under a neat sidewalk canopy, which reaches from the front door to the gutter. One walks through a short vestibule, with its hat-check booth to the right, and into a square, dimly lit room. The walls are painted a warm red, and the effect of contemporary decor is spoiled only by a couple of square columns in the center of the room that are encased in mirrors and look rather like surplus props from a 1936 Ruby Keeler musical.

A bar takes up almost the length of one wall on the right as one enters. To the left, at right angles to the bar, is a slightly raised platform, the club's bandstand. The wall behind the bandstand contains three archways leading to a kind of patio area where patrons are seated behind the musicians on crowded evenings.

9:30 p.m. The bar is full, although the relief group, the Roland Hanna Trio, is not due to start playing until 10 and Thelonious Monk's quartet not expected till 11. The bar looks familiar; it was moved from the original Five Spot, once a few blocks down the Bowery but now demolished for another of those grim, hazardous institutions known as modern housing.

According to the New York Fire Department's notice posted on a back wall, the club's occupancy is limited to 223. There are about 35 persons now at the tables and more arriving. It is mostly a young crowd, the kind one would expect during a holiday weekend. The red walls are covered with posters and flyers for artists' showings and gallery openings and for jazz concerts dating back a year or so—just like the walls of the old Five Spot.

Across the room, a lone man sits in a corner table. A waiter, dressed in a neat, red jacket that almost matches the paint on the walls, says politely, "Sorry, sir, this is a table for four." The waiter looks like a college student on a part-time job, and he is.

A couple come in and are escorted to a table near the bandstand. She is wearing a mink, and he doesn't look old enough to have bought it for her.

In the patio area, there is a jukebox. To judge from its listed contents the clientele's taste runs to the Marvellets, Brook Benton, Nina Simone, and (for goodness sake!) Moms Mabley. It isn't playing, however, but there is a piano LP being quietly piped through the house public address system. The recorded pianist is heaping up currently hip block chords at a great rate.

It isn't very much like the old Five Spot. It is cleaner, neater, bigger, yet younger, more prosperous, and business-like but still very comfortable and easy as clubs go.

Behind the bar, Iggy Termini, a stocky, blond man of medium height, and co-proprietor with his brother Joe, is polishing glasses when he isn't filling them or checking some small account books he keeps back there. He and the bar itself are the familiar sights in a relatively unfamiliar atmosphere.

The original Five Spot was a neighborhood bar and had been in the Termini family for more than twenty-five years. It was not particularly a Bowery bar, for there are many such that cater almost exclusively to the thick tastes and thin pockets of the skid-row clientele. When the Termini sons, Joe and Iggy, came out of the Army, the father Termini gradually turned the place over to them. They in turn found themselves getting as customers more and more of the Village expatriates who had moved into the neighborhood. These included sculptor David Smart and painter Herman Cherry, both of whom hounded the management to put in some live entertainment—specifically, some live jazz. The Terminis finally capitulated.

The honor of being among the first musicians to play jazz in the Five Spot belongs to the David Amram–George Barrow group, to

Cecil Taylor's quartet with Steve Lacy, to Randy Weston, and to Charlie Mingus. By that time, the future had clearly been decided, and this small East-Side bar was a going New York jazz club.

It was rather a relaxed scene in those early days. There was no cover or minimum charge, relatively inexpensive beer, and a lot of attentive listening. Too much listening in a sense; in order to handle the increasing crowds, Joe and Iggy had to take on some help and made the mistake of hiring a few younger jazz fans and hippies to tend the customers at the tables. As a result, something like the following scene was played with minor variations several times a night:

Customer: "Waiter, could I have another. . . ."

Waiter: "Shush, man! Don't you dig—Jackie is soloing? Wait a minute!"

It soon became house policy to interview a prospective employee carefully, and if he admitted the slightest interest in jazz, he probably wouldn't get the job.

The Terminis soon went after the then-legendary Monk for the Five Spot. They finally got him, and it was Monk's extended stays at the club that had as much as anything else to do with his rediscovery by musicians and critics as a major jazzman. The most celebrated of the several Monk Five Spot gigs was the first, in the summer of 1957, with Monk, tenor saxophonist John Coltrane, bassist Wilbur Ware, and drummer Shadow Wilson, a group and an occasion important enough to have become fabled within six months of its existence. And it was at this point that Joe Termini would acknowledge, in one of his relatively guarded moments, "Well, we're in show business now."

And after the triumphs with Monk? Well, the second most celebrated booking was surely the first New York appearance of saxophonist Ornette Coleman (who was also something of a fixture for a while), and there was a return engagement for pianist Cecil Taylor too.

Meanwhile, the Terminis had temporarily branched out with a second and larger club, the Jazz Gallery, a promising but ill-fated enterprise a few blocks up and across town.

Then, Charlie Mingus was back to close the original Five Spot before the wrecking crews moved in to demolish it.

Iggy and Joe acquired a corner cafeteria and tobacco shop a few blocks up the street, redesigned it, and applied for a license to operate a cabaret. They didn't get it at first, and for a while it was touch and go at the new Five Spot with legally allowable pianists, without drummers, and with some weekend sessions. They took in Hsio Wen Shih, the son of a Chinese diplomat, the former publisher of *The Jazz Review,* writer on jazz, and architect by profession, as a part of the organization. Finally there came the license and an official opening with the current Thelonious Monk Quartet, an engagement which continued for seven months.

9:55. A male voice, young, drifts up from somewhere in the crowd that is drinking, chatting, and waiting for the music to start: ". . . swimming in the nude and that sort of thing, but they've clamped down on it." Roland Hanna, looking like a kindly but officious banker who is about to explain an overdraft to a befuddled dowager, enters the clubroom through the kitchen, crosses the floor to the area behind the bandstand (this patio area is the section that used to be the cigar store), and chats with his bass player, Ernie Farrell.

Behind the bar, Iggy says softly to an old customer, "This is a quiet place. I mean there're no problems." (He probably has in mind the Bowery drunks who used to wander into the old place and try for a handout before Joe could grab them and usher them out, thrusting them firmly among the crowd of fans that usually filled the sidewalk outside the club.)

A few feet down the bar, a young man who has been nursing a beer for about an hour says to his companion, "How about that rent strike in Harlem?"

10:05. Hanna moves out of the patio area, through an archway, and onto the bandstand. He sits down on the piano bench and warms up by running through the middle octaves of the keyboard. Farrell is in place. Drummer Albert Heath also looks ready. They begin, and Hanna's banker's demeanor continues through the thick chords of his opening chorus of *On Green Dolphin Street.* The crowd continues to buzz and chat. But then

Hanna is interpolating a phrase from *Solar* and waggling his head, and the banker is a forgotten person.

There is applause as the pianist segues into a bass solo, and it is followed by a sudden burst of irrelevant laughter from someone enjoying a private joke at the bar. A young man in a heavy, black turtle-neck sweater and olive-drab corduroys crosses the room earnestly searching for the men's room door, snapping his fingers as he goes.

Hanna's right hand travels up the keyboard, and the number is over. Scattered applause.

Through the front windows of the patio, a city bus visibly grinds down the side street. At the canopy, a lone panhandler approaches a couple of arriving jazz fans.

The place is filling up, and the late arrivals are not so young as the earlier crowd.

10:20. Heath, in a long drum solo, has the eyes and ears of the crowd. At the end of the bar, a middle-aged woman looks on admiringly, and as if she knew exactly what was happening. She has a copy of the *New Yorker* and a half-empty martini glass on the bar in front of her. To her right, her escort looks noncommittal.

10:40. Hanna, into a fast blues, laughs about the tempo during Farrell's long solo. At the front door a waiter takes down the rope for a couple in their late thirties and for four youngsters on a double date. The older couple ends up at the bar, and the foursome gets a table.

10:50. Frankie Dunlop and Butch Warren have arrived, but so far no Monk and no Charlie Rouse. Hanna finishes his set and announces into the mike that he is turning over the bandstand to "Mister high priest, Thelonious Monk." Shades of 1947 press agentry! A waiter confides to a customer at a back table that Hanna tongue-tangled it into "the high beast of prebop" a few nights back.

Various beards, bulky sweaters, and Brooks Brothers suits begin shuffling around the room, table-hopping, men's-rooming, and telephoning, as silence follows Hanna's departure from the stand.

Nobody turns up the lights between sets, and the red walls smolder on the right and left, to the front and rear.

"Did you ever see Monk's drummer?" asks a fellow at the bar, loudly for some reason.

A woman at a back table giggles constantly.

"Yes, Germany and Japan were *allies* during the war—you mean you didn't *know* that?" says he to her at a table by one of the mirrored columns.

"Ya, but ze Americans zey. . . ." says she, a young, blond girl looking earnestly at her escort.

11:20. "Look out!" someone shouts to a waiter near the center of the room. Behind him the dark figure of Monk is rushing down an aisle between the tables, singular of purpose and unmistakable in his tweed hat and heavy tan jacket. He is quickly through the kitchen door at the back end of the club, headed for the dressing room beyond.

11:27. Monk comes through the kitchen door and moves toward the stand, a little more slowly this time but no less purposefully. He is hardly in front of the piano before he is playing *Don't Blame Me* solo. A burst of hard applause covers his opening notes, but almost immediately the room is silent. He plays with unrelenting and uncompromising emotion, and there is simply nothing to do but listen. Then a sudden, hard succession of clusters of tones in the bass. What did he *do?* Ah, anyway Monk is still growing. The second chorus begins with wild, sardonic trills, played partly with the inside fingers of the right hand while his outside fingers carry the melody notes. An unexpected alignment of ten notes ends the piece abruptly.

"Thank you. . . ." He taps the microphone and then slaps it lightly with three fingers. Is it on? "Thank you, ladies and gentlemen. . . ." A deep voice, followed by more tapping. "Thank you, ladies and gentlemen, and good evening to you. Now Butch Warren will play a bass solo for you." Monk goes hurriedly off the stand with a couple of right and left lunging movements that seem to contradict each other but which end him up on the patio behind the bandstand.

Warren plays a cleanly articulated *Softly, As in a Morning Sunrise.* As he begins, Charlie Rouse arrives and ducks quickly behind the bandstand. Monk paces erratically.

"And now Frankie Dunlop will warm up with a number."

About two minutes later, Monk and Warren are back on the bandstand, and Monk offers his brittle, out-of-tempo opening chorus to *I'm Getting Sentimental over You*. Just before the bridge, Monk leans to his left and looks under the piano, almost as if the next notes were down there somewhere. Then a break takes them into tempo for the second chorus, with tenor saxophonist Rouse walking onto the bandstand as he plays, and Monk really working behind him with a clipped distillation of the melody in support.

Halfway through the chorus, Monk gets up, leaving his instrument to undertake his swaying, shuffling dance. Half the crowd seems to be nodding knowingly about his eccentricity. But a few in the audience seem to realize that, besides giving the group a change of texture and sound by laying out, Monk is conducting. His movements are encouraging drummer Dunlop and Warren, particularly, to hear, not just the obvious beat, but the accent and space *around* the one-two-three-four, the rhythms that Monk is so interested in.

Warren solos, and Monk and Rouse leave the stand. Then Dunlop is there alone. He articulates the four eight-bar divisions of the piece very clearly on his drums for two choruses. The group reassembles. Anybody who can't dig the music will probably like the show.

Monk's well-known bass figure leads him to a fast *Epistrophy*, his theme. They give it a full performance. Monk accompanies Rouse with accents that are dazzling, although he isn't playing so demandingly of his theme. Then he signals musically for Rouse to come back for the out chorus.

Midnight. The piece ends; the set is over. Monk leads the way off the stand, and for a moment the piano sits empty, bathed in an amber spotlight.

At the door, two couples arrive and ask, "When will Monk be on again?"

"He should be back in an hour. Roland Hanna will be on in a few minutes."

"You wanna wait? You wanna go in now or come back?" (1964)

≈
≈
≈
≈

Ornette Coleman:
The Musician
and the Music

The major part of this profile-appreciation appeared in the
magazine *ASCAP Today* in late 1969, but I have here added
material from an article I had contributed to the *International Musician* eight years earlier.

In the music that is called jazz, "the one essential quality is the
right to be an individual."

The speaker is Ornette Coleman, a slight, soft-spoken, and
usually bearded Texan whose innovations in the music, although
they have remained controversial, have been influencing the
work of most young musicians for over ten years.

Nowadays one can hardly pick up a copy of a jazz magazine,
American or foreign, and not find in it some mention of Coleman.
This slight, modest, bearded young man has also attracted a great
deal of attention among musicians of other persuasions. An
intrigued Leonard Bernstein has attended his performances at
the Five Spot Cafe in New York, and an approving Virgil
Thomson has written of him in *Harper's* magazine. Theatrical
composers Marc Blitzstein and Jule Styne have also heard him
with interest. One man who has praised and encouraged is
composer Gunther Schuller, who works both the classical and

jazz sides of the fence, and who has also combined the two musics in several so-called "third stream" pieces in which both concert musicians and jazz improvisers participate in a single work.

Praise for Coleman from his own side of the fence has come from composer-pianist John Lewis, one of the first men to give him active support. Composer-arranger Gil Evans has said, "I like him. He swings, and he's got a good feeling for melody." Drummer Shelly Manne declared, "When I worked [with Ornette] . . . somehow I became more of a person in my own playing." Great enthusiasm for Coleman's work and high praise has come from jazz composer George Russell. Tenor saxophonist John Coltrane, one of the most currently influential players in jazz, has become deeply interested in Coleman's music and is Ornette's frequent companion. And praise has come from composer-bassist Charlie Mingus.

Nearly everyone admires Coleman as a composer. During the mid-fifties he was introduced to Charlie Parker by a mutual friend with a, by now, classic attitude: "Bird, this is Ornette Coleman. He plays alto. Why don't you let him come and play the session tonight? Of course, he's not *really* a player. He's a writer. His pieces are very, very good."

Coleman's work has also been very well received by writer-observers of the jazz scene. Nat Hentoff has declared, "I'm especially convinced that Ornette Coleman is making a unique and valuable contribution to tomorrow's music because of the startling power of his playing to reach the most basic emotions."

For Coleman, questions of individuality are inevitably tied up with questions of race. He once spoke with *Down Beat*'s Dan Morgenstern of "the anger I feel as a Negro, the true anger I have to confront every day in order to survive." But he added that the greatest anger came from "people who accept your abilities and yet disillusion you by not accepting you as a person."

The problem for Coleman echoes far back into his musical life to an incident he has related often. He was playing at a white dance, in Fort Worth, probably his first, when a guest approached him, shook his hand, and remarked that he was a wonderful saxophonist, but then added "you're still a nigger to me." It was at that dance, A. B. Spellman suggests in his book *Four Lives in the Bebop Business* that Coleman first began to hit on his innovative musical ideas.

There is another incident that Coleman often talked about in interviews. "I *do* play from memory of what I have felt and heard," he told Joe Goldberg. "One night I'd just gotten off work in Texas, and there was a white fellow standing on the corner by the bus stop, yodeling, and he was very sad. We started a conversation. He was a truck-driver, to New York and back, and he was married. One of his buddies had been makin' it with his old lady. He thought he was working to make his family happy, but he's away for three days, and. . . . Me and that man had nothing in common, but I can remember the whole feeling, the way he was singing, the tears in his eyes, everything about him. I can just think of that and re-create that kind of feeling. I felt sad for him, because he really had the blues."

So the white man has humanity too, a humanity that was expressed to Coleman partly in song, a song that has entered Coleman's song.

Ornette Coleman was born on March 19, 1930, in Fort Worth, Texas. His family could not afford to respond to his early interest in music by giving him lessons, so he tried to teach himself with an instruction book. "I thought the low C on my horn was the A in the book," and it was apparently from just such errors, which he later made for Bb tenor saxophone as well as for his Eb alto, that set him on his path. But the important thing, after all, is that he heard as correct certain tonal relationships which had not been used before in jazz, and that he arrived at them, not through training in contemporary concert music, but as logical extensions of the jazz tradition itself.

Coleman heard and admired the style of such older alto men as Tab Smith and Buster Smith (who was a major influence on Charlie Parker) in person and on records. He also played with a man named Red Connor, who had worked with Parker and who, according to Coleman, had absorbed Parker's musical language. Coleman himself attended Parker's recordings, and many contemporaries testify that in those days Coleman could give a classic imitation of his style. He still can.

After he had persuaded his mother to let him leave home, Ornette Coleman spent eight years on the road, first with a carnival band, in one of those tawdry tent shows that still tour the small town and rural South, and then with various rhythm-and-blues groups. "I had a lot of ideas that I just couldn't keep down. I kept hearing all kinds of possibilities and I wanted to play them."

When he tried to show a fellow musician some basics, the leader fired him for "trying to make a bebopper" out of him. He was stranded in Natchez, Mississippi; the police took one look at this strange, bearded black man and ran him out of town. And later in New Orleans, three patrons at a Negro dance, probably disturbed by his already unorthodox music, ambushed him outside the hall, beat and kicked him, and smashed his saxophone.

By 1950, he was again stranded, this time in Los Angeles, and, as he put it to Whitney Balliett, "in the next six, seven years, I traveled back and forth between Fort Worth and California, playing once in a while but doing day work mostly—stockboy, houseboy, freight elevator operator." In the blues bands, "they kept telling me I was doing this wrong, doing that wrong." The jazzmen with whom he tried informally to "sit in" in California were sometimes less articulate; often they simply ordered him off the bandstand. And sometimes, trumpeter Don Cherry remembers, rhythm sections simply froze and could not continue to play after Coleman's first few notes.

Coleman bore it, stuck to his convictions about music, and continued a study of harmony and theory from books while parked at a top floor when his department store elevator was not in demand.

Perhaps it was not entirely Coleman's music that put people off, however. His appearance was sometimes rather bizarre. Trumpeter Don Cherry remembers that when he first encountered him during an L.A. summer, Ornette was wearing a huge overcoat that hung well below his knees and was several sizes too big for him, which he kept on indoors and out. "He scared me,"

Cherry adds frankly. (Today, Ornette is a conservative dresser and a neat one, his only eccentricity being an unusual collection of hats, among which a high coachman's topper is a current favorite.)

What exactly had Coleman done that was proving so unorthodox to most, so disturbing to some, and so exciting to a very few, Don Cherry included? "I think you have to hear something new to play something new," he says. He had begun to intone his melodies in a highly personal manner, so much so that many players believed he could not play in tune (some still do!). In this he was simply extending the jazz tradition, however, expanding on the idea of a personal sound, of the vocally inflected tones and blues notes that jazz musicians have always used. "You can play sharp in tune and flat in tune," he explains, adding that a D played in a passage representing sadness should not sound like a joyous D. In short, Coleman has discovered the concept of microtones for jazz.

Further, Coleman's improvised melodies do not follow the traditional formal melodic or harmonic variational patterns of previous jazz improvising. They move more freely on their own, within the key of a theme, or, if inspiration dictates, straying momentarily out of it. In other words, Coleman, by passing through modality, has discovered an approach to atonality for jazz.

More important, Coleman's music involves a fresh approach to jazz rhythm, new ways of phrasing and accentuation, even a gradual variety of tempos within a performance. Louis Armstrong's innovations sprang from a rhythmic difference. So did Charlie Parker's. So do Coleman's. "My music doesn't have any real time, no metric time," he's said. "It has time, but not in the sense that you can time it. It's more like breathing, a natural, freer time."

These questions of rhythm and time enter into Coleman's compositions as well. His *Una Muy Bonita* alternates time signatures of 15/8 and 4/4, ending in 7/8. And *Congeniality* involves a duality of speeds, back and forth, in the theme statement, and polymetric displacements in his solo that defy notation, even by the loose standards that one automatically assumes when jazz is transcribed in European form. "I like to turn phrases around on a different beat," he remarks.

The rhythmic unity of Coleman's groups is sometimes quite remarkable. They can go through whole programs with no tempo signals, or even without very obvious down-beats at the beginnings of pieces. And Coleman also asks his drummers to think in terms of participating musical phrasing rather than of keeping time and of accompaniments. I once heard him in the middle of a highly informal session make the very formal announcement, "I wish it were possible to maintain the swing without making an obvious beat. I confess I don't know how to do it." And he has also said that he wishes that rhythmic patterns could be as natural and as free as breathing.

The really crucial point in his work, however, is revealed in his ready acknowledgment that "music is for our feelings." He may try out a new composition with this sort of instruction to his men: "This time, just play the melody for the *emotion*. Just play it all as quarter notes for the emotion." And then quickly, at the end of a couple of tries, "OK—*now* let's try it a little faster and watch the phrasing." Clearly, such music has no contrivance but, like all good music, is born of an emotional and expressive need. And, as his listeners seem to know immediately, it is not Coleman's subjective need, but one that many men share with him.

Many observers who are still not converted to Coleman the player, are full of praises for his pieces. "Those 'heads' are so beautiful," says one famous jazzman, adding with a shrug, "Then it's Cape Kennedy!" Indeed, it was his composing that first brought Ornette Coleman recognition. Bassist Red Mitchell heard him, liked his writing and introduced him to Lester Koenig of Contemporary Records in Hollywood. Coleman, unable to present his works on piano, got out his alto and performed *a capella*. Koenig wanted the pieces, and Coleman too, and made some records. "In my own playing and writing," Ornette says, "I'm at a loss for a category as far as the relative positions of player and composer are concerned. . . . I've written lots of music and thought about it as writing to have something to play."

Coleman was on his way. But where to? Percy Heath of the Modern Jazz Quartet was impressed. So was the group's composer-pianist John Lewis, who persuaded Nesuhi Ertegun of Atlantic Records to record Coleman. Coleman came to New York with a quartet for an engagement at the Five Spot in the Fall of 1959. He was called a genuine innovator, a genius, a promising musician ("a gang of potential," said Thelonious Monk), and a fake. Leonard Bernstein was enthralled; Kenneth Tynan appalled ("They've gone too far!"). Jimmy Giuffre declared that he could teach Coleman nothing about the saxophone because the younger man knew it all. Another musician declared Coleman's problem was that he didn't know his horn. He began to influence many including at least one of his elders: John Coltrane, probably the most advanced saxophonist on the scene until Coleman arrived.

Ornette Coleman does not necessarily improvise within the implied harmonic framework of a composition as jazzmen have regularly done for over forty years. "If I am going to run the chords, for me, I might as well write out my solo ahead of time." What is the relationship of variations to theme if one does not use the chord changes? George Russell has put it this way, "Ornette seems to depend mostly on the over-all tonality of the song as a point of departure for melody. By this I don't mean the key the music might be in . . . I mean that the melody and the chords of his compositions have an over-all sound which Ornette seems to use as a point of departure. This approach liberates the improviser to sing his own song really, without having to meet the deadline of any particular chord . . ." The musical pitch of a theme, fragmentations of its melody, implied scales and harmonics, its rhythms, and its emotion are all legitimate subjects for exploration by the improviser.

Obviously Coleman's procedures have some striking analogues to the practices in twelve-tone music. It was precisely this analogue which led Gunther Schuller to compose *Abstraction* for Coleman. *Abstraction* is an atonal, serial piece in mirror form, with Ornette Coleman freely improvising against written parts for an augmented string quartet. Schuller's comments on Coleman are instructive: "Perhaps the most outstanding element in Ornette's musical conception is an utter and complete freedom . . . Despite this—or more accurately, *because* of this—his playing has a deep inner logic, based on subtleties of reaction, subtleties of timing and color that are, I think, quite new to jazz. At least they have never appeared in so pure and direct a form."

Coleman's musical life since he first came to New York has been one of constant activity, but along very personal lines. He quit all night-club and concert appearances at one point, and emerged two years later playing violin and trumpet as well as alto saxophone. He produced his own concert at Town Hall, but was invited to a summer "promenade" performance at Lincoln Center. He wrote the sound track music for a highly provocative film (Conrad Rooks' *Chapaqua*) and the result was so assertive that it overpowered the visuals and had to be replaced. He takes nightclub engagements only intermittently, when he wants to or when he needs the income. "Six hours a night, six nights a week. Sometimes I go to the club and can't understand what I feel. . . . 'How will I make it through the night?' I say to myself. I'd like to play a couple of nights a week is all. I'd have more to say."

He undertook a tour of England and faced with union exchange restrictions on dance and jazz musicians, he composed a woodwind quartet to be a part of his program, *Forms and Sounds,* which has since been recorded on both sides of the Atlantic. He rejects enticing recording contracts to sign with smaller record companies because he likes the people he will be working with.

In the past couple of years, Ornette has invited his son Denny, now age 12, to play some jobs with him on drums. Ornette explains that when Denny was six there was a hurried, cross-country phone call about a suitable present.

"What would you like for your birthday?"

"Dad, you know I saw a gun on TV called a cannon or something like that. I would like to have that."

"Well I don't know if I can find it here. I'll try. If I can't find it, how would you like a set of drums, in case I don't find the gun?"

"Dad, you can forget about the gun, send the drums air mail express!"

Four years later, Coleman had decided to use Denny on a record date, and the test of his son's musicianship was not so much the drum technique he had acquired by that time, but that he played what he did know with feeling, and didn't try for anything he didn't feel.

"I'd rather take my chances and truly play," Ornette Coleman once said, "and see if a person really liked it—than try to figure out something that people are likely to like." And as a black American who is also musical innovator, he is perhaps qualified to add that, "the menace in America is that everyone—black or white—is enslaved in history. This enslavement tends to make you remember history more than to think of what you could do if it were nothing but history." (1962; 1969)

≈
≈
≈
≈

Three Men on a Bass

The 1960s produced several outstanding young bass players. It was as if Charlie Mingus had released the instrument in the 1950s and those who followed found their ways of exploring its new role. Here are interviews with three of them—somehow I missed interviewing Charlie Haden for print. Incidentally, within two weeks after the first of these appeared, Scott LaFaro opened at the Village Vanguard with Ornette Coleman.

1. Scott LaFaro, by Way of Introduction

"It's quite a wonderful thing to work with the Bill Evans trio," said bassist Scott LaFaro.

"We are really just beginning to find our way. You won't hear much of that on our first record together, except a little on *Blue in Green* where no one was playing time as such. Bill was improvising lines, I was playing musical phrases behind him, and Paul Motian played in free rhythmic drum phrases."

LaFaro is dissatisfied with a great deal of what he hears in jazz, but what he says about it isn't mere carping. He thinks he knows what to do about it, at least in his own playing. "My ideas are so different from what is generally acceptable nowadays that I sometimes wonder if I am a jazz musician. I remember that Bill and I used to reassure each other some nights kiddingly that we really were jazz musicians. I have such respect for so many modern classical composers, and I learn so much from them.

Things are so contrived nowadays in jazz, and harmonically it has been so saccharine since Bird."

Charlie Parker was already dead before Scott LaFaro was aware of him, even on records. In fact Scott LaFaro was not really much aware of jazz at all until 1955.

He was born in 1936 in Newark, New Jersey, but his family moved to Geneva, New York, when he was five. "There was always the countryside. I miss it now. I am not a city man. Maybe that is why Miles Davis touches me so deeply. He grew up near the countryside too, I believe. I hear that in his playing anyway. I've never been through that 'blues' thing either."

LaFaro started on clarinet at fourteen and studied music in high school. He took up bass on a kind of dare. "My father played violin with a small 'society' trio in town. I didn't know what I wanted to do when I had finished school, and my father said—half-joking, I think—that if I learned bass, I could play with them. When I did, I knew that I wanted to be a musician. It's strange: playing clarinet and sax didn't do it, but when I started on bass, I knew it was music." He went to Ithaca Conservatory and then to Syracuse; it was there, through fellow students, that he began to listen to jazz. He got a job in Syracuse at a place called the Embassy Club. "The leader was a drummer who played sort of like Sidney Catlett and Kenny Clarke. He formed my ideas of what jazz was about. He, and the juke box in the place—it had Miles Davis records. And I first heard Percy Heath and Paul Chambers on that juke box. They taught me my first jazz bass lessons. There was also a Lee Konitz record with Stan Kenton called *Prologue*."

In late 1955, LaFaro joined Buddy Morrow's band. "We toured all over the country until I left the band in Los Angeles in September 1956. I didn't hear any jazz or improve at all during that whole time." But a few weeks after he left Morrow, he joined a Chet Baker group that included Bobby Timmons and Lawrence Marable. "I found out so much from Lawrence, a lot of it just from playing with him. I have trouble with getting *with* people rhythmically and I learned a lot about it from him. I learned more about rhythm when I played with Monk last fall; a great experience. With Monk, rhythmically, it's just *there*, always."

LaFaro remembers two other important experiences in California. The first was hearing Ray Brown, whose swing and perfection in his style impressed him. The other came when he lived for almost a year in the mountain-top house of Herb Geller and his late wife, Lorraine. "I practiced and listened to records. I had—I still have—a feeling that if I don't practice I will never be able to play. And Herb had all the jazz records; I heard a lot of music, many people for the first time, on his records."

In September 1958 LaFaro played with Sonny Rollins in San Francisco, and later he worked with the same rhythm section behind Harold Land. "I think horn players and pianists have probably influenced me the most, Miles Davis, Coltrane, Bill Evans, and Sonny perhaps deepest of all. Sonny is technically good, harmonically imaginative, and really creative. He uses all he knows to make finished music when he improvises.

"I found out playing with Bill that I have a deep respect for harmony, melodic patterns, and form. I think a lot more imaginative work could be done within them than most people are doing, but I can't abandon them. That's why I don't think I could play with Ornette Coleman. I used to in California; we would go looking all over town for some place to play. I respect the way he overrides forms. It's all right for him, but I don't think I could do it myself.

"Bill gives the bass harmonic freedom because of the way he voices, and he is practically the only pianist who does. It's because of his classical studies. Many drummers know too little rhythmically, and many pianists know too little harmonically. In the trio we were each contributing something and really improvising *together*, each playing melodic and rhythmic phrases. The harmony would be improvised; we would often begin only with something thematic and not a chord sequence.

"I don't like to look back, because the whole point in jazz is doing it *now*. (I don't even like any of my records except maybe the first one I did with Pat Moran on Audio Fidelity.) There are too many things to learn and too many things you can do, to keep doing the same things over and over. My main problem now is to get that instrument under my fingers so I can play more music." (1960)

II. Steve Swallow

"I'd rather play with either Jimmy McPartland or Bud Freeman or with the Jimmy Giuffre Trio than play bebop."

This provocative statement comes from Steve Swallow, one of the best of a remarkable group of young bass players who have participated in the most recent developments in jazz.

"New thing" music (to use that graceless and even ambiguous but still necessary term) can now boast three or four outstanding reed men and three or four accomplished trumpeters at best. But the good bassists who have been involved in it! . . . Charlie Haden, Jimmy Garrison, the late Scott LaFaro, Ron Carter, Gary Peacock, David Izenzon, Chuck Israels, Swallow—not to mention a venerable progenitor like Charlie Mingus or a recent apprentice like Barre Phillips.

Swallow is not alone among younger players in having an articulate sense of jazz history and his own relationship to it. He elaborated:

"Orthodox modern jazz is difficult for me because there are so many things that are given, so many inflexible idiomatic requirements of exactly what each player is supposed to do in the music. And a man can make the music sound wrong if he doesn't meet those requirements.

"The Dixieland players know that they are part of history, and they have less concern with the sanctity of their idiom. The style is refined, but it always sounds stylized, sounds like Dixieland, in a variety of formats and instrumentations. In that sense, it is flexible.

"The basic Dixieland instruments have certain ensemble functions, but beyond that a player is free to find his own way. Drummers don't play the flow of the rhythm, for example, but its demarcation. George Wettling is superb at this. And the ensemble deals with a varied texture. Therefore, I feel free to find a sixth voice.

"Because I play with such a variety of groups, some people assume I play in a variety of styles, but I don't. Actually I'm not sure there was ever an exact place in Dixieland for the bass, and some groups, I think, sound better without one.

"And today the swing-period players can allow the same sort of freedom to a bass player in their style.

"Bud Freeman, whom I love to play with, long ago found a place for his tenor in the Dixieland ensemble. Anyway, the best things in Bud's style are bigger than category, not the things that make him an ensemble player or make him a swing-period soloist.

"By now, bebop is historical too, but many of the players don't know it yet. And beboppers still want things done only along well-established lines. Of course, some players thought of as modernists are too mature to need absolute orthodoxy. I never assume with Art Farmer that he wants me to play any way other than the way I play."

Swallow has worked, within the same month, for George Russell and Benny Goodman. And as of this writing, he is simultaneously bassist with the Jimmy Giuffre Three, the new Art Farmer-Jim Hall Quartet, and the Marian McPartland Trio. He also is likely to respond positively to any calls from Bud Freeman or Al Cohn and Zoot Sims if he can sandwich in the gig. Obviously such a multiple musical life cannot continue for him, for he simply will not have the time.

Swallow is a native New Yorker, born there in 1940 and raised just across the river in Fair Lawn, N.J. His father is an electrical engineer by profession, but as a part-time musician he worked his way through college with an alto saxophone and trombone and later continued his interest in the jazz of his own day.

Steve was a trumpet player when he was a youngster, and he wanted to play jazz.

"My father played me records by Jelly Roll Morton and Bix Beiderbecke, and I liked them," he said. "Actually, I was a rotten trumpet player. In junior high school I wanted to jam with some fellows who were playing jazz, so I got a book called 50 *Hot Licks for Trumpet* by Ziggy Elman. I learned them all right away, in all the keys, and went off to the session. I could make a solo just by stringing together my Ziggy Elman licks. The other players tolerated me.

"I can't say I ever actually switched to bass—it was just that there was always a need for a bass player, and I was a rotten trumpet player. From the beginning I seemed to get the right notes on bass, but I can't say that my time was too good then."

Swallow was sent to prep school, and there he met Ian Underwood, an exceptionally talented flutist and reed player. They had what Swallow calls "real amateurs' zeal" and used to get up early to play together before school breakfast.

The association with Underwood continued at Yale University, where the bassist became a member of the local Dixieland outfit, the Bullpups.

"They needed a bass player, and I needed the money and enjoyed the trips we made," he recalled. "That was about all there was to it really. At that point I wasn't even the zealot I had been in prep school, but I realize, looking back, what important lessons I was learning.

"The bass player that I admired most on records then was Percy Heath, but there were excellent swing-period musicians at Yale functions. I got to work with Buddy Tate, Buck Clayton, Rex Stewart, Dickie Wells. I learned especially from Dickie—he is such a clear and precise player, you know. I would often follow him and simply play his solos back note for note. He didn't seem to mind, and it was superb training for me."

The knowledge that music held more for him than an outlet for amateur's zeal or a college student's part-time job came to Swallow abruptly and fatalistically. In the fall of 1959, pianist Ran Blake, then himself a student, held his second jazz festival at the small Bard College in New York state. Blake invited one of his favorite pianists, Paul Bley, to participate, and Bley got Paul Cohen, then a good drummer and now a young Pennsylvania lawyer. Cohen recommended Swallow.

"I had no idea how Paul Bley played," Swallow said, "and I

hurried around trying to find one of his records. They were out of stock every place I went. The afternoon of the concert, we held one rehearsal. I was deeply impressed with Paul's music but seemed to get nowhere playing it. That evening on the program we followed the Gospel singing of Prof. Alex Bradford, which of course the audience loved. When we started to play, my back was against the wall, and I found that I was managing to produce a real affinity with Paul's music. It was a very strong experience, the whole thing. I was physically sick afterward, but I knew then that music was going to be my life.

"I left Yale before midterm exams. I went to New York, and I just called Paul Bley, asking if he needed a bass player."

Bley said that he did. It was rather a lean time for them, but they had a job at Copa City with blues singer Big Miller, and Swallow had the Dixieland and mainstream contacts he had made at Yale, particularly Jimmy McPartland and Freeman.

"Paul set me the most important challenges," Swallow said. "He set all the fast tunes slightly faster than I could play and all the ballads slightly slower. In four months he whipped me into shape. I had gotten through the instrument, I had learned the bass. He felt that the instrument itself simply has to be gotten through. And I played it the same afterward, until Jimmy Giuffre got hold of me."

Swallow had arrived in New York in the winter of 1959, in time for Ornette Coleman's first Five Spot engagement with Don Cherry, Charlie Haden, and Billy Higgins in his quartet. Swallow was quickly introduced to Coleman's music by Bley, in whose group Coleman had played in California. So, besides the workouts with Bley and the Dixieland jobs, there was frequent attendance at the Five Spot.

In the summer of 1960, Swallow went with Ian Underwood on a European trip that included a long stretch in Germany.

"We played nothing but Monk tunes and Ornette tunes," he said. "Learning the Monk repertory is the only meaningful training in composition I have had, by the way, except for some brief study at Yale with Donald Martino, an ex-jazzman who is now a serial composer. That and knowing Carla Bley's music."

Back in New York there were frequent weekend sessions at the Phase 2 coffee house. These often included, besides Paul Bley and his wife Carla, trumpeter Don Ellis and pianist Jaki Byard.

It was at these Phase 2 sessions that the players began to change tempo and key, and leave chord structures altogether, to keep the young, amateur beboppers out of the jamming. Shades of Gillespie and Monk at Minton's! The effort of the Phase 2 players was not to disparage Gillespie and Parker or the achievements of bop. Rather, they wanted to acknowledge that the musicians of their own generation had to stop walking in Bird and Dizzy's shadows—after nearly twenty years of modern jazz—and find their own way.

Paul Bley had already joined Giuffre by the time Swallow had got back from Europe, and Swallow went with Bud Freeman. But when Giuffre's regular bassist was caught in a traffic jam, Swallow made a rehearsal. He soon found himself having to choose between Bud Freeman and Giuffre, and he says, "It was a hard choice."

"At first the Giuffre book was full of simple song forms," he said, "but gradually Jimmy's ideas began to emerge, and they made sense to me. He has been a big influence, chiefly by making it clear that he would not accept common practice—although, of course, he does not want to avoid it just to be avoiding it.

"We approach a piece phrase by phrase rather than setting a tempo first and keeping it. All of my own playing is related to a tempo, but when the Giuffre trio played that extended job at the Take 3 coffee house last spring, we really managed to break through. Tempo still exists in our music but in a way that permeates—if that's the word. I still play in reference to it, not because the tempo makes the music swing—tempo doesn't—but because a consistent proportioning of the time establishes relationships. To put it another way, each musical phrase takes its own shape, and it may deny the time and the tempo.

"These things have become so fundamental to us that Jimmy didn't realize that on *Spasmodic* and *Divided Man* on our *Free Fall* LP, there are stretches in strict tempo. And of course, that's good, because it means he was thinking in terms of musical phrases."

Swallow finds a further challenge in the work of players past and present, not all of them bass players. He will mention Pete LaRoca, Marian McPartland's drummer, as having "the ideal solution for drums." And he found Art Tatum's virtuosity a fundamental personal incentive for a while.

But on his own instrument "if someone says that I remind him of Charlie Haden, I have to admit that I remind myself of Charlie Haden. I have decided to let my sources rise to the top and be obvious because that is the best way to assimilate sources. Charlie's influence is clear to me, but the others are less clear because they aren't directly related to the bass. But I know that I listen to Django Reinhardt's records for instruction as well as for pleasure. I think you can hear the effect of his sound in my playing, but I am also fascinated by the way he used triads. He used them in part to organize tonality, and I am not interested in that aspect of it, of course."

Swallow says that he used to be able to play faster than he does now, but he is not talking about rapid tempos, as will be seen. The admission brought him to some remarks on fellow bassist Gary Peacock, who, he says, has been a very big influence.

"I tried for the concentration, the density, of his playing, and I just couldn't do it," Swallow remarked. "If I hadn't been exposed as strongly to the style through knowing him and hearing him, I could have spent a long time trying to play that way and got nowhere. I am very thankful there are important differences between me and such an extraordinary player as Gary.

"His concern with velocity is fundamental to what he has to say. With Bill Evans, he will inject, in a single moment—even between Bill's rapid phrases—a finished idea. I need half a chorus to develop an idea most of the time. That's why I say I play more slowly now."

The admiration for Peacock is mutual, and the latter especially credits Swallow with exploring the range of tone and sound beyond that supposed to be legitimately possible on the bass.

A lot is said about the new jazz as a "free" music, but Swallow declared, "The word freedom is really meaningless to me—musically I don't even consider it. I am a member of an ensemble, and most of what I do is in reference to the other music being made on the bandstand." (1963)

III. Gary Peacock: The Beauties of Intuition

As recently as a year ago, few persons would have numbered Gary Peacock among the more proficient young bassists in jazz. Today there are few who would not.

Scott LaFaro's unexpected death was a loss in several senses, not the least of which was regarding his contribution to development of the future role of the bass in jazz. Peacock's recent spurt of development is a gain for much the same reason. His playing has come far indeed from that heard on a Bud Shank record released about two years ago. He is sure, incidentally, that "although you may have an idea of where you are in your work, a record will show you where you really are—you and anyone else who hears it."

Truly contemporary bass playing probably can be said to begin with Charlie Mingus—and perhaps Wilbur Ware and Red Mitchell. The most provocative young bassists do not play a quarter-note walk, 1-2-3-4/1-2-3-4—they do not play "time"—and they do not necessarily play a harmonic part. And the horn players know that they do not need them to keep time or provide changes, harmonic reminders. The newer bassists do not merely "accompany" others and take an occasional solo but participate more directly in the music.

In their various ways, truly contemporary bass players are melodists—percussive melodists, lyric melodists, or in LaFaro's case and Peacock's, virtuoso melodists. Furthermore, like the young horn men, they explore their instruments even beyond what is supposedly their legitimate range and function.

The Peacock who suddenly burst through on recordings with Clare Fischer and with Don Ellis and Paul Bley is a Peacock who is learning to make his way in the most advanced groups and among the most challenging young players in jazz.

He was born in Burley, Idaho, in 1935 and grew up there and in Washington state and Oregon. He studied piano for about six months when he was thirteen, and in junior high and high school he was a drummer in student bands. He heard a great deal of so-called western-swing music, which is very popular in the Northwest.

One of his earliest conscious exposures to jazz came when he was sixteen. "A trumpeter I knew played me some of those early records by Bird and Dizzy—*Salt Peanuts* and those things," he said. "I was really amazed, and I asked him who the second alto player was! I could hardly believe him when he answered there was only one."

Peacock left home at seventeen and spent a year in Los Angeles, studying vibraharp for several months at Westlake College. From 1954 to 1956, he was in the Army, stationed in Germany. It was then that his interest in music really began to take shape. He found himself the leader of a group in which he played drums or piano, and occasionally vibes. But then his bass player left, and Peacock picked up the instrument.

Suddenly things were different: "My hands went down right almost from the beginning. The instrument seemed to fall under my fingers. I never really tried to learn bass—it was as if I just started playing it."

After the service, he went back to Los Angeles, went on the road with Terry Gibbs, and subsequently worked with (as he puts it) "every group in the area except Red Norvo's—Harold Land, Art Pepper, Dexter Gordon, Bud Shank. . . ." In the course of it, his whole approach to the bass changed from the old one to the new.

"I don't know exactly when it happened," Peacock said. "It must have been gradual. Before I realized it, I was there."

It definitely happened later than one evening he remembers when he chanced to end up on the same bandstand with Ornette

Coleman. ("When he started to blow, I just froze; I couldn't play.") But it happened.

Then he no longer had any trouble with groups that improvised freely and no longer had to work only with players who go through every piece cyclically and harmonically, ever repeating the basic structure.

"Only for about six months in 1959 did I put in any extra time practicing and exploring my instrument. I had begun to hear things I couldn't execute properly and had to find a way to play them. The rest of the time I learned on the job, just by playing and listening. I grew quite unsatisfied with playing the time. It became redundant, a strait jacket. Along with several other people, I found that if a tempo is simply allowed to exist, you don't need to play it—it's even redundant to play it.

"But it is a personal thing. If it's right for a given player to play time, okay. But if it isn't, it won't feel right to him or sound right to his listeners."

This latter observation reflects an attitude that several of the young players seem to have: an awareness that what is right for them to play or to search for is not necessarily right for everyone. Peacock, for instance, talks readily of his great admiration for Al Cohn and Zoot Sims and for the Modern Jazz Quartet. But the MJQ holds still another lesson for him, for theirs is truly a group music, and future jazz will be truly group music.

"You know the title of that LP of Ornette Coleman's," he asked, *"This Is Our Music?* I think that tells the story. I think, in the future, we will hear a group music by equal participants. Each member is going to have to be a leader to some extent.

"It will have to be that way. In my own experience, we work now with a kind of psychic communication. We just know when a drummer has finished a phrase and when he has finished a solo. We know when a horn player has finished developing his ideas.

"Perhaps this is only the first stage, and we will have different ideas later on. Perhaps we will have more conscious reasons for what we do, but for now, things are evolving this intuitive way."

Peacock has thought about the dangers, delusions, and contradictions in a freer music, however.

"The pitfall in the concept of freedom is that *total* musical freedom invites chaos," he said. "And I think we should also remember that freedom isn't necessarily valid unless it produces something. Also, so-called self-expression is not necessarily musical or artistic. I think we should keep those things in mind when we play. And most of all, we have to know when to stop. We must know when we have said it all, or when it isn't happening.

"But for myself at this stage, I know that generally my best playing comes when I don't think too consciously about what I'm doing, and frankly that doesn't bother me too much. You can be specific about logical causes and about emotional causes, but about intuition there are no reasons. You just do what the intuition says. Incidentally, I think Ornette Coleman plays by intuition, too, not just feeling, as some people say. Anyway, I think that now we just have to play out the intuitions and see what happens. After all, if you go so far wrong, you'll eventually get back to what's right. And the only way to find out about some of the things we're working on is just plunge in and do them."

About the attitude that it is up to each player to explore the possibilities of his instrument, Peacock said, "Musicians tend not to regard their instruments as a whole. They take only a section of what can be done. The bass has two worlds. At the bottom, it affects everyone, especially in rhythm. At the top, you are into the piano's range and are more of a horn. There you can't upset the time and rhythm.

"The thing to do is ask, 'What can I do with texture? Dynamics? Timbre? What can I do with one note? What can I do with the whole range? And can I extend it?' These ideas are reaching a lot of players, and particularly bass players—especially, I should name Steve Swallow in this. They are asking these questions, and asking how the answers affect the group music. But a player should work these things out at practice, not on the job. A job is a place to play, not experiment.

"Take Ornette Coleman. He takes a note, bends it, twists it, even spits it out. It's beautiful; it gives the instrument a new life. Jimmy Giuffre is doing the same sort of thing with the clarinet."

Peacock has substituted for Swallow in Giuffre's current trio on a couple of occasions and considers the experience among the most musically exciting he has had. "Jimmy and Paul [Bley] don't need anyone keeping time—in fact, it would get in their way. But playing with them is very exacting. They have really broken through recently. Their new Columbia record tells the story."

If Bley is not working with Giuffre, he and Gary Peacock can probably be found together. They worked recently at a Sunday session at New York City's Five Spot, with trumpeter Don Cherry and drummer Pete LaRoca, after which Bley moved over to the Take 3 coffee house to take his place with Giuffre and Swallow. Peacock and Bley also have made a television appearance on New York's educational Channel 13, and Peacock recently played a weekend with tenorist Archie Shepp and trumpeter Bill Dixon. But players of their persuasion don't get much of the work yet.

Nevertheless, it is very important to Peacock to be in New York now. "It only took me one day here to know that this is the place," he said. "In Los Angeles, the first thing you think of doing is relaxing. In New York, we play things and work things out— things that need to be worked out. This is the place—the music, the quality of the music, and the interest in it." (1963)

≈
≈
≈
≈ Pharoah's Tale

Pharoah Sanders was born in 1940, and, somewhat surprisingly, that is young enough so that among his earliest musical idols were John Coltrane, Eric Dolphy and Ornette Coleman.

Sanders was born in Little Rock, Arkansas, in 1940, and although his given name has sometimes been confused in print, it is Pharoah.

"My grandfather was a school teacher; he taught music and mathematics. My mother and her sisters used to sing in clubs and teach piano. For myself, I started playing drums in the high school band. Then I played tuba and baritone horn, clarinet and flute. In 1959, I started playing tenor saxophone, still in the school band," he says.

"At the same time I was listening to Jimmy Cannon, my band teacher, who played jazz. Richard Boone, the Count Basie trombone player—he's from Little Rock too. He would sometimes sit in with the concert band.

"In my own playing I was more or less into rhythm and blues. I liked Earl Bostic a lot."

At the same time, Sanders had become interested in art and wanted to be any kind of artist, painter or commercial artist, just to do art work.

"When I finished high school in 1959, I was supposed to take either a music or an art scholarship. I didn't want to stay in Little Rock so I left for the West Coast. I went to Oakland Junior College for a couple of years, and then moved over to San Francisco. I majored in art. But I was getting some rock 'n' roll gigs playing tenor. I also played alto, flute, clarinet, and baritone whenever possible, but I had fallen in love with the tenor.

"On those blues jobs, I played mostly by ear, but I had some private lessons in Oakland which taught me about harmonics.

"By this time I was listening to Sonny Rollins, who was a big influence at first; John Coltrane, who was a later big influence; and Ornette Coleman, Eric Dolphy, Booker Ervin, Hank Mobley and Horace Silver's group. I loved Benny Golson on *Moanin'* with Art Blakey.

"When I heard Coltrane's *Blue Train* LP, I really didn't know what he was doing. I had never heard anybody play tenor like that before, with that range. Most of the guys played just in the middle register.

"When I first heard Ornette's music I liked it—*really*, it was something! It seemed so natural, as if he weren't limiting himself, as if he wanted to let himself just go to the music. I remember talking to Ornette in 'Frisco. I don't know whether he remembers me from then.

"By that time I had begun to try to play that way myself. Sonny Simmons, and a lot of people I was playing with in Oakland at the time, were playing a lot freer. They had been playing that way before I came to California. They heard me and invited me to come down and play sometime. I was kind of skeptical about it because up to that point all I had been playing was rhythm and blues. What they played had a good feeling, but I was wondering, what are they doing? Were they crazy? But it felt good. So, I just fell in with it too," he said.

"Later, I started playing jazz more conventionally and studying the basics—getting my chords and my scales."

The mention of the basics sets Sanders to reflecting. "Actually I have never had a jazz gig of my own long enough to see what I can really do on conventional tunes. I would like to get one for at least six nights a week so I could try to express myself fully 'inside' and see both sides of it. I still take different kinds of jobs. I play rock 'n' roll for dances, usually in Brooklyn. It's a big help financially, and my profession is music, so it's my business to be able to play any kind of music."

Returning to his days in the Bay Area, Sanders remembers, "Once when John Coltrane came out to San Francisco, he was asking around about mouthpieces. So I told him that I had a bunch of mouthpieces, and that he could try them. I also said I would take him around to the different places in town if he wanted to try some more. I never thought he'd take me up on it, of course—he was a giant to me then. But he showed up one morning, saying, 'Are you ready, man?' I was really shook up! At the time, my own horn was in the repair shop and he offered to pay the bill so I could get it out. All day long we went around to pawn shops and more pawn shops, trying out different mouthpieces."

Sanders arrived in New York in 1962. He had driven across the country with a couple of musician friends in a car which constantly broke down, but somehow they made it. He had absolutely no money. "I slept in the subway—the police didn't bother me—or in tenement hallways under the stairs. And I pawned my instrument," he recalls.

"I think my first gig in New York was one in a coffee house in the Village called the Speakeasy, with C Sharp and Billy Higgins . . . We made $8 a night. The job lasted almost a year. I used to live on wheat germ, peanut butter and bread—I still carry a jar of wheat germ in my instrument case. It's good food.

"I began seeing a lot of Billy Higgins. We would play together, talk, eat; might be together all day long. If he wasn't playing on his drums he would play on the table, or glasses with spoons or whatever else he found.

"I took some other jobs. Once I was a combination cook, waiter and counter-man, and all I got was what I ate. Then I caught on that I should be paid, and I split. I was trying to survive, and it is harder to survive in New York than in Oakland or San Francisco. If I wasn't thinking about trying to survive, I was thinking about music. I didn't think much about commercial art by this time.

"A friend of mine who lived in Brooklyn, someone I had known in San Francisco, invited me to stay at his place. That's where I met Don Cherry, and we began rehearsing and playing together.

We got one job at Pratt Institute in Brooklyn. There was an exhibition of student art work and they wanted some of our kind of music along with it. I had to get my horn out of hock for that one, and the other guys in the group helped me by putting up the money.

"When I play, I try to adjust myself to the group, and I don't think much about whether the music is conventional or not. If the others go 'outside,' play 'free,' I go out there too. If I tried to play too differently from the rest of the group, it seems to me I would be taking the other musicians' energy away from them. I still want to play my own way. But I wouldn't want to play with anybody that I couldn't please with the way I play.

"Anyway, Don Cherry seemed to like what I was doing. I was getting different sounds out of the horn then. For my part, I was just trying to express myself. Whatever came out of the instrument just came out, as if I had no choice.

"Naturally, you have elements of music and musical skills to work with, but once you've got those down, I think you should go after feelings. If you try to be too intellectual about it, the music becomes too mechanical. It seems that for me, the more I play 'inside,' inside the chords and the tune, the more I want to play 'outside,' and free. But also, the more I play 'outside' the more I want to play 'inside' too. I'm trying to get a balance in my music. A lot of cats play 'out' to start with. But if I, myself, start off playing 'inside' and then let the spirit take over, wherever it goes, it seems better to me.

"I'm not trying to do something that is over somebody's head. My aim is to *give* people something. When I give them something they can give me something, the energy to continue."

The first time Sanders played with John Coltrane was at the Half Note in New York. "We had become pretty close¹ and had been talking a lot. He would call me and we would talk about religion and about life. He was also concerned about what he wanted to do next in his music, about where he was headed.

"We got pretty close and sometimes he would say, 'Come on down and play something with me tonight,' almost as though we were continuing the conversation. So I would just come down and start playing.

"By that time, I thought of him not just as a great musician but also as a wise man. But I was still a little self-conscious and wasn't sure what to do with him musically. I thought maybe I was playing too long, and on some numbers, I wouldn't play at all. And sometimes I would start to pack up my horn. But he would tell me not to. Anyway, I'd never play as long as he did because, you know, he might play for an hour on one tune."

Sanders says he was never asked officially to become a member of Coltrane's group. He would just play with Coltrane from time to time, whenever he was asked to. "Then later, he might say, 'I have a job down in Washington for a week. How about coming on down with me?' Or, he'd say he had a record date coming up and would I like to play on it too.

"Always, it was like a communication through music, like he knew some things that I wanted to know that he could express musically, and that I maybe had some things to contribute too. It's hard to talk about it, except in spiritual or religious terms, actually.

"Still, he had a lot of things on his mind musically. He wanted to decide what he should turn to next, and he needed time to find out. He was a perfectionist, and he wanted to grow, always. Whatever he did, he wanted it to come from inside himself, and he did not want to hold anything back, or hide anything he found there. Good or bad, it had to be expressed. Once he asked me what I thought he should do next, what he should work on—how could he create something different. I told him maybe he should try to better some of the things he had already done, go back and try again on older tunes. I don't really know if that was any help to him; I don't know whether that was what he was looking for or not."

Returning to the subject of his own playing, Sanders says, "In a group, I like to play with anyone who really wants to play, who really wants to put out the energy. If the players don't put out the energy it takes away my own."

If he is asked about the meaning of his music, Pharoah Sanders replies, "I don't like to talk about what my playing is about. I just like to let it be. If I *had* to say something, I would say it was about me. About what *is*. Or about a Supreme Being.

"I think I am just beginning to find out about such things, so I am not going to try to force my findings on anybody else. I am still learning how to play and trying to find out a lot of things about myself so I can bring them out." (1968)

II

JELLY ROLL
AT THE LIBRARY
OF CONGRESS

In 1938, Ferdinand "Jelly Roll" Morton was managing and performing at a small club in Washington, D. C. In May of that year, Alan Lomax began recording him for the Library of Congress's Folklore Archives, playing piano, singing, reminiscing, theorizing, bragging. Reputedly, Lomax undertook the sessions without proper approval and for the job, he purchased at his own expense the Presto portable home disc recorder he used.

The rights to issue these fabled performances were acquired from the Morton estate by Rudi Blesh's Circle Records in the late 1940s, and the material appeared in twelve 78 rpm and twelve LP volumes. In 1958, Riverside licensed Circle material and reissued the Morton albums. It was for that Riverside release that the notes that follow were written.

Morton's Library of Congress records are indeed a national musical treasure, but a treasure not without its problems. Riverside followed Circle's original programming, which gathered the material under a number of rather loose headings—and which had a performance of *Original Jelly Roll Blues* beginning in Volume 1 and ending in Volume 10!

As will be occasionally evident in these notes, Lomax's tendency to treat the relatively sophisticated composer-pianist as a "folk" figure did not always work to the full credit of either man. And as a final problem, the Presto recorder's turntable moved at a consistently slow speed on some occasions, a condition which neither the Circle nor the Riverside releases sought to correct.

Yes, I agree, if any body of American music needs and deserves new transfers with speed correction and a fresh, more valid programming and general availability, it is *this* body of American music.

≈
≈
≈
≈

Boyhood Memories

The story goes that in 1938 the Washington, D.C., police picked up two men trying to break into the Library of Congress. The men turned out to be record collectors and they wanted to get into the Library's Folklore Archives to copy the Jelly Roll Morton collection. Probably the story is true: Marshall Stearns gives it in his *Story of Jazz*. Perhaps some other jazz students were more successful: I heard the fascinating demonstration of the evolution of *Tiger Rag* which begins this collection on a scratchy acetate "dub" (of a dub of a dub, in fact) in the apartment of a collector about ten years ago. I remember, too, feeling that some of the themes of the original quadrille sounded like the worst aberrations of the lady next door pounding away at the parlor upright on Saturday night, and how the mere act of Morton's syncopating and swinging them with his subtle sense of time seemed to make them infinitely more musical.

This record introduces the unique series well, for it presents Morton in all the roles he assumed and expanded. One is immediately struck by Morton the speaker who can win us with what is (despite the painful delusions, the fabrications, and the over-blown rhetoric) an authentic poetic quality. Morton the historian of jazz is here, of course, Morton the autobiographer (which is so often Morton the "semi-fictioneer"), Morton the entertainer—"one night while working *ad lib* on stage doing comedy . . ."—and Morton the singer, a new role to most of us since he had previously recorded only one vocal chorus.

Most important of all is Morton the musician; without that role the others would mean very little. And Morton the musician transcends his historical and his influential importance.

It is particularly fitting that *Hyena Stomp* is included in this first volume, because it gives a clear picture of the kind of music which Morton created. The piece is uncharacteristic of him in that it has only one theme and that is a very simple one—but the simplicity is a help.* Morton recorded it twice: besides this version there is a rather different orchestral one and a comparison of the two give, as we shall see, a further insight into Morton's conception.

The theme, as I say, is simple. The basic idea is stated in the first two measures. That statement is harmonically modulated through a chorus of sixteen bars which serves as an introduction. There follows the second sixteen-bar chorus in which the melody is again stated in bare form. In these first two statements the harmony (full, unusual for its time, and beautifully appropriate) is necessarily made clear, and there are occasional hints of the kind of rhythmic variation that is to come. There follows a series of six variations. Each is based on a musical idea which Morton works out, each is related to what precedes and what follows, either as contrast or complement, and each is a part of the total pattern of the whole performance. The variations are primarily melodic: the kind of jazz which makes harmonic variations, "blowing" with only the chord sequence of a tune as a point of reference, was more than unusual for Morton.

Before we examine the choruses, we should bring up the aspect of Morton's approach which the band recording of *Hyena Stomp* brings out. The variations here are instrumentally and orchestrally conceived; Morton once said that the basis of jazz piano style was in its imitation of an orchestra.

The first variation is primarily rhythmic—an appropriate contrast to the careful harmonic emphasis of the theme statements. He simplifies the melody and harmony drastically (preparing to rebuild it). It is a kind of "barrelhouse" variation in which a swinging rhythmic momentum is first introduced. It is

---

* It is typical of him, however, in that the piece is built on the chord structure of the main section of his most famous piece, *King Porter Stomp*.

another passage for the whole band, with the work of the rhythm section, the trombone, and the accents of the horns above them. The next chorus is an elaborate lyric transformation of the theme, lightly dancing after the heavier motion of what preceded it. Obviously Morton had the clarinet's lower register in mind. This chorus is melodically the most complex. From this point on, as we gradually return to and build on the rhythmic momentum set up in the first variation, we hear an increasing melodic simplification and dynamic building. The third variation is an excellent stroke. It still refers to the melody, of course, but also transforms (by simplification) the previous variation. (It is the clarinet in the upper register.) It thus forms a kind of two-chorus unit with the preceding. The next chorus is a contrast, but one which has been subtly prepared for. It is a variation made in the bass; Morton's left hand imitates the polyphonic line of a trombone (a rather complicated one for the time) under his treble. And notice that in the preceding chorus there had been much activity in his left hand, readying our ears for this one. In the fifth variation, we are reminded of trumpet figures, and these gradually build into an ensemble variation in the sixth. Morton leads into and makes his climax, the dynamics and the sonority continue to build excitement, the rhythm swings freely and simply. This chorus shows that special quality of excitement completely articulated, never frenzied, of which Morton was a master, and the performance justly ends with a restored calm.

There is a lot of music made from that simple theme, made in a way that is so widespread in all kinds of music that one is tempted to believe that Morton is in touch with something implicit in the nature of music itself. But if I may ask you to hear this apparently simple piece again, I think that we will see Morton even more deeply involved with possibilities in the material he chose and in his sense of formal structure. Our chorus unit here is sixteen measures (the structure of the march and of ragtime). But, as we have seen, Morton has used variations which have a close continuity across two choruses, in variations 2 and 3 (the two "clarinet" choruses) and in variations 6 and 8 (the "brass" choruses). At the same time, each chorus by its nature may readily fall into two eight-bar units. These in turn may fall into units of four bars each. Then there is the fact that we began with: that the basic melodic content can be stated in two bars. Morton takes some interesting advantages of these things during the performance. Notice, for example, that the final chorus (variation 6) consists of a continuous eight-bar line, followed by two four-bar units. Notice, too, that the first statement in the introduction does not really state the melody exactly—there is a slight, improvised change of meter in the first two bars which is "corrected" in what follows. And notice the contrast in the two "clarinet" variations. The first of these is based on a parallel repetition of two-bar units, the second begins with an improvisation which makes contrasting two-bar units. Thus Morton makes a strikingly effective use of what some might see as, necessarily, a melodic limitation, and makes it one of the basic conceptions and chief virtues of his playing. He builds variations in a continuity within sixteen-bar choruses, he combines some of these into double choruses, and within this, he works out smaller structures of two, four, and eight bars which contribute by contrast, parallel, and echo to the total development and form.

Morton's command of the materials and devices which he used was that of an artist. Still, jazz was for him a performer's music and he could project emotion spontaneously and immediately. However, I believe that once a listener understands that ordered, frequently subtle melodies or thematic variation is essential to Morton's music, its excitement and its beauty and its uniqueness will possess the listener even more strongly and lastingly.

≈
≈
≈
≈

The Animule Ball

The title of this volume comes from the two tracks herein in which Jelly Roll Morton presents himself as the entertainer, but the dominant figure here is Morton the speaker, quite personally, and with musical examples, re-creating the life in New Orleans—or that colorful stratum of the life in New Orleans in which he lived and worked, and in which jazz music flourished. As he says during the discourse on funerals, no musician in New Orleans made much money but the pianists. Morton was a pianist and that meant he worked in the "sporting" houses. He knew the musical life of the rest of the city, however, usually at first hand, and from that he made *his* music, a very personal development of New Orleans jazz.

Morton's remarks on *The Animule Ball* (or *Dance* as he also calls it) are characteristic of him: he first admits that the song is "ages old" (which it certainly is), he then immediately claims to have written it. In Volume 1, we heard him claim *Tiger Rag* (a composition claimed, adopted, and stolen by many) just after showing how it came from a "traditional" quadrille. Morton so often seems the kind of boaster or downright liar who really is not sure that he expects to be believed. He does not claim to have been the first "scat" singer in jazz, but gives the credit to Joe Sims of Vicksburg, and says the New Orleans musicians got it from him. Since singing "nonsense" syllables is almost universal in highly rhythmic vernacular music, the question of who "invented" it is rather irrelevant as such—but Morton didn't claim it.

The first part of *Animule Ball* begins with some of Morton's "comedy." Like almost all of his comedy, it is very bad. Among those musicians who knew him, and those who respected his musicianship most, there is singular agreement that Morton was a dreadful comedian and that the closest he ever got to showing a sense of humor was in an unself-conscious cheerfulness and good spirits. The song itself may fascinate a folklorist, perhaps one especially interested in "songs of derision" or even a historian of minstrelsy and vaudeville. His playing—with the voice as a part of it—is more to the point here; it is a clear demonstration of his outstanding ability to swing. Unquestionably a part of the effectiveness of the brief performance comes from his use of his voice as a solo line while behind it his piano makes a polyphonic line based on a "riff" pattern. Notice also the wonderfully effective use of breaks. (Morton has much to say about both breaks and riffs, musically and theoretically, in Volume 3.)

Morton's *Scat Song* is a two-chorus demonstration on one of his typical sixteen-bar sequences. His scatting is in his most melodically and harmonically simple styles—rather like one of his final "brass" choruses. The nonsense syllables he scats with are apt to make the singing sound more old-fashioned than it should.

Shooting the Agate begins with a reference to a mysterious "Mike," whose identification was unfortunately cut in the original editing of these sides. No matter, the description is of the dress and the carriage of the "swells" of the waterfront and Storyville. One of the first things which strikes one about this series, no matter how well he may think he knows Morton's music, is what an interesting talker the man was. His vocabulary and structure can be quite pretentious. (Morton's style has been compared to the purple rhetoric of the New Orleans "Blue Book"—the directory of the ornate brothels and bars of the city.) Despite this and despite his delusions, there is an undeniably poetic quality about his speech. Even on the level of cadence, listen to the way it falls:

> *They got something when they could,*
> *And when they couldn't,*
> *They would work out*
> *In the yards.*

or (and note the irony too):

> *Well every night*
> *The boys would hang around.*
> *Some of 'em would even go so far*
> *To meet their Sweet Mammas.*
> *St. Charles Street was quite a way off,*
> *But sometimes they would brave it and walk*
> *To where their sweet Mammas were working.*
> *And of course sometimes*
> *It was okay for them to go into the house.*

When we realize that part of the total effect of this comes from the quiet self-accompaniment, a comparison to ancient and "bardic" poetic performance becomes inevitable.

See See Rider, a blues with a widespread and complicated heritage, follows. Morton heard it sung by one "Josky" Adams, as he says "behind his sister's and mother's back," obviously because it is uncompromisingly about sex. The first chorus:

> *See, see, Rider, see what you have done,*
> *See, see, Rider, see what you have done:*
> *You made me like you, now your man done come,*

has given transcribers trouble for years. They have written it C. C. Rider, among other things. And the version of the blues which begins "Easy Rider" has been written E. C. Rider. (One critic has even called the "Rider" the singer's guitar!) Obviously Morton means, "Look, look, Rider." He concludes his version of it with two of his favorite salacious stanzas—ones which will show up on various blues in this series. According to singer Big Bill Broonzy, in the book *Big Bill Blues*, the women singers learned their blues from their men, their "Riders," in just such evening exchanges as Morton describes here.

This leads Morton to an account of the many social clubs that these "boys" belonged to in New Orleans, and this leads him readily to funerals. In describing the "wake" and its feast, Morton sings a spiritual (*Steal Away*) and a hymn (*Nearer My God to Thee*). I once heard a student of Afro-American music claim that all Negro religious music was casually, spontaneously polyphonic until the popularity of the Mills Brothers in the middle 1930s convinced many that close harmony was more "enlightened." It is obvious from the beginning that Morton is imitating a harmonized performance here. And when he remarks that the singers picked their harmonies so that just anyone couldn't "jump in and sing," we are immediately reminded of the events in Minton's in Harlem in the middle '40s when "Dizzy" Gillespie and Thelonious Monk would work out unusual changes to keep the amateurs out of the jamming. It may also remind us of the persistent insistence from some quarters that early jazz used none but the barest harmonies. (Those who make the claim intend it as a value judgment, which it could not be. They also show ignorance of the music, and have not heard for example the fat Wagnerian ninths in one of Morton's simplest blues.)

The New Orleans funeral has unfortunately become one of the big "show biz" clichés even with more or less authentic New Orleans bands. Morton's description was among the earliest. In his hands it is much less an engaging anecdote about a bunch of "colorful" (and perhaps a bit naif) old-timers than a very real part of a complex way of life.

"Rejoice at the death and cry at the birth: New Orleans sticks close to the scripture."

≈

≈

≈

≈
Discourse on Jazz

This record is about two things: (1) ragtime and the relationship of Jelly Roll Morton to ragtime, and (2) some elements of Morton's music itself.

Ragtime was, first of all, a separate movement in Afro-American syncopated music; it is not a kind of crude pre-jazz, although it made important contributions to jazz. It is, in several respects, a polished and formal music. It may derive some of its themes and a few of its devices from Negro folk songs, spirituals, etc., but it has a close relationship to "Western" march music, dances and their melodies. It is primarily melodic: its rhythms are fairly tight and one kind of syncopation frequently dominates it.

Ragtime compositions (and they *are* compositions in the strictest sense) were made of several equally important related themes.* The simplest structure was ABCD; equally frequent was ABACD; cyclical and rondo forms were also used. Scott Joplin's *Maple Leaf Rag*, which Morton uses here, has the ABACD form. Morton first plays it quite authentically, by the way, aside from a couple of strange mistakes in fingering and his occasional inability to resist improvising in his own style. Although ragtime performances may have involved some improvisation (undoubtedly there was much embellishment), variation and improvisation were not a part of the nature of this music. At the turn of the century, it had become *the* dominant popular music in America. Of course, it was then drastically simplified, commer-

* My remarks on ragtime are indebted to Guy Waterman's two critical essays in *The Record Changer*, Vol. 14, nos. 7 and 8.

cialized, and exploited. It also became a kind of showman's piano for rapid displays of technique. It soon attracted inferior composers and performers and, with some important exceptions, its creativity as a movement was spent by about 1910. One exception was Joplin, who worked until his death extending, polishing, and refining his music—raising (and sometimes solving) some problems which modern jazz is faced with today. Meanwhile, a new musical movement had replaced it. That movement was called "jazz."

Morton once claimed to have invented this new jazz music. Whether he did or not, his music shows a crucial transition. Take the very exciting version of *Kansas City Stomps* on this LP. It is built, like a rag, on several themes: its form is basically ABACA—a rondo, notice. It uses several kinds of syncopation with great rhythmic freedom and relaxation, uses both played and suggested polyrhythms, "odd" harmonies and polyphonies, but most important its substance and effectiveness depend on variation and improvisation. Morton's music combined the form and melodic approach of ragtime (and its partial analogue the march) and dances and songs—music of European origin—with the rhythms, melodic devices, polyphonies in blues, work songs, spirituals, etc., and produced something new. Like many social or vernacular musics, these blues and spirituals used improvisation of some kind. However, there are two things in particular to notice. First, Morton made variation crucial in the music he produced (and it need not have happened that way: it didn't in ragtime). The second is that if Morton's musical sensibilities and ability to make variations had not been outstanding, his music would mean little and his importance would be nil.

Morton was a modernist in his day, an innovator. That is why he so frequently ridiculed "ragtime men." He was part of a movement which saved Afro-American syncopated music from degeneration at the hands of pseudo and second-rate ragtimers, and continued its development. (He obviously respected the *best* ragtime and its composers, however.) And that is also why he frequently scorned blues pianists, "one tune piano players." His work was more sophisticated, formal, knowledgable, resourceful, varied—more *musical* than theirs. At the same time, it is interesting to speculate on what banal rhythm-making jazz might have become if it did not have the formal melodic conception of ragtime in its background. At the same time, one shudders to think what might have happened if the deep passion, the freedom, the poetry and rhythmic variety of Negro folk music and blues had not replenished it, as it were, from below.

When Morton is asked here for his theory of jazz, he gives, of course, not a theory but some basic things about it which were important to him. Some are obviously directed at your old Aunt Sallie who thinks that jazz is loud, fast, and disorganized.

Notice that Morton says that he worked out his style at medium tempos—almost all of the innovations in jazz have originally been worked out in the same way. (Hear the recordings made at Minton's in the early '40s, hear Armstrong's "ballads" in the '30s.) His first point is the famous "always keep the melody going some way." He acknowledges that melodic variation is his way, but notice also that this remark is really a part of his insistence on continuous, proper, and interesting harmonization.

His next remarks are on riffs. Much has been made of his insistence that they are for background (and after the powerful demonstration he uses here, small wonder), but Morton himself did not always use them that way: several of his tunes have riff melodies and the very one he uses in the bass here is the last strain of his band recording of *Georgia Swing*. At any rate, one could hardly question the great, continuing effectiveness of riffs behind a soloist.

His third point, that a pianist should imitate an orchestra, at least has historical confirmation; almost every piano style in jazz (from Hines through Garner, Morton through Powell) has been derived from the imitation of a band or a horn style.

As Morton puts it, "breaks" are "one of the most effective things you can do in jazz." In a sense they are the culmination of the syncopation and the rhythmic resources in jazz (unless "stop time" carries things a step further), yet they are almost a lost art. Charlie Parker's famous break in A *Night in Tunisia* became a fable immediately after his record of it was released. But today breaks are often made at the beginnings of choruses, where they are possibly least effective. Certainly Morton's subtle sense of time and suspense in making them is the bane of his "revivalist" followers.

Complete with pretentious arpeggios, comes the just assertion that jazz can be soft, sweet, and slow. To this day, many a jazz band wisely tests its ability to swing by trying to do so at a pianissimo whisper. And the problem of swinging at slow tempos is one which has plagued many jazzmen in all periods—and is plaguing members of the "funky" school now. Notice the break Morton uses in this demonstration: it is in double time, a cornerstone of styles from ragtime to Charlie Parker's.

His performance of *King Porter Stomp* (the first of two in this series) is quite different from any of the several others that he recorded. For one thing, it contains more improvisation on the basic pattern. Variation on the third theme is always a part of it, of course, but here he passionately improvises on the whole piece in this pattern: A,A,B,B, interlude, C,C,C,C. Its rhythmic momentum is compelling indeed, but as a final irony, Morton does here precisely the thing that he was damning Randall, of *Randall's Rag*, for doing as this LP began: he gradually increases his tempo.

≈

≈

≈

≈

Creepy Feeling

The subject of this album is what Jelly Roll Morton called "the Spanish tinge" in jazz—or in his jazz—but in a sense it misrepresents that element in his music. The six of his own pieces which it contains are "jazz tangos," but the influence of what is called "Latin" music on his music and on New Orleans jazz is both more general and more deep than the fact that he wrote several jazz tangos.

"New Orleans was inhabited with maybe every race on the face of the globe. And, of course, we had Spanish people, plenty of them . . . ," Morton says. "Spanish" music was a part of the city's musical heritage and life. The tango and what was called the "Mexican serenade" were also a continuing part of the popular music of the day. Unfortunately many of the discussions of the constant flirting of jazz and Latin rhythms quickly become a matter of listing tunes: several of Morton's; *St. Louis Blues;* Armstrong's *Peanut Vendor; Monteca; Barbados; Un Poco Loco; Senior Blues,* etc., etc. (They might also mention the "samba" qualities in some ragtime, Scott Joplin's tango rag *Solace,* and some others.)

According to recent opinions of musicologists, the habañera was of Hispanic-Afro-American origin, not directly African, as was once thought. It came from Cuba, as its name indicates. In the poorer sections of Buenos Aires about 1900, the habañera was combined with the milonga to make the tango, became a popular dance, and spread. It is not supposed to have been syncopated

141

there before 1905, but I have the feeling that it was syncopated in New Orleans before that.

But what is the relationship of early jazz to the tango? Is it only a matter of a man like Morton having written tangos of a special kind? Is it a matter of using tango themes as a part of certain compositions (as in *Fickle Fay Creep* here)? Is it a matter of occasional rhythmic effects? There are several records by King Oliver's Creole Jazz Band wherein Lil Armstrong will spontaneously break into tango rhythm behind the polyphony of the horns. She may be quickly joined by Bill Johnson and Honoré Dutrey, or she may continue alone, playing against everyone else's beat. The effect of this is exciting and the possibilities for rhythmic variety are obvious. Morton will frequently do much the same: often in his band records we hear him suddenly inject tango rhythms against the prevailing beat, with a kind of sublime intuition about just when to do it and how long to keep it up. We also hear this sort of thing in his solo piano, of course. One can hear it, too, in Baby Dodds' drum solos and accompaniments. Modern drummers (and other instrumentalists) similarly found a source of rhythmic variety in Latin patterns. (One might even say that modern drummers *re*-discovered their polyrhythmic and melodic role, one which swing drummers largely neglected.)

Thus we can perform jazz tangos, we can use tango themes and interludes, we can use tango rhythms for, as Morton put it, a "seasoning." But it goes further than that, I think. Just as Dizzy Gillespie's trumpet phrasing frequently shows his keen ear for trumpeters in rumba bands, certain of Louis Armstrong's phrases come from the melodic-rhythmic manner of the tango. It may even be that both of the latter were encouraged to play so markedly behind the beat not only by their apprenticeships as second trumpeters but also by the delayed pulse of tango phrasing. The same kind of thing shows up constantly in Morton's playing and composing. For example, the "trio" strain of one of his most successful pieces, *Wolverine Blues*. The placement of the notes there corresponds to the placement of the heavy beats in a tango. The result automatically plays one rhythm against another.*

In his demonstration on *La Paloma* here, Morton goes at the problem the other way around. He does not show tango effects in a jazz piece, or play a jazz tango, but remakes a well-known tango into jazz. Notice that one of the chief musical points he makes is rhythmic and metric, but that the one he talks about is his use of "blue" notes and the effect of the juxtaposition of the two rhythms. Morton made two other piano versions of *Mama 'Nita* (sometimes called *Mamanita*), but the improvisation on this one can make the others sound rather pallid. The piece has three themes; actually the second becomes more interesting when he alters it, and the third is almost a variant of the first. Notice that Morton performs on them in cyclical form. One point that immediately strikes one is the wonderful alliance he makes here between the tango bass and his characteristic use of trombone-like polyphonic bass lines; these two elements usually become one in his work.

I can find no other version of *Spanish Swat* under any title either among Morton's published scores or his recordings. That is just as well, for although it is an unusual piece for him, being in the thirty-two-bar "popular song" form, it is a rather poor melody and his "variations" here are really decorative embellishments.

Morton's *New Orleans Blues* (or *New Orleans Joys*) is the second of two versions of a piece quite celebrated in certain quarters for the masterful way he drops behind the beat. It is a twelve-bar blues-tango and, the way he has organized it, two themes emerge. He plays them thus: A,A,B (introduced by the bass figure); B,B,B (the bass figure has risen to treble; this is the "behind the beat" chorus, by the way); A,A (the last two choruses drop the tango effect and, as Morton put it, "stomp").

Morton did not record his *Creepy Feeling* until 1938 and then made this and another version. It is the inventive *tour de force* of

---

*What I did not say here, and certainly should have, is that it was the Americanization of the habañera-tango-bolero rhythm, with further syncopation, that produced the Charleston rhythm, still a crucial element in jazz.

this set; Morton plays on its three themes as if his ability to improvise variations is inexhaustible, and they flow out of him as easily and naturally as breathing. Notice how he prepares for the third theme in his development of the second, and in his development of that third how he uses blue dissonance for surprise—an idea he uses again in *The Crave.*

The Crave is another piece that Morton recorded only late in his career. He plays its two themes in cycle: A,A,B,B,A,B,B, etc. The "blues" break which introduces the second theme is one of the delightful strokes in all his music—and the variations he makes on it manage to top that stroke. Morton's inventiveness is still flowing.

Fickle Fay Creep has an interesting history. In the twenties, Morton called it *Soap Suds* and recorded it obscurely in St. Louis with a rather amateurish band called the "Levee Serenaders." He made another version for orchestra in 1930 on his last record date for Victor. The first theme is a tango; the second is certainly not a great melody, but notice that as he develops it he uses tango rhythms—not in the bass, but in the treble. The third theme is very Mortonesque but he has put similar material to better use elsewhere—in *Mister Joe,* for instance.

≈
≈
≈
≈

Georgia Skin Game

"Yes, it was some terrible environments that I went through in those days, inhabited by some very tough babies."

One of the great clichés of jazz commentary in America has been Jelly Roll Morton, the colorful character, and I think there has been more than enough of it. Not only is it unfair to the human being behind the music, but it also stands in the way of our seeing his music for what it is. That is not to say that I think an honest approach to his life, his way of life, his shifting world, to be beside the point, but the "colorful character" concept often confuses and even destroys such an approach.

Morton was an exasperatingly contradictory man; a puzzlingly complex man. One can grasp at what seems to be enlightening, but there is much that we can merely wonder at. The ultimate point, however, is the music. Our knowledge of his life and his world is important only as it enlightens us on the music. But, hearing that music, we so often feel that it says much more about the man and his real feelings than his public masks, his pride, and his pontifications can ever tell us.

Morton made these records for a folklore collection and he obliged with many tales and many indigenous songs. In quietly singing the blues about Aaron Harris, he gives the line about the "hoodoo woman" and explains it a bit when asked afterward. Hoodoo, Voodoo, Vodun—it has echoes in several directions. The original slaves brought to New Orleans were Dahomeans, and Vodun was their worship. According to Marshall Stearns' book, *The Story of Jazz*, West African influences survived for years in *laissez-faire* New Orleans and gradually blended with European music in "private vodun ceremonies and public performances in Congo Square." Vodun is a powerful and continuing fact and New Orleans is its center in the United States. Morton himself was a Catholic. However, he described his aunt as a hoodoo witch who, during his childhood, had used Vodun to cure him of an illness. Later (in New York in about 1930), Morton burned his clothing and "spent thousands of dollars trying to get this spell taken off of me."

The blues about Harris has what might seem an "irregular" second verse if we are too used to a more formal kind. It has the same line three times and its ironic comment is hung almost casually between the second and third:

> *Killed his sweet little sister and his brother-in-law,*
> *Killed his sweet little sister and his brother-in-law.*
> *About a cup of coffee, he killed his sister and his*
> *   brother-in-law.*

The fact that the song about Robert Charles and the Robert Charles riots was forcefully suppressed indicates how explosive an event those riots were. They are usually said to have signaled the final step in the gradual installation of formal segregation in New Orleans. The history of caste, class, and color line in that city is complex. As Dr. Edmond Souchon has described the situation that existed in his youth, a time when Morton was still in the city (*Record Changer,* Feb. 1953), "Jelly Roll's attitude was in no small measure due to his complete rebellion against the strict Jim Crow laws of the South, but he also presented a very interesting subject for investigation by a psychoanalyst. Jelly Roll was the victim of his own particular 'cult' or 'social group,' if you will; for in New Orleans the self-imposed color line between the light and the dark Negro is much more marked than is the Jim Crow line between white and colored."

There were three classes in New Orleans, then, and as "the prejudice" came, these Creoles of Color, proud families, often landowners, small businessmen, often educated abroad, were hit hard. Stearns gives the background in his book: "The Black Code of 1724 made provision for the manumission, or freeing, of slaves. Children shared the status of their mother. When a white aristocrat died . . . his will frequently provided that his part-African mistress and slave should be freed. His children by the same woman were automatically free. A class known as Creoles of Color grew up with French and Spanish as well as African blood in their veins."

There is no doubt that in his own attitudes, a part of Morton was the victim of the snobbery of this class. His attitudes were defensively complicated by the fact that his family was not a particularly prosperous one in the Creole community and the fact that he himself was not really sure (so it seems) of his own legitimacy or parentage. He had many masques. At the same time, remember his reverence of his teacher Tony Jackson, his praise of King Oliver, his elevation of Buddy Bolden. But more to the point and more revealing of his inner feeling is what we hear in his music, or what the artist in him knew and spoke of. Whether he admitted it to himself or not, he had in effect already rejected the bourgeois Creole world (no matter how often it clung to the face he showed), before that world rejected him because of his music.

Morton's account of it is given in the book *Mister Jelly Roll*. "My grandmother gave me that Frenchman look and said to me in French, 'your mother is gone and can't help her little girls now. She left Amede and Mimi to their old grandmother to raise as good girls. A musician is nothing but a bum and a scalawag. I don't want you around your sisters. I reckon you better move.' My grandmother said all this and she walked up the path to the white columns of the front porch, went inside, and shut the door."

That way of life rejected him, and he it, but its snobbery remained a part of him—perhaps because of the very nature of that rejection—to be reflected often enough in the proud face he turned towards the world. And, as is so often the case, the snobbery of this Creole family may have been at least partly due to uneasiness about an older skeleton in its closet. Many years later, Morton's uncle Henri Monette was quoted by Alan Lomax on the subject of Morton's father: "That's where music came into this boy. Listen—Ed La Menthe was a trambone player! Played a slidin' trambone! I didn't think of that . . . That's where Jelly got his music. Ed could cooperate pretty well in a band. Slidin' trambone too, at that . . ."

Jelly Roll Morton led us to believe that he found work and a high income in Storyville. But is that where jazz was born: in the "houses" of the "district"? In an interview with Countess Willie Piazza, "The First Lady of Storyville" (*Record Changer,* Feb. 1951), Kay C. Thompson quoted, "Where jazz came from I can't rightly say, but . . . I was the first in New Orleans to employ a jazz pianist in the red-light district . . . In those days jazz was associated principally with dance halls and cabarets . . . Jazz didn't start in sporting houses . . . it was what most of our customers wanted to hear."

Before his grandmother had shut the door on him, Morton had cast his lot with a music that had captured him. And he was true to it even as he wandered, gambled, pimped, pursued the diamonds and the Cadillacs. He knew where it came from and he called you to hear it. The delusions fall away, and the best that was in him came out in his work. Hear the way he re-creates the *Georgia Skin Game.*

The song is like a work song, the slap of the cards is the stroke of the laborer's hammer. Its melody suggests the spiritual *Motherless Child.* The loving passion with which Morton sings its beautifully haunting blue notes shows how deeply he felt about this music, for this kind of music, however he might act or whatever he might say on another day and to a certain man. And the dramatic vividness with which he re-creates that scene is not only evidence of a talent but of a passionate apprehension and wondering admiration of the human beings involved. If his art can help us to see as his deeper self could see, he will have served all men well.

At this point the reader will probably find it useful to have a summary of the main points of Jelly Roll Morton's discourse on jazz.

"Always keep the melody going some kind of way," he

insisted. Or, as we might put it, make your variations by embellishing or ornamenting or simplifying the theme itself.

Morton said that ragtime had tended to be played faster and faster by its pianists, without their changing the music essentially or adding very much. For jazz, finding the right tempo so that variations and embellishments would flow naturally was essential.

He insisted that riffs, short one- or two-bar ostinato figures, make the music more exciting and effective, but they should be used as backgrounds, as accompaniment figures, not as a substitute for main melodies.

He said that a jazz pianist should initiate a jazz band.

Morton insisted on "breaks," momentary suspensions of a stated pulse, usually for two bars, during which a soloist's line takes off as if suspended in mid-air. "Without breaks, without good, clean breaks, you just don't have jazz."

Jazz can be soft, sweet, slow, melodious, but with "plenty of rhythm." And Morton wanted a good use of dynamics as a part of this. "You can't make *crescendos* and *diminuendos* when everybody is playing *triple forte.*" He used the image, if a glass of water is full, it's full. You can't add any more.

And finally, "Without 'the Spanish Tinge' you just don't have jazz." That is to say, without a coming-to-terms with the habañera or tango rhythm, with its behind-the-beat syncopations—as contrasted with ragtime's mostly ahead-of-the-beat syncopations—you just don't have jazz. And I have added that it was the further syncopation of the habañera-tango which produced the very American (and quite essential) Charleston rhythm.

≈
≈
≈
≈ # The Pearls

About the time that this series of records was being made, a young pianist (who has since become a very famous one) went with some friends to hear "an old-time piano player" they had vaguely heard of at a Washington club. They went quite frankly to build up their own egos and convictions about jazz at his expense; they came away full of respect and admiration. He had even done things they admitted they couldn't do. The pianist they heard was, of course, Ferdinand "Jelly Roll" Morton.*

The Pearls is one of Morton's best compositions, but aside from two piano versions, a band version, and an interesting piano roll by Morton, and a 1938 record based on one of its themes by Mary Lou Williams, it was a somewhat neglected piece.

There are three themes to *The Pearls,* plus a four-bar introduction, an interlude before the third, and a four-bar ending. The first two themes are each sixteen-bar melodies, both in G. The third is a thirty-two bar strain in C—not the usual "popular song" thirty-two bar sequence, but the kind based on a doubling of the sixteen-bar form. Thus the basic structure is ABC. Morton's way of handling these strains in his previous versions of the piece (and all are quite different) was A,B,B2,C,C2. Here his joyous and pensive flow of ideas makes it A,A2,B,B2,A3,C,C2,C3,C4,C5.

Morton was not well when these records were made, and he occasionally makes mistakes in fingering which show it. At the same time, he was clearly showing off for posterity and he never made records which show his invention so tellingly as these do.

* And the young visitor was pianist Billy Taylor.

He had plenty of time; he had only to interrupt himself while the acetate blanks were changed on the portable recorder. And he could pick his tempos as he wished, not in order to get everything in three minutes. *The Pearls* particularly gains by a slower tempo here.

One of the things which makes *The Pearls* one of his best pieces is that it has three good themes with a developing relationship and emotional range which show Morton's musical intuition operating at its best. The crisp first theme, the strong song and harmonic emphasis of the second, are followed by the gentle lyricism of the third, main theme and its harmony. (If there is a defect in this performance it is that his initial statement of that third theme does not bring out its implicit lyricism; improvisation seems to have possessed him.) The third theme is then transformed chiefly by a kind of gradual simplification (but with several internal returns to complexity) into a kind of bravura statement, a brass-like crescendo, a reminder of the quality of the first strain.

Variation is essential to Morton's music; if we strip it down to the level of composition only, variation on the final theme is there. And even on that level his music reflects a step in the evolution of jazz. However, it is clear that in performance, improvisation as well is a part of his work. If hearing the way that he spontaneously operates on *The Pearls* here will not convince us of that, we need only compare the various versions of it. At the same time, I do not believe that his performances leave him with only the historical or academic status that such descriptions of what he did would seem to indicate. His performances have an intrinsic merit on their own terms—if for no other reason than because they are unique. They also deal with questions of form and development which jazz has been constantly faced with. And one of Morton's ways of dealing with the problem of form was, of course, his use of melodic, or thematic, variations.

Morton's approach is rather like the one we hear in James P. Johnson, in Fats Waller, or today in Erroll Garner or in the way Thelonious Monk operates on a ballad. Morton, as I have said, makes thematic variations in sets, approaching each separately (or in parallel pairs) and building in a "classic" form. This practice is so common among post-ragtime styles, in James P. Johnson, in Willie "The Lion" Smith, in their "pupil" Waller (all of whom, I believe, would have used pretty much the same style and approach as they did whether or not there had been any New Orleans jazz) that one can only wonder at its origin. Playing on chord sequences alone is indigenous to blues, altering a line in performance is characteristic of much music, however uniquely beautiful and exciting it may be in American Negro folk music. On the other hand, these "classic" sets of melodic variations which approach choruses separately, which build, contrast, echo, parallel—where did this approach come from? Any bar-room pianist makes embellishments of course (sometimes through sheer ignorance) but what is the genesis of these ordered transformations of melody from *within* its structure which involved so much melodic-rhythmic invention? We can be sure of one thing: it takes a musical sensibility to be able to make them well, whether one arrives at the procedure himself or adopts it from a "source"; and in jazz, Morton could do it surpassingly and uniquely.

Pep has two themes. The first is stated as an harmonic sequence and its basic melodic material can be reduced to a two-bar phrase. (Lest anyone think that Morton could not use long lines, let him remember *Shreveport Stomp,* or let him catch the hint in the second theme in *Pep.*) It uses the kind of harmonies usually called "haunting," again quite "advanced" for their day. Morton puts it through five two-handed variations. Following an interlude, he plays three choruses on his second theme, again showing the rhythmic and architectonic resources of his playing—including the way that his key phrases and melodic segments blend and develop without choppiness. This performance of *Pep* is superior to the original record in several respects, not the least of which is that it swings more.

Whatever its merits and defects, Morton's playing and casual scatting of four choruses on Fats Waller's *Ain't Misbehavin'* make an interesting comparison (rhythmic as well as melodic) to any of Waller's own versions, and a comment on our discussion above.

Chorus four begins with a fine counter-melody, and notice the motif of thirty-second note runs he introduces in the second. One immediately thinks of Parker, then of Hines and Tatum. And in Morton's playing, the device has a clear reference to his "Spanish tinge."

Morton's tribute in *Bert Williams* to the great comedian is apparently nominal because we know that when he wrote the tune in his early California days (1917–22), he called it *The Pacific Rag*. It has three themes in the basic ABAC form, here used AABBACCC, and the kind of lightly swinging, loose rhythm that clearly gives the "rag" in the original title the lie if we took it literally. The variations on B again show what interesting use Morton can make of his most casual, almost incidental second themes. The third strain has an echo-like structure of which Morton takes knowing advantage.

Jungle Blues is a deliberately archaic, harmonically "primitive" blues. Morton played it here as a part of his criticism of Duke Ellington, something about Ellington playing "jungle music" and his having made that kind of music before him. (Morton's criticism of Ellington seems to miss the point as much as Ellington's often-quoted attack on Morton.) It may sound like a kind of improvisation on blues chords, but it is not; the basic sequence and development were compositionally pre-set. I think one of its nicest effects is the way Morton will keep one kind of rhythm going to the brink of monotony and then shift his treble to a counter-rhythm—the kind of relieving contrast wherein Morton's instincts seldom failed him.

For any jazzman or theorist confronted with the recurrent problems of developing structure and integrated rhythmic variety, Morton's music can stand, I believe, as a precedent and example. At any rate, it can be a source of emotional instruction and delight to us all.

≈

≈

≈

≈ Mamie's Blues

Morton's demonstrations of honky-tonk blues and the ragtime-esque "kind of tune that Albert Carroll used to play for the girls" here juxtapose two important influences on his own playing and dramatize his music as a transition (a *leap* might be more accurate) from ragtime into jazz. But there is much more to be said, of course. One of the clichés is that its essence is "New Orleans polyphony." But Morton's first orchestral records before 1926 abound with solos and even unison passages. I have often been puzzled by commentators who make polyphony a part of their credo: what do they do with piano solos, with Morton's duets (the one with Oliver, say), or with his clarinet trios? The answer that says Morton "originated" something which Benny Goodman used later is hardly to the point (and unless one hung out at Pete Lala's or Dago Tony's in Storyville, or many other such places in many other cities, is on shaky historical grounds to say the least). Morton's earliest Victor records use polyphony (a beautiful polyphony) but, in a sense, use it sparingly. They use unison and harmonized passages and they are full of solos. At the same time they have a harmonic and melodic sophistication which by comparison can make many of Oliver's early recordings seem, in a sense, no more than the work of a highly skillful blues band.

All this and more is implicit in Morton's piano style from his first recordings. His records have some passages which are in effect harmonized section work which swings—before Don Redman is supposed to have solved that problem. At the same time, they show a range of devices and attitudes from one composition to the next and within each composition which can make many another group sound like it is playing the same number over and over all night long. *Shreveport Stomp* uses a long continuous line—a problem which few dared to take up again until the time of Charlie Parker (its germ is in several rags). Later, Morton met the challenges around him of more extended solos, of orchestration into larger sections, of working more often with a single theme, of extending the range of the blues mood, and on and on.

If Morton's boast, "Listen, man, whatever you blow on that horn, you're blowing Jelly Roll" is taken to mean, "I *originated* everything in jazz and everybody got it from me," it is obviously not a little absurd (and the ghosts of Scott Joplin, James Scott and the rest might throw the words back in his face). But one can say that Morton raised or reflected many possibilities for jazz (obviously borrowing some, undoubtedly arriving at others for himself) and solved many of them well. One might say that on a *technical* level alone, he cuts across years of development in jazz. And I am not raising any of these points here to make any claim for him as an influence on others.

Some of Morton's remarks here on Tony Jackson and the inclusion of *All That I Ask Is Love* raise the question of how he felt about his music. They raise, too, the whole question of jazz as "entertainment" or as "art" and that other one about "popular art" and "fine art." Without going into that problem, we will assume that jazz goes beyond "cabaret" and most "popular" and "folk" music, and turn to Morton.

"Everybody had their own style," he says. So Morton developed his. Whether he "originated" it, borrowed it, or stole it, is ultimately beside the point. The point is that it released his creativity and the music within him came out.

Tony Jackson was his "teacher" and Jackson was "the world's greatest single-handed entertainer." And undoubtedly Morton thought of himself as an entertainer. He became a lot of other things too, and he often looks like a pool shark or gambler using his music to cover up his real purposes. Then he was a procurer (a "higher up," he said), and also a patent medicine salesman.

"Morton," as Whitney Balliett has said, "gave the American Dream an awful pummelling before it finally cut him down." But through it all there is a constant return to his music and a devotion to it. And this return goes more deeply and much further than can be accounted for by any desire to cash in on something that was more or less popular.

He may top his cutting of a Benny Frenchy by giving the crowd a new Irish-tenor ballad (why not?) but it showed neither the kind of music *he* offered nor finally wanted to be judged by. During the whole course of his recording career his musical integrity is constant and admirable indeed. One suspects a gradual realization that he was part of a movement that was terribly important, that had spread widely, and whatever else he was in it for, he was in it to contribute (though he may not have put it that way), to keep things on the track, to try out things that might work within it, to show what would work. In his violent arguments later in Harlem with Chick Webb and his musicians, whatever we hear of ego and perhaps of jealousy, we hear also a devotion to the principles of jazz that he stood for and a rejection of tendencies he did not believe in. His "theories of jazz" (so often misunderstood, I think) are not his effort to portray himself as hot stuff, but rather an attempt to explain practice and to defend the integrity of a music against public misunderstanding, against exploitation, and against tendencies within it which to him were wrong ones.

Morton knew very well that jazz was a music with an identity and heritage that was unknown or badly misunderstood. At the same time, he did not want it to be esoteric or cultish. At times one feels he believed he could communicate his music to *anyone.* Perhaps he was right at that, but the point is that the communication was to be made in his terms, not theirs, and the music was to say what it said, not what they wanted to hear. Whatever his delusions about wealth or boasts about his position, there is an integrity to his craft and art which came back to him in his most adverse moments. Even at those times in his wanderings and in his myriad of enterprises when Morton seemed almost to be fighting off his destiny as a musician, the music seemed to triumph.

Mamie's Blues was at first an almost incidental part of his reminiscences about New Orleans. He later developed it into one of the most touchingly beautiful blues, with a delicacy and gentleness that is unique. Here it is a more robust piece, a mood more appropriate to the afternoons when he overheard Mamie Desdume play it. The bass again shows tango tending toward what later came to be called boogie woogie, and the stanzas are a combination of practicality, pride, and feminine feeling.

His really joyful demonstrations of honky-tonk and barrel-house blues of the time show what a keen ear and respect Morton had for a kind of music that he went beyond. Some, especially *The Game Kid*'s, are very like pieces which Cripple Clarence Lofton, Cow Cow Davenport, and Speckled Red later recorded (but often with "eight beat" basses), and if we did not know that such things could be heard all over the South and Southwest, we might conclude that *everything* started in New Orleans. And if Benny Frenchy is typical (which he probably isn't) perhaps it was all played better than elsewhere.

If the blues chorus that he attributes here to Buddy Carter sounds familiar it is probably not only because its first few notes are like those in *Muskrat Ramble* (*notice:* more Spanish tinge) but also because Morton had a strain rather like it in *Sidewalk Blues*. This *Crazy Chords Rag* is not the same as Morton's own *Crazy Chords*. And we will hear again from the theme with which Morton demonstrates Benny Frenchy's amateurishness in Volume 9.

≈

≈

≈

≈

The Murder Ballad . . .

The "colorful old character" approach to Jelly Roll Morton has done him disservice, but an equal if not greater disservice has been done to his music by the kind of indiscriminate blanket praise that every note he ever wrote or played has received in some quarters. Such an attitude can do nothing but harm to any artist, be he Honoré Daumier or George Herriman, George Balanchine or Fred Astaire, William Shakespeare or Charlie Chaplin. Morton wrote some poor themes, produced some second-rate pieces, played some bad piano, and made some bad records. Unless one admits that any discussion of his music is going to be at least suspect, any evaluation of it a little absurd . . .

Wolverine Blues is deservedly one of Morton's most successful pieces. I think that this version of it contains some of the very best things in this series, but at the same time it has one strange lapse and he plays a part of it better on his other versions. *Wolverine Blues* isn't a blues, neither an eight-, twelve-, or sixteen-bar blues. Why is it called one? The answer to that lies in W. C. Handy's great success and to bring up Handy is to bring up another of those strange, wonderful, but exasperating events in Morton's later life. In 1939 a Ripley "Believe It or Not" broadcast represented Handy as the originator of jazz, stomps, and blues. Morton was furious and pointed out what Handy himself had in effect acknowledged often, that Handy had simply written down and more or less formalized blues that were "in the air." But about this time Morton was beginning first to hint, then to claim that he "invented jazz in 1902." *Down Beat* published his articles, his letters. According to his friend and publisher Roy J. Carew (*Record Changer,* Dec. 1952), Morton meant he invented *piano* jazz. Morton's cards did read "originator of jazz and stomps"—but if that means that he composed material of those types, who could argue? And remember that he begins this series, "Jazz started in New Orleans . . .", *not* "I started jazz."

Handy's first success (beginning about 1912) came as the public vogue for ragtime was waning and before jazz from New Orleans began to be widely successful. He performed an invaluable service in setting down material he had heard and which otherwise would surely have been lost, and he kept a compelling syncopated music before a wide public. (I am not saying that Handy may not have been a composer as well, but am merely trying to characterize his contribution in general.) His blues were, like rags, made up of several themes, and certainly the musical intuition which juxtaposed the strains of *Memphis Blues, St. Louis Blues, Beale Street Blues* so aptly was a sure one. (Morton might have agreed, since he recorded *Beale Street* for Victor.) As a result of Handy's continuing success, writers and especially publishers put the word "blues" on tune after tune and continued to for many years. Hence, Morton's *The Wolverine* (named, one story goes, for a friend's barber shop in Detroit) became *Wolverine Blues.*

In the first volume we heard Morton call his *New Orleans Blues* (which also forms the basis for the accompaniment to the *Low Down Blues* verses here) the "earliest playable composition." He means, I believe, that it was the earliest blues written down and passed around on paper in the city. Morton's blues are always compositions (as were Handy's); the idea of playing on blues chords (or other chords) as a public performance was foreign to him. He composed (or borrowed, to be sure) themes, composed and improvised variations on these themes. Handy can be judged almost as a folklorist with some fine musical instincts, Morton as a composer-arranger-performer-improviser.

Wolverine Blues is a composition in three themes, published as A(16 bars), B(16), A, C(32 bars). Here, Morton plays A and one variation on A with a rather stiff beat. Theme B (which is rather like several other tunes) is then used as a basis for two choruses. Following, Morton starts a return to A, but changes into the interlude that leads to C. But for some reason Morton uncharacteristically begins this trio with some trite scatting and follows with another chorus in which he toys with the rather inane words the Spikes brothers wrote for a song version of the piece. At this point the original acetate record had run out. When Morton comes back, he is a changed man: organized, swinging, improvising, creating. He begins C again in effect, first stating the series of harmonies which are its theme, plays a first variation with a clarinet-like line, follows with a compelling two-handed contrapuntal variation, scats brass-like figures, makes a flowing but exciting climax.

The rest of the selections in this set are vocal blues: by request, Morton was giving the music he had heard, performing only one of his own things. Before he made this series, he had sung on records only once, although he had been known as a singer among certain musicians at times. I think we discover a remarkably effective singer here and at the same time a side of Morton's character that one might not suspect.

Michigan Water Blues (Clarence Williams wrote this one down) is a part of Morton's account of Tony Jackson. The accompaniment is based on a descending figure, modulated through the changes. The solo choruses demonstrate a "single run bass" (a crawl or four-beat walk, we might have called it in the '30s) and a "double running bass" (an eight-beat walking bass to others). The stanzas that Morton sings seem to have no particular continuity, apparently just ones he happened to call up at the time.

This lack of continuity is hardly true of *The Murder Ballad,* and in it Morton shows he had decided to call things as they were (and perhaps the "lady present" who had inhibited him on an earlier record had left). Something seems to have been cut off the beginning and end, and we begin, quite effectively, with a scene in the girl's cell. It is quite a poem in its way, and unfolds with a series of telling, rapidly shifting scenes, speeches, facts, and memories which give us character and narrative with striking economy and force. The light Spanish-tinged accompaniment is rather like Jimmy Yancey's way of playing blues. (Perhaps the last line here should have had the judge say, "I'm *not* sure I can").

This version of *Winin' Boy,* very different from the pensive one which will end this series, is a swinging, humorous, frankly salacious medium-tempo blues with a rather unusual "refrain" verse form. As to the title (which became Morton's early nickname), well, whether it's a fellow who drinks wine, a fellow who can make them whine and moan, a fellow who can wind it as Stavin' Chain could shake it, or something about a "Winding Ball" (whatever that is—probably a colloquial corruption), I leave to the lyrics to indicate. If you think you hear censorship-at-source in a couple of skipped beats in the last stanza, you're right.

The Low Down Blues begins with an almost literal statement of what Morton was doing, "I could sit right here and think a thousand miles away," and that stanza came to him often as he made this series. The "low down" of the title seems this time to mean what your prudish aunt thinks it always means. Morton strings earthy stanzas (several of which he liked enough to use often in these recordings) to show what they sang when they sang blues like these. (The fine little figure that he introduces as a transition after the second stanza may give a hint as to why Morton admired Bob Zurke's work, by the way.)

Thus, by request, Morton was performing much here that was a part of his background and his life, but not, as such, of his own music as we know it. But these blues show some of Morton's best singing on the series, I think. He showed his fine ability to alter a line beautifully, and with a deceptive simplicity—take the first and, especially, the lovely fourth stanzas of *Winin' Boy.* Also, the singing here does not strain his range and he was in good voice on the days these were done. Among the numbers here there is a variety of mood and emotion, despite the recurrent subject of sex. But most important is the care and love with which the sophisticated Morton, pulling old stanzas and stories out of his memory, re-creates an authentic beauty of line and sound, and, with honest, unaffected emotion, brings these scenes and these people to life.

≈

≈

≈

≈ # Jack the Bear

There is a passage in *Life on the Mississippi* in which Mark Twain remarks on the number of Negroes who traveled: it was as if they had decided to make up for all the years when they and their forebears could not travel.

Morton traveled. He traveled the way we think of an itinerant blues singer traveling. And for much of this record he reports on his travels. In the book *Mister Jelly Roll*, Alan Lomax writes: "After 1904 he was constantly on the prod, using New Orleans only as a base of operations and nurturing ambitions mortal strange. . . ." The "Jack the Bear" episode here begins in Jackson, Mississippi, and moves to Memphis; we go to St. Louis, and the song *Alabama Bound* carried Morton through many early wanderings around the Gulf Coast and elsewhere.

Morton's memory of *Salty Dog* here is for me one of the minor delights of the series, because, although no great shakes as a composition or improvisation, it shows a side of his way of playing easy to lose sight of. The "Benny Frenchy" episode, given in Volume 7, actually followed the Memphis part of this "Jack the Bear" story when Morton told it, and he showed Frenchy's ineptitude on this same little *Salty Dog* theme. The tune reminds him of Bill Johnson and therefore of Freddie Keppard. Keppard's Original Creole band (with the same instrumentation, and some say style, as the later successful Original Dixieland Jazz Band) was formed in 1908, toured widely from 1912 (Los Angeles, 1914, Coney Island, 1915). Keppard never recorded with the group, of course—either because he refused to put his ideas out where anyone could steal them (many New Orleans men played with cloths over their horns so others couldn't watch their fingering) or because the record companies were frightened by this then-strange style. Keppard's later records, made (musicians say) after his power and technique were much diminished, show a still-strong, precise trumpeter with a beat and attack quite like Morton's or Mutt Carey's (and rather unlike Oliver's) and an approach to improvising involving chorus-by-chorus variations like Morton's, like Bunk Johnson's, like, according to testimony, Buddy Bolden's. Morton had played with Keppard in New Orleans and once called him "my protégé." Bill Johnson, Morton's brother-in-law, joined Keppard on bass, as he indicates here, but *Salty Dog* was a thing he played with his trio. By saying that Johnson played "bad" chords here, Morton may mean "low down" or "blue," or he may simply mean very good—as musicians today use "terrible" to indicate approval.

Salty Dog (not, by the way, Charlie Johnson's blues of the same name, which Keppard recorded) is a lightly swinging riff tune with a beat quite unlike the one Morton usually shows on his own compositions. The compelling rhythm that he achieves at this middle dynamic level, and the easy flow of his playing is another lesson on the power of swing versus the power of fortissimo. Part of the reason for this rhythmic flow is, of course, Morton's imitation of Johnson's bass line with his left hand. Anyone who insists that the bassists in those days did nothing but monotonously pluck or slap out two beats to the bar on two chords should attend. On a two-beat pattern he makes a constant reference to a four-beat pattern, and displaces his accents as well.

There are, of course, many melodic lines in early jazz (and in ragtime) which are really riffs. Jimmy Blythe's *Adam's Apple* is a handy example since it is another Keppard record, but the riff did not really dominate jazz melody until late Fletcher Henderson and early Count Basie arrangements. There is a striking similarity between the light swinging quality of Morton's performance here and that which the Basie band achieved.

* * *

By the time Morton came to St. Louis (about 1912), its greatest days were past, but his familiarity with the pieces of Scott Joplin, James Scott, and Artie Matthews is a testament to its illustrious past in American syncopated music. As Morton described it, "The people were prejudiced also in St. Louis. But they had a lot of good musicians in St. Louis because there was a publishing company by the name of Stark and Company that published Negro music special. They were also publishers of Scott Joplin, known throughout the world as the greatest ragtime writer that ever lived." By this time, Joplin was in New York, working on extending his music (*Euphonic Sounds, Magnetic Rag,* and the opera *Treemonisha*). Of those who remained, Matthews was one of those whom Rudi Blesh and Harriet Janis, in their valuable history *They All Played Ragtime,* included in "the third and last of the St. Louis ragtime generations." The fact that Matthews became a successful teacher of the classics in Cincinnati, where he moved in 1918, is a good comment on the nature of ragtime. On one of Morton's earliest band records, made in 1924, he performed *Weary Blues,* which had been written by Matthews for John Stark in 1915, in response to W. C. Handy's success. We don't know how good the musicians were whom Morton was playing for in St. Louis. We *can* hear that Morton does not pretend he was sight reading but admits that he was playing things that he had practiced and knew. He must have been telling the unadorned truth that time.

With Morton's version of the *Miserere* the point is not to compare its aesthetic effect with Verdi's—if one does he can easily take offense in several respects. The point is to notice the nature of the transformation of familiar material—the thing that ragtime composers and jazzmen were doing and are doing, each in his own way and according to the practices of his craft.

In the first place, there is the form of what he makes. Morton takes themes from the "imprisonment" scene and the "Anvil Chorus" and produces a jazz piece in the ABC modified ragtime form. The first strain of the Verdi *Miserere* becomes a thirty-two bar sequence A, the second strain of that duet a sixteen-bar section B. When Morton then follows with a variation on B, notice that the musical-rhythmic character of what he is doing becomes more valid and more interesting. The basis for his sixteen-bar C, "trio" section is, as he says, the "Anvil Chorus." This is the most successful part of the performance: the rhythmic statement is there and Morton is making rhythmic-melodic variations on it before he begins his second chorus of this section.

Morton says he wrote *I'm Alabama Bound* around 1904. "So I kept on traveling around the different little spots, singing my new tune." The tune, of course, is very old and very widespread. Some of us know Leadbelly's version of it, essentially the same piece but with a slightly different melody line than the one here, and if we know such things as Danny and Blu Lu Barker's *Don't You Get Me High*, we've heard it there, too. The second of Blind Boone's *Rag Medleys,* called "Strains from Flat Branch" contains *I'm Alabama Bound.* Boone's own story, as reported by Blesh and Janis, makes another comment on the nature and appeal of ragtime: he led a spasm band (tin whistles, jews-harp, triangles) when a child, had a firm classical training, often fled from it into the back alleys of ragtime, often returned to a successful concert career, published rag themes in his later years.

When Morton was asked to record his "New Orleans Memories" for General Records in 1939, he included a *Don't You Leave Me Here,* obviously based on *Alabama Bound,* with a slightly altered melody. The verse which gives the latter tune its title is the third here, an expression of humorous practicality:

> (*She said*) *Don't you leave me here.*
> *Don't leave me here.*
> *But* (*Sweet Papa*) *if you just must go,*
> *Leave a dime for beer.*

After a little more reminiscence (during which a question seems to have annoyed him), Morton returns to more piano and more stanzas—undoubtedly he could remember, adapt, or invent any number of choruses of lyrics to it when he was using it as his specialty in those days.

≈
≈
≈
≈ # Original Jelly Roll
Blues . . .

There is a story (it may well be true) that in the late 1930s Jelly Roll Morton was in the audience when a large and successful swing band began to play his *King Porter Stomp*. He was upset by their version and went up to the stand, halted them, berated them, and sat down at the piano to show them how they should have been doing it.

This set contains, along with four other solos, versions of two of Morton's most famous pieces. The *Original Jelly Roll Blues* was Morton's "specialty" during early visits to the North as "the earliest published jazz composition." *King Porter Stomp* was, and is, Morton's most successful single piece. It is also a work through which his conception (or part of it) has had, I think, a direct, identifiable, widespread, and continuing influence on jazz. Present also is another of his demonstrations in transformation: *My Gal Sal* here belongs with the *Tiger Rag* of Volume 1 (a French quadrille into jazz), *Maple Leaf Rag* of Volume 3 (ragtime into jazz), *La Paloma* of Volume 4 (a tango into jazz), the French songs of Volume 11, and "The Marching Bands" of Volume 11 (Sousa into jazz).

Sweet Peter is a composition in two themes (the second reminiscent of the popular song *All of Me* among other things). Morton recorded it for Victor in 1929 in a version for seven instruments, and, as far as we know, it was written about that time. The copyright year is 1933. Morton plays it here: introduction, A (in a march-like interpretation, 32 bars), B (more lyric, 32 bars), B (a rhythmic version of the lyric strain). It is interesting because it gives a clear, almost simplified, statement of Morton's use of his left hand and his way of gradually adopting its rhythmic emphasis into a forceful two-handed climax.

State and Madison is a curious inclusion: I can find no other recording of it by Morton. It was published in Chicago in 1926 by Charles Raymond during the period when Melrose Brothers were bringing out Morton compositions with much success. Its first theme is dull. The second, with its descending chimes figures, is a better one, and the third is a much improved echo of the first. For some reason (and perhaps this is the real cause of the dullness involved) Morton plays his two choruses of each theme without much swing* and in almost straight ragtime style until toward the end of the performance. It is odd that this number was originally played, at the 1938 recording sessions, between *Wolverine Blues* and *The Pearls*, which contain some of his liveliest and soundest music in this series.

Freakish is, like *Crazy Chords* and *Pep*, one of Morton's "far out" pieces—a statement that might have more meaning if it weren't true that, even in 1957, Morton's structure and some of his rhythmic devices are still, in a sense, very "far out." He recorded it as a piano solo once before, in 1929, on his second record date in New York. This version swings more, I think. It must be called a study in rhythmic and harmonic "experiments" in an ABAC form, with a "tag" that hints of a rondo return to A.

A good many people who have never heard of Jelly Roll Morton (unless they have run across the "funny name") have heard *King Porter Stomp*. It is (with its three themes cut to two and with one of these never really stated) the most recorded and performed, most popular (unless *Wolverine Blues* beats it), and most influential of his pieces. Yet Morton himself (who made it four times as a piano solo, once as a duet with King Oliver, and once on a piano roll) never recorded a version with a band.

---

* James Dapogny suggested in 1982 that Morton was reading from his Library of Congress copyright deposit manuscript.

In Volume 9, we heard Morton say he had known a pianist named Porter King in Mobile in 1905 who "was considered a very good piano player" and he acknowledged in Volume 3 that King's technical knowledge of music was greater then than his own. He and King wrote the piece together (it may originally have been King's piece, of course) and, according to S. Brunson Campbell, sent it to Scott Joplin in St. Louis for help. But, Campbell added, Morton changed and reworked it later, naming it for King. It was first copyrighted in 1906, first recorded and published in 1924. Many have played it since, and many have used it as a basis for "originals."

In the published version, *King Porter* has three themes with two variations on the third: A,B,C,C,C. In the faster version in Volume 3, Morton played on it A,A,B,B,C,C,C,C almost in a rhythmic study. Here he performs it A,A,B,B,C,C,C. There are differences among all his versions, but the differences between the two in this series are striking, for not only does one hear differing improvisations but an almost complete change in tone and quality. Here, at a slower pace, an almost medium easy-rock, there is no lack of rhythmic interest, but there is a lyric, a melodic-harmonic note that is unique to this version. These two versions give succinct evidence not only of Morton's way of improvising but of his ability to articulate a mood and emotion musically.

In 1944 William Russell wrote an analytical review, for the magazine *The Needle,* when Morton's "lost" recording of his *Frog-i-More Rag* was released, which I think is the definitive essay on Morton's music. "Jelly Roll had a more formal musical training and background than many New Orleans musicians. Perhaps this fact is reflected in the formal construction of his compositions. At times the close-knit design is marked by an economy of means that amounts to understatement . . . Jelly took great pride in his 'improvisations' [on the theme] . . . Jelly's performance is a revelation of rhythmic variety by means of such devices as shifted accents, slight delays, and anticipations. Of course, to some of our European trained 'critics' this is only a bad performance by a pianist unable to keep correct time, of a piece any third-grade conservatory pupil could play right off at sight. Curiously, as raggy as Jelly's performance . . . is, it is nevertheless in perfect *time;* the regular pulse can be felt throughout with no loss at all in momentum . . . The melodic invention of this finale is as notable as its immense rhythmic vitality . . . Jelly's rhythmic impetus and melodic embellishment give the effect of a fantastic and frenzied variation. Actually each bar is directly related to its counterpart in the first simple statement and all of Jelly's most characteristic and fanciful 'figurations' are fused with the basic idea as though they belonged there originally . . . With Jelly Roll, no matter how exuberant rhythmically or varied melodically . . . there is never any doubt of their musical logic and that every note grows out of the original motive."

I have noted my belief that we can see in *King Porter* a direct and clearly identifiable influence of Morton's work on jazz. One could gather a lot of other evidence of influence, of course. You can point especially to the many mid-western or Kansas City musicians who have said they were influenced by his records and scores; and Kansas City groups recorded a number of his pieces. But in the variations on the trio of *King Porter,* figures which Henderson used, passed on to Goodman and all the others, I think we hear a kind of scoring for brass (and Morton clearly had brass in mind in these choruses) which set a pattern, and which influenced almost everyone during the "swing" period (even Ellington: hear *Bojangles* for the clearest instance). And one can hear it continuing to operate in the arrangements of Ernie Wilkins and others.

This collection also contains another version of *Original Jelly Roll Blues,* actually a continuation of the one which was given in part in Volume 1. James P. Johnson remembered Morton playing it on a trip through New York in 1911. It was first published by Will Rossiter in Chicago in 1915. Morton recorded it once before as a piano solo and later in a band version. In Volume 1, we were cut off after his remarks on the chitterlings suppers tapered off (and as the original acetate side ran out) and Morton had been showing off his treble technique again, as he seldom did on his records before these. He resumes here with tango choruses (I especially like the third and the descending figure at its end, and the fourth), then slows down for an account of the words, which he sings with more blues than he uses in the playing.

Morton also remarks on something anyone will notice immediately when he hears this series—the clicking of his heel as he plays. He did it on four beats—yet many think of his favorite rhythm as "two beat." Even when he clearly uses 2/4, an often subtle suggestion of four, plus ever-present tango rhythms and devices, will often account, I think for some of his rhythmic variety—but not all of it. And his rhythms are really, as Russell says, part of his melodies and his developments of his themes.

≈

≈

≈

≈

Buddy Bolden's Legend

"One of my pleasantest memories as a kid growing up in New Orleans was how a bunch of us kids, playing, would suddenly hear sounds. It was like a phenomenon, like the Aurora Borealis—maybe. The sounds of men playing would be so clear, but we wouldn't be sure where they were coming from. So we'd start trotting, start running—'It's this way!' 'It's this way!'— And, sometimes, after running for a while, you'd find you'd be nowhere near that music. But that music could come on you any time like that. The city was full of the sounds of music . . ."— Danny Barker in *Hear Me Talkin' to Ya*, edited by Nat Shapiro and Nat Hentoff.

The Negro community of almost any Southern city or town will have several men's clubs, but in New Orleans there seemed to be more of them than anywhere else. Jelly Roll Morton sometimes rattles off the names of these clubs with the impatience of a man asked to name the commonplace. They all needed music, as a part of the celebration, for outings, dances, funerals, and for parades. Those wonderful New Orleans parades. "Yes, they'd have lots of fights. Well here's the way some of the bands would play" and he begins a version of *Stars and Stripes Forever* strange and exciting, in a style that soon became familiar (in some version or other) around the world.

There is at least one existing photograph of Charles ("Buddy," then "Kid," then "King") Bolden's band. There are six pieces: Bolden's cornet, Willie Cornish's valve trombone, two clarinets, a string bass, a guitar. There is *no* tuba, *no* banjo, *no* drummer

171

(he added one later, Bunk Johnson said), and, of course, there is no piano. A pretty "far out" group isn't it? This, according to many, was the first jazz band. (The instrumentation alone might suggest the kind of rhythmic flow that could make a jazz pulse out of the more clipped rhythms of orchestrated ragtime.) However, you will notice that on these records, Morton does not call Bolden the first jazz musician, but says he played *ragtime.*

Charles "Buddy" Bolden was born about 1878 and died in 1931, but the last twenty-four years of his life were passed in the Louisiana State Hospital at Angola, his diagnosis reading "dementia praecox, paranoid type."

How did he play? He played lots of blues and they say he liked to play them slowly and often quietly. That doesn't sound like ragtime. Albert Gleny, once his bassist, has said he was "the best for ragtime," but for years the New Orleans musical style was called by the name of that Missouri style that had become a national craze. And Willie Cornish said that when they were playing the rhythms might cross "three times at once." Bolden probably made disk records and at least one cylinder, but none of these have been found—yet. Bunk Johnson recorded demonstrations of the way Bolden played (*American Music* 643) on which he seems close to the beat, and with a beat rather like Morton's or Freddie Keppard's or Mutt Carey's. But those demonstrations show variations (which are improvised) that use a rhythmic complexity, and which approach the piece chorus by chorus in a gradually evolving development of a theme. Bud Scott said that Bolden got his music from church; Mutt Carey said: "that music was swinging all the way back in Bolden's time and before him in the Holy Roller churches he got it from." That speaks for rhythmic complexity and for improvisation certainly. Bolden couldn't read and apparently had a superb ear and that speaks both for improvisation and for an imitation of the voice unknown in ragtime.

According to all reports, Bolden was a very powerful trumpeter. He was fantastically idolized. Bunk said: ". . . his band had the whole of New Orleans real crazy and running wild

behind it." Clarence Williams said: "It was after I heard Buddy
Bolden when he came through my home town, Plaquemine,
Louisiana, on an excursion, and his trumpet playin' excited me so
that I said, 'I'm goin' to New Orleans.' I had never heard
anything like that in my whole life before." Bolden was a barber
by trade and he ran a scandal sheet called *The Cricket*. One of the
essential points about him has been made this way: he and his
musicians were a part of the community life, not in any class
apart called "musicians."

Perhaps Mutt Carey's phrase, that Bolden was "the man who
started the big noise in jazz" is the most accurate; he was
powerful enough, good enough, and popular enough to establish
the music's identity and to draw creative people to it who would
continue it, as, say, Armstrong and Parker were to do later.

Morton says that the tune here called *Buddy Bolden's Blues* was
written by Bolden and later stolen by the author of *St. Louis
Tickle* (Barney and Seymore, 1904). The research done by Rudi
Blesh and Harriet Janis for *They All Played Ragtime* indicates that
it was an old ribald levee song, heard all along the Mississippi.
One early publication was in 1899, as a part of Ben Harney's *The
Cakewalk in the Sky*, in which several rhythmic variations on it
were present. Morton's performance here is rather different
from the two slower ones he did later.

The two tracks on "Marching Bands" here were recorded after
the body of the Library series and where a piano was not
available, to fill in some gaps. When Morton says he played
drums and trombones in parades, no one who has heard his left
hand will be much surprised. In the second part, we get the
conversion of Sousa and the *Stars and Stripes Forever* into jazz very
clearly and wonderfully. When he calls out the "next strain," he
gives, of course, a chorus of melodic-rhythmic variation. Anyone
who has ever heard a Negro band in a parade in any Southern city
has heard something approaching this music. Notice also the
remarks on the trombone's improvisation. I once heard a man in
Virginia say that in his early band, which played orchestrated
rags, the trumpet and clarinet read harmonized and unison

passages, but the trombone felt free to "clown," as he did in parades.

Morton's remark (his second such) that ragtime players would keep increasing their tempos because a perfect tempo hadn't been picked for that style has puzzled many and will continue to. Jazz players can increase their tempos, too (Morton may himself), and a blues pianist like Will Ezell does it in a way that makes it seem intentional. The device is standard in many musics, including West African, of course. Morton once said that he hit on his style because he couldn't make fast tempos at first, and then discovered that he could incorporate rhythmic variety, embellishments, and variations of many kinds at such speeds. Certainly if a player uses a simple ragtime bass he may well tend to speed up, and if he is building in his performance by rhythmic-melodic variation, he will not need the false climax of merely increasing his speed.

The question of American Indian music and its influence on jazz reminds one of a theory about jazz which had some popularity at the time of these recordings and was neglected thereafter until bassist Oscar Pettiford (born on a reservation in Okmulgee, Oklahoma) raised it again—strongly, to say the least—at a summer round table in 1956 at Music Inn in Lenox, Mass. One can be sure of one thing: Indian music is analogous to African in several ways, and such an analogue can be an encouragement to creativity. Morton's apparently accurate memory of a Mardi Gras ceremony he had known as a young man (which may have been very mixed with *vodun* music by that time, of course) seems to show that the music made an important impression. A couple of notes appended to Hally Wood's transcription of *Ungai Ha* in Alan Lomax's book, *Mister Jelly Roll* are interesting: "This is written longer than the singer actually sang it. Barely anticipate the beat without any hurried feeling and you will have it." "Not sung as a full tone change, but more as an emphasis on this beat." The descriptions might apply to so much of jazz, to so much of Morton.

The Creole Song, which Morton plays very simply, later showed up in part as a *Creole Song* about two gossips which Kid

Ory later revived. One can readily imagine it as a French song, with a rhythm at half time to this, in a heavy 2/4.

The melody of *If You Don't Shake* could also easily come from a European "nursery" or folk song. If you have any trouble supplying the censored words, maybe you'd better not be listening to this one in the first place.

≈
≈
≈
≈

The Storyville Story

One thing to be kept in mind when hearing this series is that Jelly Roll Morton was not only giving an account of his own music and of his life. He was also being a source of information on the early days of jazz, on life in New Orleans, and on the music he heard there and in his travels. On this LP, for example, besides reminiscence, there are some eight good pieces of music. All of them were close to Morton, all are enlightening and represent the kinds of things which in some way contributed to his music, but only two of them are a part of his music as such.

Another thing to remember is that these records were not made at a regular recording "session" in a professional studio, and there were *no* second takes.

The form of *Levee Man Blues* may sound strange at first. We should not think of any blues as "irregular" because it does not fit the "regular" eight-, twelve-, or sixteen-bar blues patterns we are used to. Some folklorists consider (wrongly, I think) that such things as bars and chorus lengths and "regular" forms impose a formal conception that is not only irrelevant, but quite inhibiting, on a music that is free and spontaneous in pattern and form. There is also the suggestion in this piece of that kind of blues one sometimes hears which begins on the sub-dominant. I suspect that another factor may be involved as well: Morton may have been avoiding a melody line too close to his "specialty," *I'm Alabama Bound,* one which was sung by roustabouts all along the river, and to which these words may fit with little modification or change. The verses also call to mind the one Bud Scott sings on King Oliver's *Snag It:*

Captain, Captain, I mean you must be cross,
I said captain, captain, you must be cross,
It's twelve o'clock and you won't knock off.

No matter how often one hears about it, he is repeatedly struck by accounts of the remarkable cross-section of life which operated so freely in the Storyville district. People from every class, every race, every economic group, and from all over the world came there. To re-create the kind of music that Tony Jackson played for the naked dances in the houses, Morton here plays three choruses. The memory was, like many other in this series, later modified and expanded into a fuller performance. The basis is here: a series of ragtime riffs, varied and modified from chorus to chorus.

Apparently part of the "true story" which inspired *I Hate a Man Like You* was cut out of the beginning here. Morton had recorded the song before, in 1929, accompanying Lizzie Miles. I think this performance, with its ironic acceptance of emotion as a part of reality, has far more blues feeling than Miss Miles, with her hints of vaudeville and torch singing, gave it. I would call this one of Morton's most moving vocal performances in the series. The gently Spanish-tinged accompaniment reminds us of another of Morton's talents: if he had been nothing else, he would have been one of the most sensitive, effective accompanists in early jazz. His orchestral-instrumental conception (a sort of trumpet-clarinet treble, trombone-string bass-drums bass) often accounts for his sound approach to the problem, but only a recognition of his own artistic instincts can account for his success at it.

The "Honky Tonk Blues" selections here supplement those Morton performed in Volume 7. Sometimes the casual descriptions Morton gives of the *milieu* of this music almost lead one to believe that anyone might sit down at a piano in a New Orleans barrelhouse and come up with some such blues—an inaccurate but rather wonderful picture! Here we get a slow vocal blues (a rejected lover stoically restores his confidence), a medium blues with an "eight-beat walking bass" (or as Morton called it earlier a "double running-bass") on which he starts some nice trips in the steady walk toward the end. The remarks on the "days in the Market" (prisoners cleaned up the French Market) remind us of one of the verses he used in *Buddy Bolden's Blues* ("I thought I heard Judge Fogarty say/'Thirty days in the Market./Take him away'") and how the songs of the city were very naturally and realistically about the life in the city.

Both *If I Was Whiskey and You Was A Duck* and *Winin' Boy* may call for some comment. The former song has many versions and many titles, of course (notice that Morton doesn't claim it). It is often called *How Long Do I Have to Wait?* and its most famous version is as the verse of W. C. Handy's *Hesitatin' Blues,* first published in 1915. Instrumental versions of the same or similar sequences are quite common, but one interesting one is Johnny Dunn's record of *Dunn's Bugle Call Blues,* made in New York in 1928. Morton played piano on the date and one hearing will convince one that he was arranger and probably leader as well. The *Bugle Call Blues* is almost a medley of familiar themes. The second is quite like *If I Was Whiskey* and the third is like the *Tiger Rag*-like trio of *Milenberg Joys,* probably Morton's contribution to that piece, which is credited to Paul Mares and Leon Rappolo of the New Orleans Rhythm Kings as well as Jelly Roll.

It is interesting to note—and the note belongs at about this point—the way Morton has begun to be coy, almost seductive, about his reluctance to sing some of the "dirty" words to the song.

We knew the *Winin' Boy* theme as the basis of the second strain of Morton's *Tom Cat Blues* (later called *Midnight Mama* when words were added), but this older blues-song version was first recorded for the Library Archives. The one chorus of quiet humming on this performance can convey the emotions of all the years of loneliness and achievement: all the beautiful and bitter memories of the New Orleans boyhood and youth and the travels, all the brava, all the wonder, and all the loneliness—and all the love of music, of his own and of the music that helped him make his own.

*   *   *

As a sort of coda to the series, I asked several musicians, "Would you advise a young musician to study Morton's music?" These are two of the most pertinent answers—

Wilbur de Paris: "That's comparable to asking me if I would advise students of the classics to study the masters. My approach to jazz can be told in the cliché that says that the height of elegance in anything is simplicity, and I hear that kind of elegance in Morton. Jelly's contribution, as far as I'm concerned, is priceless and anyone who studies his compositions will realize the wide variety of forms he used and the great differences among his pieces. And I think they could be a source of inspiration and of ideas to anyone, not to imitate or copy, but to learn from."

Bob Brookmeyer: "He is a stimulating man. One can learn the essentials of writing, arranging, time, and improvising from him. He was one of the earliest articulate voices in jazz and the forms they used then were more complex than those we use today. I also remember his voice, ringing with pride: pride in his music, in his achievement, in himself as a man, as a gentleman. I hear that pride in his works, too. It is a rare quality; you don't hear it often nowadays."

There is one other tribute one wishes Morton could have known about. It was composer-arranger Bill Russo's decision to use the Melrose stock arrangement of *Hyena Stomp* in his class in the "big band" at the first session of the School of Jazz in Lenox, Mass., in the summer of 1957.

But perhaps the best personal tribute to his spirit is the recovery in his song:

> *I'm a poor boy, a long way from home.*
> *I'm a poor boy, a long, long way from home.*
> *Long way, I'm a poor boy from home.*
> *I'm gonna try to never roam alone . . .*
> *I'm the Winin' boy, don't deny my name!*

III

PROGRAM NOTES

≈

≈

≈

≈
First Recordings:
Quintet of the
Hot Club of France

In 1968 Prestige Records, with Don Schlitten as producer, licensed the earliest records by guitarist Django Reinhardt and violinist Stephane Grappelly. Re-reading these notes, I realize that I should have made more than I did of their version of *Dinah*. One comment below on Gus Kahn's *I've Had My Moments* comes about because its melody resembles Gershwin's *A Foggy Day*. The catalogue number here was Prestige 7614.

A major musician in the jazz idiom who was not an American, who visited the United States only after he was well established, and then only briefly and abortively?

Impossible of course. Yet it is true. For between Lonnie Johnson and Eddie Lang, who emerged in the 1920s, and Charlie Christian, who emerged in 1939, Django Reinhardt was *the* jazz guitar soloist. He learned his jazz first from phonograph records imported from the States, yet by the mid-1930s, he had played with the best visiting American jazzmen, including Louis Armstrong, Coleman Hawkins, and Benny Carter, all of whom were respectfully delighted. And Reinhardt's own records attest not only to how well he had learned his lessons, but also to how lastingly delightful are his solos.

183

The key to his artistry lay, I think, in his perceptive understanding of one of the first requisites of jazz: learn to express what you are. Django Reinhardt was a Belgian-born, French-raised gypsy musician in love with American jazz, and he sounded like it. He was, above all, a unique individual named Django Reinhardt. And he sounded like that too. He did not simply imitate. His playing was not merely derivative. And he certainly did not repeat some "hot licks" in a jazzy style. He went to the heart of the matter, and he made a music.

This LP collects some of the earliest recordings on which Reinhardt soloed. In its first three titles, it offers music from the very first recording date by the group which was, in effect, assembled to feature his talents, the Quintet of the Hot Club of France.

The make-up of that ensemble is interesting. I would be less than frank if I said that its two rhythm guitarists and its bassist made an ideal rhythm section, either in its instrumentation or in its personnel and their performance. The group is a modification of the sort of string ensemble that one associates with the continental European restaurant, café, and bar from the late nineteenth century forward. And there is no question in my own mind that Reinhardt performed differently with them than with the more distinctly jazz-oriented instrumentations and ensembles with which he recorded. Such differences, with a musician of Reinhardt's stature, are important. At the same time, there had been the groups of Eddie Lang and violinist Joe Venuti, and the duets of Lang and Lonnie Johnson, most of which Reinhardt probably knew from records.

The Quintet actually grew out of Reinhardt's desire to lead a string group, and out of backstage jam sessions with Stephane Grappelly—the very first of which took place on *Dinah*, the violinist remembered.

Reinhardt, born in Liverchines, Belgium, in 1910, was at first a proficient violinist who also played banjo and guitar. He was seriously burned in a fire in his caravan in 1928, so much so that the doctors wanted to amputate his left hand. Django refused and during the next year recovered and taught himself to play guitar again, using only three fingers of his left hand on the frets.

The Hot Club of France was an association of enthusiasts founded in December 1932 to organize concerts and promote jazz, and it was "hot" because the word *jazz* had been so abused by its association with derivative and merely jazz-influenced dance and concert music, that a modifier was taken on to indicate the real, improvisational idiom.

The recordings were made for the Ultraphone company in a huge studio that had once served as an organ factory. The musicians gained their confidence by playing a bit, and once recording itself was under way, the session went well. The only mishap can be heard at the end of *Dinah* where Grappelly's bow accidentally hits his bridge; the engineers wanted another take but the musicians like this one.

When the records were released they received the attention of reviewers and listeners who had never before taken jazz seriously. And Reinhardt, although he remained a true Bohemian to the end, himself knew that his reputation was established. The recordings have been in print on a variety of labels, in a variety of countries, since.

It is appropriate that the LP begins with *Tiger Rag,* for its third theme was one of Reinhardt's favorite vehicles for in-person improvising, and he recorded it many times. One knows immediately on hearing his two breaks in the second theme that one is hearing an exceptional guitarist; his solo choruses bristle with ideas, and his accompaniments also amply confirm one's first impression.

On *Dinah,* Reinhardt begins with an invention and obliquely introduces a fragment of the melody only in his second phrase. His nicely paced choruses show how well he had learned his lessons from some of the great jazz hornmen. And he evokes a whole band in his accompaniment to Grappelly. Similarly, on *Lady, Be Good,* Reinhardt lets us glimpse the theme only here and there among phrases of his own invention, almost in Armstrong's manner. And notice, too, how cool Reinhardt's second entrance is; a second-rater would undoubtedly have tried for the big come-on at this point.

On *Avalon,* we get a chance to hear both Reinhardt and Grappelly improvise with a jazz brass section behind them, riffing in fine style. The trumpet soloist is Arthur Briggs, who came to France with the Will Marion Cook orchestra in 1919 (Sidney Bechet was the star soloist of that ensemble), and he had obviously been keeping up with things since. The brass continues on *Smoke Rings,* which has a lovely, ornamented solo by Rein-hardt. Notice that it is Grappelly who comes in to "boot it," as they used to say in those days—with Reinhardt's help beneath him, to be sure.

Blue Drag is not a blues, but a blues-influenced piece in song form, and a fine vehicle for the guitarist. Reinhardt's sensitive solo is a paradoxical combination of delicacy, personal mystery, and strong assertiveness that makes it his early masterpiece, in my opinion.

Swanee River, for me, indicates again Reinhardt's apprentice-ship in its sax-like (which in 1935 means Coleman Hawkins-like) accents. *The Sunshine of Your Smile* (still identified in most discographies by its French title, *Ton Doux Sourire*) has a knowledgeable accompaniment and showy solo by Reinhardt.

Ultrafox (presumably an Ultraphone fox trot) is Reinhardt and Grappelly's own theme, and in his solo Reinhardt shows clearly that he had the basic attribute of a first-rate jazz improviser: he was a melodist. But he was at the same time an instrumental melodist who understood that the guitar had properties and resources of its own.

I've Had My Moments opens with a Grappelly statement in his best ballad style, sweet and full of sentiment, as the violin can be, but not really schmaltzy, as the violinist can also be. The tempo rises for Django's eventful solo, for an invention by the violinist, and for some riffing figures and breaks. (If it occurs to anyone to ask about it at this point, Gershwin's *A Foggy Day* appeared two years later, in 1937.)

The venerable *Sheik of Araby* is a vehicle for the more-than-able reed work of Alix Combelle, who makes a record-fast switch from tenor to clarinet along the way. Very much in the background of this performance was the fact that Coleman Hawkins was in Europe at the time, and had recorded with Reinhardt and Grappelly. He would soon record with Reinhardt and Combelle as well. Django's accompaniment is exceptional: he is, one might say, rhythm, brass, and reeds—all spontaneously.

The official billing when these records were first released was "Django Reinhardt et le Quintette du Hot Club de France avec Stephane Grappelly," which in a sense gives the violinist the last word. Critic André Hodeir once called Grappelly "a genuine improviser," which is the kind of remark that is as important for what it does not say as for what it does. But listen again to *Smoke Rings*, and listen to him on *Ultrafox* and on his later entrance on *I've Had My Moments*. Reinhardt's accompaniment helps, of course, but on this toughest of jazz instruments, Grappelly had (and still has) the attack of a jazzman. (1968)

≈

≈

≈

≈

Dinah Washington: "The Queen"

The appearance of Mercury MG 20439, and the invitation to write some notes for it, allowed me to say something about Dinah Washington, her roots, and her very contemporary style.

There is now still another reason for the younger jazz musicians and listeners to be discovering Dinah Washington as their older brothers did: many of them are apt to be of a "funky" persuasion.

The musicians of the mid-'50s school felt that certain tendencies in the cool style might be robbing jazz of its emotional heritage and, to correct the matter, these men turned to gospel music and to the blues as a means of replenishing their playing. In such music, besides many of melodic forms and rhythmic devices, they knew there was confirmation for the kind of shout and passion they wanted to employ.

Dinah Washington knows about these things, and the way she sings has always shown that she does. As one man has put it, "People talk about how all these young rhythm and blues singers are now using a churchy style. Why, Dinah Washington has always used one. She's more sophisticated, sure, but sometimes I think she sounds like she just walked out of a Baptist church, stopped by the Brill building just long enough to pick up a copy of a tune, and started to wail."

She did beat the funky players to a kind of direct gospel-jazz, and her biography confirms what our ears will tell us about it.

Dinah Washington (born Ruth Jones—but if you have heard of one singer by that name, imagine how many others there might be) was almost raised on religious music and was accompanying a church choir on piano before she was fifteen. She became a jazz singer by winning an amateur contest, let a lot of people know she was one when she worked with Lionel Hampton, let everybody know it when she became her own boss some twelve years ago.

In a recent interview, Washington said that she strongly objected to her usual billing as "Queen of the Blues." I don't blame her; she sings a lot more pop songs than she does blues. And she always has, although her first record was *Evil Gal Blues* and although she continues to sing blues—there are four on this disc. On the other hand, you could reasonably say that she sings nothing but blues, because no matter what the song she usually turns it into her kind of gospel-style blues, and that fact reveals one source of her effectiveness.

The blues is more than 8- or 12-, or 16-bar musical forms; it can be an attitude toward life. It always involves a kind of humor, and Dinah Washington is innately equipped for it. I don't mean just the kind of salty joke with which she embellishes the words to *All of Me* here, "Since you took the best, why not come back and support the rest"; it is a deeper kind of wit. It shows in her concluding stanza after she has described the destruction and turbulence of *Back Water Blues,* "But if I ever get my nerves settled down, Lord, I'll be a mean so-and-so." That song comes from Bessie Smith, and Dinah Washington shares with the blues singers of the '20s that ironic way of seeing things. It is never nihilistic but is affirmative, and always affirmative of the individual consciousness and of its right to see and accept things according to its own lights.

Take *I Thought About You.* The tune itself has an excessively four-square quality, but one would hardly know it from this interpretation. From the first phrase it is obvious that Dinah Washington is not an obedient servant to that tune as it is on paper but will break through the mechanical quality of its contours. She alters melody and meter to make music out of banality. One source of what she does to it, melodically, rhythmically, and emotionally, is certainly her kind of churchy-blues. And one thing that makes her ability to do it her own way is the ease with which she handles her rhythm. She always swings, of course, but she sings around the mere mechanics of the beat easily; she does not have to remind herself of where she is rhythmically and doesn't have to risk rhythmic monotony.

Or take *Lingering*. One thing that keeps it from being the sentimental and rather effete thing that another singer might have made of it, is, again, the fact that Dinah Washington refuses to sing those lush lines the way they are written. Like a good jazz singer and musician, she sees how the tune can be converted into an honest comment on reality and proceeds to make it into one.

Another of her resources shows particularly on *I Remember Clifford*, her ability to use dynamics—the way she can move swiftly from a near-whisper to a near-shout without sounding like she is pulling off a mere vocal trick or performing a stunt for a dull audience. She can show the knowledge that such things need to contribute to quality and development of a performance or, in the long run, they come to nothing. And she can carry her audience without talking down to it.

As I say, there are four blues here. The newer ones—*Show Time* and *Bad Luck*—both use in part the kind of "refrain" blues form that has four bars of stop-time plus a repeated refrain that ends each stanza. Washington has always done this kind of blues and because she handles that stop-time so well, she helps keep the form alive in jazz-blues singing.

Trouble in Mind (an eight-bar blues) and *Back Water Blues* both date from the '20s. This new version of the latter is a very good example of her sense of pace. By restraining and a gradually revealing vocal intensity and building her emotional pattern, Washington transforms a narrative into an individual's dramatic monologue, and the final stroke of the line I quoted above (one that Bessie Smith did not use in her version) is surely a delightful, almost sublime, example of release-of-tension, restoration-of-order, and human nature triumphant.

One more thing that Washington shares with the great blues singers of the past and perhaps all good singers is her implicit ability as an actress. I do not mean the kind of actress that the movies have made us all too familiar with who is really a "performer" or a "personality." I mean the kind of actress who uses her resources to fulfill her role, not her role as an excuse to dramatize herself.

I have saved this new version of *Somewhere Along the Line* for last because I think that so many of Washington's virtues as a singer come together in it in exceptional balance. It is a mature performance by a singer-actress. What she can do with her voice and with her emotions is beautifully disciplined and channelled toward an almost delicate exposition of a song and mood. Lest my exposition of some details of her craft lead you to believe that she is capable only of a kind of tasteful bravura or of exhibiting certain appropriate resources and effects, by all means hear this one and let it change your mind. And let it show you how when all the details of her craft melody, rhythm, meter, dynamics, embellishment, improvisation, emotion are granted, then they must all mysteriously come together and become one thing. (1959)

≈
≈
≈
≈

The Weary Blues and Other Poems Read by Langston Hughes

The jazz-and-poetry phenomenon was a relatively short-lived one of the late 1950s, which started—as one might expect—in the Bay area. Leonard Feather had the very interesting and appropriate idea of recording Langston Hughes, a writer whose work had a special relationship to the blues and jazz, with two groups, a "traditional" ensemble including trumpeter Red Allen, trombonist Vic Dickenson, and others; the other, nominally led by pianist Horace Parlan, and including Jimmy Knepper and other members of Charlie Mingus's Jazz Workshop, including the leader himself, and using some of his music. Had I been reviewing the album rather than annotating it, I would have felt obliged to add that, unexpectedly, Hughes proved to be a bit less than perfect as a reader, with a somehow less-than-perfect rapport with the rhythm section. The recording appeared on MGM E3697.

As one who has had strong misgivings about what Nat Hentoff has called "this jazz-and-poetry hopscotch," let me assure that this record is a different matter.

It should be fairly well known by now that the current interest in poetry readings to jazz music began last year in San Francisco. Some of its leaders have said that the original suggestion came from Dylan Thomas. At any rate, by the spring of 1957 in "The Cellar" club, the poets were reading, reciting, and rolling their abdomens and the musicians were playing. The word spread, and New York's Half Note installed a regular poetry night (which often reached a rather noisy climax about one a.m.) and the Five Spot had hired a poet.

(Anyone who has been exposed to a course in American poetry, will remember that Vachel Lindsay had at least comparable ideas in the 1910s and 1920s for the combination of poetry and a music, which if it wasn't really jazz was often of the more rowdy popular variety.)

Probably these activities were an inevitable outgrowth of the nature of the artistic Bohemia in these cities in contemporary America, and of the downright *fan*-ish way in which its poets and painters listen to jazz.

However, there were some strong *buts* voiced. The first was that, despite the opinion of the poets, their works (and the works of the French "decadents" and Americans of the twenties which they also used) really did not have enough in common with jazz to prevent a strong incongruity. Another was an old lesson that had been learned in previous efforts to meld the arts. Poetry is an art, and the partisans of jazz at least insist that jazz is one, and a constantly growing one. The usual result of such blendings is that one experience predominates, the others become a functional part of it. We can call opera a union of music, poetry, dance, design—but it is clear that opera is essentially a musical experience and the librettist soon learns (perhaps to his dismay) that he must restrain himself at the level of a respectable versifier. Thus, if this poetry was going to be poetry, this struggling art of jazz was going to come off second.

One other objection was perhaps more to the point: jazz has a poetry; it is called the blues. In blues lyrics lie some of the finest "folk" poetry in English. If anything is going to happen with any jazz-and-poetry, why not try to develop things from that point, the vocal blues, where part of the work had already been done and where the development might be a more natural, less artificial one?

The blues singer is a poet and, like the ancient bard and the medieval minstrel, he keeps his melodies and accompaniments simple and functional. However, within the medium of vocal blues, there had been a striking development: a kind of blues singing in which the poetry remained poetry, but the instrumental accompaniment and interplay had enlarged in both size and scope. Thus, Ma Rainey and Bessie Smith and the other women blues singers of the twenties used not only sizable groups but outstanding soloists like Joe Smith and Tommy Ladnier, but even a virtuoso of the time like Louis Armstrong. And in the thirties one could hear Joe Turner with a small ensemble, Billie Holiday with select instrumentalists, and Jimmy Rushing singing not only with Lester Young, Dickie Wells or Buck Clayton in response, but with the entire Basie band. And some of the first bop music reached records as accompaniments by Dizzy Gillespie and Charlie Parker to blues singing.

Such activity, if it was not on a level with the balanced equating of poetry and music one finds in German *Leider,* was at least full of latent possibilities. Why not start at that point?

Now there is at least one American poet who had taken the devices and conventions of blues and of gospel-spiritual music as the basis from which he developed his own poetic voice, and begun it as long ago as the twenties. His name is Langston Hughes. Here was a poetry that had deliberately sought to extend traditional forms and had as its subject the life in which those forms grew and flourished.

At his public appearances, Hughes often tells with irony the story of how he became a poet—he was elected one in grade school when it was the only position left open in the election of class officers. He also has become a novelist, short story writer, historian, biographer, children's author, librettist (he wrote *Street Scene* with Kurt Weill), and the chronicler of Simple.

Some of the poems on this record go back to the twenties and the musicians who work with him on some of those blues and songs were selected because of the sympathy of their styles with those works.

Henry "Red" Allen is in some ways the most advanced member of the New Orleans trumpet school which had produced Buddy Bolden, King Oliver, Tommy Ladnier, Louis Armstrong. Stylistically, Allen may be said to represent a kind of "missing link" between Armstrong and Roy Eldridge. From his first appearances in New York with Luis Russell and Fletcher Henderson it was evident that his was one of the leading trumpet voices of the thirties and, especially as a result of some recent recording work, he is lately being rediscovered as one of the true individual jazz stylists.

Vic Dickenson, two years Allen's senior, had been in many "southwestern" bands before he came to prominence with Claude Hopkins, Benny Carter and Count Basie. His individual emotional projection and vocal tone make him too one of the strong individualists on his instrument.

Sam "the Man" Taylor has turned the "rock and roll" gig into a career for himself in the past few years, but he has long been a jazz tenor saxist, his favorites having been Coleman Hawkins and Ben Webster.

The piano of Al Williams is evident throughout the first side of this record. He has been associated with Allen since 1943 and his flexible style has also been heard on records with Sonny Stitt. And anyone who has purchased over four jazz LP's made in New York in the last few years must have at least one with Milt Hinton and Osie Johnson.

Like the other members of the second instrumental group, pianist Horace Parlan has been a member of Charlie Mingus's Jazz Workshop Quintet which he joined in October 1957. Parlan suffered an attack of polio during his childhood in Pittsburgh and through the encouragement of bassist Wyatt Ruther and his teacher Mary Alston, he developed a predominantly left-hand piano style. His playing alone might tell us that one of his favorite pianists is Horace Silver; his others include Bud Powell and John Lewis, and, like Silver and Lewis, Parlan is also a composer-arranger.

Charlie Mingus has said of the music of this group that it comes from Duke Ellington, Charlie Parker, church, and the lives of its players. Clearly it too shows the results of the movement in Eastern jazz of the fifties which has set musicians to examining their roots in the basic blues and church music and not only has modified their work but introduced a new set of terms like "funk" and "soul."

Trombonist Jimmy Knepper has been called by one commentator the first original trombonist since J. J. Johnson (and, incidentally, he lists Vic Dickenson as one of his early influences). And Shafi Hadi (Curtis Porter) is one of several current Eastern reed men whose playing is both contemporary and a reflection of an apprenticeship in rhythm and blues bands.

This, as I began saying, is different. A poetry which has its roots in blues, in jazz, and in the life in which these musics grew, read with just such music. A meeting on ground that is common and has been fertile for a very long time. (1958)

≈
≈
≈
≈

Art Blakey's
Jazz Messengers
with Thelonious Monk

Atlantic's recorded collaboration of Blakey and Monk, two
artists with whom the label was not regularly associated,
was issued on the label's LP 1278. It came at a time when
Blakey had acquired a sizable audience, but when Monk
was only beginning to do so.

I think that this collaboration of Art Blakey's group and
Thelonious Monk dramatizes important events in jazz in the late
1950s for, although each man has been heard from for years, each
has recently been listened to probably more attentively than ever
before, and each is a man in whose work we see jazz doing what it
must do as a music with an identity of its own—finding, not
borrowing, its way by developing the implicit possibilities in the
materials which are its substance.

Now that the "cool" conception of the early fifties has ceased to
be a fad, it should be clear which of its arrangers, its instrumentalists, and its groups have been and are capable of genuine
creativity within that idiom, and of exploring it further, and
which are capable only of a kind of derivative hack-work. The
fashion as such has passed and the real artists and craftsmen can
be counted.

When the pendulum swung, it swung almost violently, and the style it swung to soon acquired a name or two: "funky" and "hard Bop." Art Blakey has led groups of messengers for years, but the group he introduced in 1954 proclaimed the "funky" style. These men wanted to incorporate as much of the quality, as well as the devices, of blues and church music in their playing as they could. Inevitably, they were called regressive and even crude, but their conception was actually neither *naif* nor reactionary. It implied that if jazz got too far from the kinds of music in its background, it might not only be in danger of a contrivance and preciocity, but of losing something essential—indeed, even of losing its identity. Such an attitude is not merely conservative, and the style not for another reason: as I have indicated above, I think it is bringing about some stylistic changes in jazz. (For a precedent, we can remember how the dominance of the almost classic ragtime conception at the turn of the century was supplanted by what has been called a "blues craze," and how a combination of elements of these two was worked out in New Orleans.)

Some of Blakey's earliest records were made with Thelonious Monk and the two collaborate excellently. It has been said of Blakey that he took the bop style and reduced it to its elements. When such a thing happens, one had better be watching for changes.

The bop drummer both simplified his basic accompaniment and expanded it by adding to it a spontaneous series of accents and replies to the soloist's improvisations, with bass "explosions," snare and cymbal strokes, etc.

Listen to Blakey behind Bill Hardman's trumpet solo on *I Mean You.* Clearly he not only accompanies but directly leads the trumpet into ideas and motifs. It is a dangerous role for a drummer, demanding constant discretion and sympathy with the soloist. The second change is illustrated in some of Blakey's solos: probably more directly than any other drummer, Blakey saw the possibility of sustaining polyrhythmic lines and he can keep several rhythms going with an unusual kind of continuity. But the most important point for me is the one we can hear illustrated by what he does on the opening chorus of *I Mean You.* He carries the accompanying 4/4 pulse, but, at the same time, he improvises a parallel percussive line which interplays with both the melody and the fundamental time: the jazz drummer becomes an improvising percussionist on a plane almost equal to that of the horns.

Rhythm is fundamental to jazz and if one develops its role soundly, one develops jazz along the way that its own nature implies that it should go. Such an obvious thing, and yet how brilliant. In the forties, Paul Bacon, probably the only American critic who understood Thelonious Monk, said of him in *The Record Changer* that he had looked at jazz, seen the gaps and, sacrificing the obvious things that everyone could do, proceeded to fill in those gaps. The same kind of thing might be said of Art Blakey.

Almost anyone knows that Monk is supposed to have been one of the founders of bop. Undoubtedly he made important contributions to the style, but it should be clear by now that what this strikingly original musician has been working on all along is something different.

Monk is a virtuoso of time, rhythm, meter, accent. He has played versions of "standards" which are little more than sets of unique rhythmic variations directly on a melodic line, with an evolving pattern of displaced accents and shifting meters—a conception at once more basic than the groups of melodic variations Jelly Roll Morton, James P. Johnson, and Fats Waller produced, and more "experimental" than the harmonic variations, which improvise new melodic lines of the late swing and bop instrumentalists. At the same time, he may play melodic variations, and his solo here on *In Walked Bud* interplays the melodic line of that piece with contrasting motifs. And notice his rhythmic and harmonic experiments with the sparsely suggestive and obviously difficult tissue of notes that is *Evidence*, both in his own solo and behind John Griffin's.

Monk's harmonies, always a part of the picture, are not innovations in themselves—it is the sequence and pattern of alteration in which he plays them that is unique. In this and in simultaneous accentual shiftings, there is an almost constant element of humor (even sarcasm) that his wonderful, deliberate dissonances often point up.

Monk also plays harmonic variations, and these may seem quite simple, even casual, on the surface. His two choruses here on *I Mean You* show the kind of inner logic they can have. The first chorus is based on a descending motif variously altered. The second on a brief and contrasting riff figure which is turned several ways, subjected to a counter-riff or two and, in the end, complemented by a descent which alludes to the first chorus and ties the two together. And, lest anyone doubt that Monk can improvise a lyric melody, let him hear the solo on *Blue Monk*.

Monk's style, like Lester Young's in the late thirties, depends on surprise. It does not, like the work of earlier "stride" pianists (yes, Monk, like Count Basie, is really a member of that school), depend on the expected. He can also be one of the most exciting and original accompanists in jazz, as his work behind Bill Hardman on *I Mean You*, both horns on *Rhythm-a-ning*, and behind Griffin on *Purple Shades* illustrates. The last example seems to me one of the best things I have ever heard him do on records and, notice also that both his solo and his accompaniment on that piece are based on similar ideas and patterns, giving that performance a fine continuity.

I think that on the whole, Monk's compositions place him with the great jazz composers, but I will confine myself to a few points which the selections here illustrate. Whereas Ellington often leans heavily on the "show tune" tradition, Monk is more directly instrumental in his conception, even when he uses the 32-bar, AABA popular tune form. Monk, himself, has made the point about the integration of the B, bridge, melody; notice that the bridges of *I Mean You* and of *In Walked Bud* are both developments of bits of the final phrase in the A melody. It is not Monk's habit to base his compositions on "standard" chord sequences, but he may, and three of the tunes here do use slight alterations of bass lines we all know. That is almost bound to be true of any 12-bar blues, of course, but notice the structure of *Blue Monk*'s melody. Most blues have an open space of about three beats at the end of each four-bar unit. There are "modern" blues which deliberately fill this hole, of course, but the deceptive simplicity with which this melody unfolds makes for neither a trick nor a contrivance, but an inevitability that flows like life.

Monk does indeed "fill in the gaps." (1957)

≈
≈
≈
≈

Solo Monk

Columbia CS 9149 was Thelonious Monk's third solo piano album.

Here's Thelonious Monk, once considered the most far out of jazzmen, opening this solo recital with a version of *Dinah*. And his left hand strides with an *oom-pa* beat that might have come directly from the 1920s. Monk's light-hearted spoof is a burlesque of the past, perhaps, but it never ridicules or degrades. It is funny, and if you have any doubts about the humorous intent of this *Dinah*, listen to Monk's jingling ending. At the same time, the performance bristles with Monkian melodic ideas and Monkian rhythmic delays, which means that the humor is always intrinsically musical.

On the other hand, there is *I Should Care*, a starkly original succession of piano sounds. Groups of notes sing out sustained, others are abruptly dampened. Left-hand figures trip by lightly and briefly even while previous right-hand notes are still ringing out. *I Should Care* is the work of a man whose pianistic technique and control are as striking and as musically effective, it seems to me, as those of any pianist in any music.

Perhaps *I Should Care* holds the key to Monk's formidable reputation as a pianist and musician. His point of departure is a superior popular song; but as he transforms it, it is no longer a song—intended to be sung—that happens to be played on a piano. It becomes a two-handed piano work which Monk has recomposed in terms of the keyboard, recomposed in terms of his own original pianistic techniques. Yet for all its originality, its subtlety and its musicality, Monk's *I Should Care* is still as accessible to almost any listener as the original song itself.

How many jazz pianists—how many artists of any kind—would expose themselves so openly as Monk does here in an unaccompanied piano solo album? Perhaps one should approach this recording as Thelonious Monk's tersely individual history of jazz piano. From the point of view of the completely uninitiated, there is definite pedagogical pleasure, for Monk once again revives the traditional idea of basing his variations and improvisations directly on the melody. While it is hard to lose the melody in these performances, it is just as easy to realize that—by leaving out a note here, adding a note there, delaying another note or a phrase, or adding a whole handful of notes—Monkian alchemy can transform the most watery musical idea into gold.

Similarly, Monk carries on the idea of a traditional, pulsing *oom-pa* left hand in several pieces. He strides in *Dinah* almost like Fats Waller or James P. Johnson as he does on *I Hadn't Anyone Till You*. And he uses a kind of light abstraction of stride bass on *Sweet and Lovely* and *Everything Happens to Me*.

There are the two pieces here in traditional blues form. Typically, Monk reassesses the most basic blues ideas in the most remarkably unexpected manner. Yet I am sure that what he does in *North of the Sunset* would have pleased an older blues man like Jimmy Yancey. Speaking of technique, in *Monk's Point* is one of the most refined examples I have ever heard of Monk's way of *bending* a piano note—not of slurring together two successive notes, but actually producing a continuous curve of sound—an "impossible" technique Monk achieves by a careful manipulation of piano keys, pedals, fingers, and hand positions.

For further contributions to tradition by T. Monk himself, notice the hefty clusters of notes on *I Surrender, Dear*. They are not always "harmonious" in the traditional sense, but they are deliberate and effective, including the frequent use of an obvious, quasi-amateurish bass note. Such things save Monk's complex chords from any sentimentality and overripeness. Take

Sweet and Lovely, one of several unexpected revivals Monk has placed in the jazz repertory. Here the pianist's crisp attack sings the theme so that it is both sweet and lovely but never sentimental; it is not merely pretty, it is beautiful. Or listen to *These Foolish Things* and hear how Monk's obliqueness has transformed what might have been a self-pitying torch song into a wise and witty blues.

Fortunately, Thelonious Monk has included two of his own best melodies: *Ask Me Now,* which he here plays with a ringing lyricism, and *Ruby, My Dear.* Monk wrote the latter when he was still in his teens, I am told, and has played it many times since. Yet he performs it here as if he has just discovered it. This is a rare performance, uncompromisingly emotional and, in the end, truly majestic. Monk's piano sings starkly, passionately, in one of those miracles in which human emotion triumphs fully over the mechanics of the keyboard and its hammers and strings. The final touch comes as Monk drops his steady tempo at just the right moment for an *ad lib* conclusion, without losing musical momentum.

Ruby, My Dear is the work of a man whose technique is placed at the disposal of music. But he does not dazzle us; indeed he does not "show" us anything. He has the true artist's ability to involve us with him so that we seem to be working things out together. He can take the simplest note and make it count in every way because he knows the musical worth of each sound he makes and each silence he allows. In the passion of the moment, he may even strike a note in mistake (as did Schnabel playing Beethoven), but we all know none of this detracts.

Monk is a jazzman, surely, and a supreme one. But he is a rare musician for any music. (1964)

The Art of
John Coltrane

As the text which follows will indicate, Atlantic SD2-313 was a two-LP retrospective drawing on John Coltrane's years with that label, 1959–61.

He has been dead since July 1967. We know that we miss him sorely; we have known that for a long time. And yet, I wonder if we really know how much we miss him.

For John Coltrane's talent was a rare (if not impossible) combination. He was a leading jazzman, leading not only because of his abilities, technical and imaginative, but also because he was one of the most advanced musicians around. He was into things that all musicians and true lovers of the music believed were breaking new ground and outlining the future.

And yet this avant gardist was a popular figure with a following both avid and, in jazz terms, sizable. That following attended his every public appearance and bought his recordings. Coltrane even had a hit record (again in jazz terms) and you'll find it in this album.

From his popularity, everybody benefited; his following spilled over and fell on almost everybody in jazz, and the music benefited.

Popular figures are important for any art. They keep up a public interest in the activities of many men involved in that art.

But widely popular figures are almost never the men who break new ground, who open up new emotional and technical possibilities for an art.

But John Coltrane was such a figure. And his audience was largely young and often black, let us remember. Perhaps too, a segment of that huge audience that otherwise went to such figures as Ray Charles and James Brown and the Supremes came to him.

For those who come to his music for the first time through this album, and for those who would like a refresher, it might be good to summarize Coltrane's career briefly.

John Coltrane was born in Hamlet, North Carolina, on September 23, 1926. His family moved to Philadelphia and there Coltrane took up E-flat alto horn, clarinet, and, later, saxophone in high school. He continued musical studies at the Granoff Studios and Ornstein School of Music in Philly (obviously he was now serious about music) and played his first professional job in 1945.

Later that same year he was in the Navy in Hawaii playing in the band. By 1947 he was on tour with singer Eddie Vinson, "Mr. Cleanhead," in a rhythm-and-blues unit, and the kind of experience in the basic blues which that experience provided is important to any jazzman. Coltrane was hired by Dizzy Gillespie in 1949 and was with him until 1951, but he did not attract very much attention with Gillespie either among fans or musicians.

Subsequently, it was back to r & b with Earl Bostic in 1952–53. Then, in 1953–54, he joined the group of the resplendent alto saxophonist Johnny Hodges, who had left Duke Ellington— temporarily, as it turned out.

In 1955 came the job that brought 'Trane his first strong recognition and gave his work its first sense of identity for listeners. Miles Davis got it all together for himself and formed the quintet that was to establish him as a star jazzman, and Coltrane was his saxophonist (although he was not, the insiders said, Davis' first choice).

Casual listeners and casual reviewers were then hearing

Coltrane as another "hard" tenor man, and he was often compared to Sonny Rollins. The resemblances were somewhat superficial, as we shall see, but in any case, he was already a strong, involved (if sometimes hesitant) technician, and a superb foil to the leader, then a trumpeter of detached and apparently simple lyric style.

During the summer and fall of 1957, 'Trane was a member of the quartet of Thelonious Monk for a historic stay at the old Five Spot Café in New York, and a small but tenacious public heard an alliance that trombonist J. J. Johnson described as the most compatible and fruitful he experienced since Charlie Parker and Dizzy Gillespie worked together in the mid-1940s.

It was a powerful experience, and in that small Bowery bar were taking place musical explorations that would have repercussions literally all over the world.

For Coltrane, it was a learning period, personally and musically. He was going through a personal crisis, a period of self-exploration, from which he emerged pretty nearly triumphant, and he spoke readily at the time of how much he was learning musically, night after night, playing with Monk.

Early in 1958, John Coltrane returned to Miles Davis' unit and was with him, somewhat intermittently, until April 1960. But it was his real intention to go off on his own, make his own music, and it was at this period that this series of Atlantic recordings began.

A word about Coltrane's style. Coleman Hawkins was the father. He played what a classical musician would call an *arpeggio* style; a vertical style, we might call it. Hawkins' most brilliant follower was Don Byas, who spent most of his life after the mid-1940s as an ex-patriate living in Holland, away from the life that his native country handed both him and his native art. But meanwhile, there had been Lester Young, whose sound was lighter and whose style was much more directly oriented in melody than Hawkins'—more horizontal, let's say. And, subsequently—most tenor men had combined the two approaches—Dexter Gordon was a leader in this approach and Sonny Rollins was, in a sense, his successor.

Coltrane apparently went through a Gordon-inspired period. But when his own style emerged, he had become a kind of updated Hawkins or Byas, expanding on their approaches in various ways—moving them from arpeggios to full scales, for one thing, to spread out those passionate "sheets of sound," as Ira Gitler called them.

Then there was his saxophone sound. It extended over a full three octaves of the horn and, wonder of wonders, was equally strong in each of them.

The music here carries Coltrane from his role as a sophisticated harmonicist, ingeniously playing the chord changes, through his incantatory "modal" playing and into his role as an avant gardist, playing "outside" the old, established intervals. I won't comment at length on all of it (as though anybody needed to), but I will single out some pieces as a kind of guide to the sketch above of his explorations during the important years this album covers.

My Shining Hour and *Like Sonny* are echoes of the years with Miles Davis, and they use his rhythm section of that time. The former is a ballad taken somewhat "up" in tempo and swinging— a time-honored practice in jazz at which Davis, 'Trane, and the pianist here, Wynton Kelly, are exceptional. The Rollins dedication is a tribute to the structures and practices favored by the fellow tenormen, and not to his style.

Giant Steps is perhaps the full expression of Coltrane the harmonicist. An ingeniously constructed obstacle course of chord changes to the musician (and an almost perfect instruction piece for the student), it is also a gracefully exciting experience for the listener. Coltrane explained when it was recorded that "the bass line is kind of a loping one. It goes from minor thirds to fourths, kind of a lop-sided pattern in contrast to moving strictly in fourths or in half steps." Notice also, the openness which Tommy Flanagan, a virtuoso pianist when he wants to be, wisely uses in his solo as a contrast to what Nat Hentoff called Coltrane's "intensely crowded choruses."

Countdown may perhaps be said to carry things even further than *Giant Steps* structurally. It is rather like a piece called *Tune*

Up (of which Miles Davis was very fond) with *Giant Steps* laid out on top of it.

The attractive *Syeeda's Song Flute* reminded the composer of "a happy child's song" when he wrote it, so he named it for his daughter, then ten years old.

McCoy Tyner's *Aisha* is worthy of comment here, not only for the fact that it offers Coltrane's unique disciplined way with a lyric melody, but also for his modesty. He leaves much of the improvisation to his sidemen—to Freddie Hubbard, his new and very important companion, to Eric Dolphy, and to the pianist-composer.

On *Central Park West,* Coltrane takes a similarly direct approach to relaxed melody. And he plays *Body and Soul* (a tenorist's ballad from Coleman Hawkins on, of course) in easy long-metre over the tempo.

Blues to Bechet looks both backward and forward. It is evidence that when Coltrane took up the soprano saxophone, a very difficult instrument in terms of intonation and range, he returned to the master, Sidney Bechet, and played a blues tribute to him. But he did it very much in his own, haunting, suspended style.

That haunting suspension is very much evident on *Mr. Knight,* conceived in the incantatory, modal style that Miles Davis introduced in his *"Kind of Blue"* album, most meaningfully on the piece called *So What?* It is, in any case, a direct contrast to *Giant Steps,* for it does away with the obstacle course and allows Coltrane's sophistication to explore a piece with very few harmonic signposts.

And that leads us to Coltrane's *My Favorite Things,* a hit that was in no way a compromise for him, a piece with a simple, folk-like lyric melody, very little chordal movement, and an invitation also to give a direct, basic 3/4 waltz rhythmic treatment in a jazz concert. As *How High the Moon* was to Charlie Parker, *My Favorite Things* was to Coltrane.

Then *The Invisible,* Ornette Coleman's early, somewhat tentative, piece. And Coleman's later "free" jazz (make no mistake about it) became an important influence on 'Trane. It is done with two Coleman associates, Don Cherry and Ed Blackwell. Percy Heath had originally recorded with Coleman, and bassist Heath was an early champion of Ornette's music.

For myself, I vividly remember Ornette Coleman's first New York concert appearance. It was in an "all star" package evening at Town Hall and while Ornette was on, Coltrane stood attentively in the wings, catching every note. He was, at that stage, the only musician who did.

I said above that it was almost impossible for a man to be as much of a technician, artist, and explorer as Coltrane and still have the kind of popular following that he had. What did he tell the audience? In what new and meaningful things did his music instruct them?

I don't know, of course. And perhaps as a white man, I can't know. But I would venture a suggestion. I don't think Coltrane spoke of society or politics. I think that like all artists, he spoke of things of the spirit, those things by which the soul of man survives. I think he spoke of the ways of the demons and the gods that were always there, yet are always contemporary. And I think he knew that he did. (1973)

≈
≈
≈
≈

National Jazz Ensemble

The National Jazz Ensemble, founded and directed by Chuck Israels, was an effort to establish a repertory orchestra to play classic works from the full range of jazz history. It raised all of the problems implied by jazz repertory and, except for its approach to the New Orleans classics (one of Morton's in this case, which was re-orchestrated for large ensemble), faced them in provocative, frequently fruitful ways. It therefore paved the way for a musical activity which, I am sure, will be an important part of jazz's future in the United States. And if I know Israels, he may yet revive his own effort. The recording for which these comments were written was Chiaroscuro CR 140.

Jazz has always depended for its survival and growth on the activities of its young players, groups, and composer-orchestrators, those who perceived what needed to be done next and proceeded to do it. One generation of musicians after another has taken care of such business for over six decades and a rich body of music has been built and preserved chiefly on recordings.

That superb body of music needs something more than record collections for its survival; it needs performance, and the recent arrival of the professional jazz repertory orchestra is a significant event in American music.

The National Jazz Ensemble is unique. Here is one orchestra, one single assemblage of jazz players that undertakes everything from Jelly Roll Morton's *Black Bottom Stomp* through Horace Silver's *Room 608,* from early Ellington through Bill Evans.

211

The whole question of jazz repertory is fraught with problems, most of them stemming from the fact that jazz is an individual player's and improviser's art. Shall jazz repertory use improvisation? And if so, how much and what kind, and what shall it do with the "original" improvised solo? It is entirely to its credit that the National Jazz Ensemble undertakes every possible approach to such problems.

A good jazz soloist is, after all, a spontaneous composer, and many a recorded solo is a jazz "classic" in itself. Shall one interpret a recorded solo *as a solo* exactly or almost exactly? Well, yes, as Jimmy Maxwell does to George Mitchell's trumpet on *Black Bottom Stomp* or Dennis Anderson does with Barney Bigard's climactic moments on *Harlem Air Shaft*. Or shall a solo be scored out as section writing? Well, yes, as is Hank Mobley's solo on *Room 608*, or Johnny Hodges' second solo, and Bigard's on *Hot Feet*. Or shall we score a part of a solo to set up the tone for a new improvisation, as a few bars of Kenny Dorham's *Room 608* solo sets up Tom Harrell? Or shall the soloist himself set things up with heavy allusions to his point-of-departure, as Sal Nistico does to Lester Young, moving into the main section of *Every Tub*?

Should improvisers undertake perhaps the heaviest task of all, the attempt to *improvise* strictly within the style of the originals as both Maxwell (for Cootie Williams) and Anderson (for Bigard) do so justifiably on *Harlem Air Shaft*? Or shall we give an earlier piece of music a really heavy test and try solos and accompaniment in a style more contemporary to ourselves, as Sal Nistico and Harrell do on *Every Tub*?

This is a repertory orchestra also in the sense that it is a flexible host to eminent guest artists, to Bill Evans on *Very Early* and Lee Konitz on *Solar Complexes,* in both cases for fresh treatments of established pieces by the Ensemble's leader (and former Evans sideman) Chuck Israels. And it is an orchestra also open to new works like *Understanding Depression*, Dave Berger's very contemporary extended treatment of the traditional blues.

The question for now is not so much how well the National Jazz Ensemble does such things—but of course it does most or all of them commendably—as that the members of this orchestra undertake all these approaches with a dedicated creative integrity.

I am convinced that for such reasons alone, the future in American music will be in their debt. For the only task is to listen—listen, enjoy, delight and respect. (1976)

≈
≈
≈
≈
Art Pepper:
"Gettin' Together"

As the notes below explain, Contemporary M/C 3573 paired Art Pepper with the Miles Davis rhythm section of early 1960.

The square's question about jazz may not be such a bad question if you think about it. I mean the one that goes, "Where's the melody?" or "Why don't they play the melody?" We could borrow the famous mountain climber George Mallory's answer, "Because it's there." But a more helpful one might be, the melody is whatever they are playing, or to put it more directly, they don't play it because they can make up better ones. And if I wanted to introduce the square to that fact, one of the people whose work I could use to show it would be Art Pepper.

This album is a sort of sequel to the earlier *Art Pepper Meets the Rhythm Section* (Contemporary C3532, stereo S7018), a set I would call one of the best in the Contemporary catalog. That one was made in 1957 and the rhythm section of the title was the very special one of the Miles Davis quintet of the time: Red Garland, piano; Paul Chambers, bass; Philly Joe Jones, drums. This one is made with the (again special) Miles Davis rhythm section of February 1960. Paul Chambers is still there, Wynton Kelly is on piano, Jimmie Cobb is on drums. That former session was made under pressure, for not only was the section available only briefly,

Pepper himself had not played for two weeks before the night it was done. For this one, the Davis group was again in town only briefly, and again, there was only one recording session. In fact, the last track, *Gettin' Together,* made because Art wanted to record a blues on tenor, is just Pepper, Kelly, and the rest playing ad lib while the tape was kept rolling.

All of which obviously does not mean that either session was made with the kind of haste that makes waste.

I began by saying that I could use Art Pepper's playing to convince our square friend that jazzmen can make up better melodies than the ones they start with. (There are many others I could use, but let's stick to the subject here, Art Pepper.) And I could well begin with an Art Pepper record like *Softly, As in a Morning Sunrise,* for Pepper states that theme with none of its usual melodramatics and proceeds to make up melodic lines spontaneously that are superior to those he began with. And I might also use it as an example of the emotional range he can develop within a solo from a very limited point of departure, and without eccentricity or crowding.

Pepper is a lyric or melodic player (those words are vague but when you have heard him, you know what they mean). Very good test pieces for such qualities are slow ballads—and many a jazzman of Pepper's generation wanders aimlessly and apologetically through such tests. There are two ballads here. *Why Are We Afraid?* is a piece Art Pepper plays in the movie *The Subterraneans. Diane* is named for Art Pepper's wife; he has recorded it before but he prefers this version. So do I. It especially seems to me an *emotionally* sustained piece of improvised impressionism, and Kelly also captures and elaborates its mood both in his accompaniment and solo. Unlike many comparable players of his generation in jazz, Art is not so preoccupied with making a melody that is "pretty" that he falls into lushness or weakness in his melodic line. What saves him is a kind of rhythmic fibre and strength that some lyric and "cool" players decidedly lack. (*Softly, As in a Morning Sunrise* is again a very good example.) For that reason, it should surprise no one to hear him, particularly on the tracks where he plays tenor here, absorbing some rhythmic ideas from the better players in the current Eastern "hard" school. And to show how well they fit and are assimilated, that ad lib blues, *Gettin' Together,* is prime evidence. Surely one of the things that makes jazz so unsentimental and fluent an art is the jazzman's rhythmic flexibility, and that is something Art Pepper has always been on to.

The events of Art Pepper's biography include the fact that he took his first music lessons at nine, but had been passionately interested in music even before that. In his teens he was fully committed to jazz and playing nightly on Central Avenue in Los Angeles with Dexter Gordon, Charlie Mingus, Gerald Wiggins, Zoot Sims, and at eighteen he was a regular member of Lester Young's brother Lee's group. Subsequently he was with Benny Carter and achieved his widest recognition when he joined Stan Kenton on alto for the second time, from 1946 through 1951. When these tracks were made he was, with Conte Candoli, one of Howard Rumsey's Lighthouse All Stars at Hermosa Beach. If *Bijou the Poodle* (Pepper's dog, by the way) and Thelonious Monk's *Rhythm-A-Ning* have a somewhat more prepared air to them than the other tracks, it is because Pepper and Candoli (whose past includes trumpet chairs with Woody Herman and Kenton) were playing them regularly at Rumsey's club.

As I said, Chambers (who is surely as innately a jazz musician as any man ever was) has been with the Miles Davis groups since 1955. Wynton Kelly's past is illustrious enough to have included work with the other major trumpeter in the modern idiom, Dizzy Gillespie; he has also accompanied Dinah Washington and Lester Young, among others. Jimmie Cobb was brought into the Davis group at the suggestion of Cannonball Adderley in 1959.

It should come as no surprise that Art finds playing with a rhythm section picked by Miles Davis such a pleasure and stimulation. It is true that those two hornmen "use the time" (as musicians put it) differently; Pepper is closer to the beat in his phrasing for one thing. But Miles Davis is a unique combination of surface lyricism, concentrated emotion, and has a decided, but not always obvious rhythmic flexibility. (He has been called a man walking on eggshells; a man with his kind of inner emotional terseness would surely crush eggshells to powder.) The sections he picks for himself might therefore be ideal for Art Pepper, for, although I don't think they convey emotion in the same way, they have many qualities in common. Miles' rhythm sections have been accused of playing "too loud" by some people. I am not sure what that means exactly, but I am sure that they are *never* heavy and always swing at any dynamic level they happen to be using, and that is a very rare quality. Their swing always has the secret kind of forward movement that is so important to jazz. (A handy explanation of "swing" might be "any two successive notes played by Paul Chambers.")

There are several other things on this record that gave me pleasure that I would recommend you listen for. One of the first is the unity of Pepper's solo on *Whims of Chambers* and the way it builds. (You cannot make a good solo just by stringing phrases together to fit the chord changes—but nobody admits how many players don't try to do much more than that.) The unity is subtle, but it is not obscure, and once grasped it becomes a delightful part of experiencing the solo. For instance, if you keep the phrase he opens with in mind, then notice how much of the solo is melodically related to that phrase. And also how much of it is related to Chambers' theme. Such unity is never monotonous because Art Pepper gets inside of these melodic ideas, finds their meaning, and develops them musically—he is never just playing their notes or playing notes mechanically related to their notes. The curve of the solo is also a delight. In a very logical way, more complex lines of shorter notes begin in Art's third chorus (that is the one where Kelly re-enters behind him). They reach a peak of dexterity in the fourth, tapering to a more lyric simplicity at its end. There is a very effective echo of those more complex melodies at the end of the fifth chorus, as the solo is gradually returning to the simpler lines it began with. (There is nothing really difficult or forbidding about following these things; if you can follow a "tune" you can follow these melodic structures, although they are far more subtle and artful than a "tune" is. And following them gives the kind of pleasure that digging deeper always does.)

Thelonious Monk's *Rhythm-A-Ning* may sound like only a visit to that "other" jazz standard (other than the blues, that is) which its title indicates. It isn't just that. And the best part is the "middle" or "bridge." Most popular songs are written with two melodies and if we give each a letter to identify it, the form of them comes out to be AABA. That B part of *Rhythm-A-Ning* is an integral part of the piece because its melody is a development of one of the ideas in the A part. The other thing is the way it is harmonized. You can easily hear that it is unusual when they play it the first time. Hearing what they do with it in the solos I leave to you to enjoy. I was also intrigued with the idea that Monk would get a smile out of Pepper's writing on *Bijou*.

A musician friend who had recently returned from California and was answering my questions about Art Pepper said, "I think maybe Art knows now that he plays not to win polls or be famous or any of that, but just because he has it in him to play and he just needs to."

If a man has come to that insight, I think you can hear it in the way he plays. I think I hear it here. (1960)

≈

≈

≈

≈ # Ornette Coleman's Crisis

The LP discussed below, Impulse 9187, was recorded at a 1969 concert at New York University. It was issued with a then-fashionable, quasi-political cover photo of the Bill of Rights in flames—probably not Coleman's idea, by the way. I had reviewed the concert for *Down Beat,* and the LP assignment gave me the rare opportunity to re-hear the music and, in a sense, re-write myself. However, for liner-note purposes, I left some things unsaid, and the reader will find the original *Down Beat* review below on p. 286. Incidentally, on the record and the liner the titles *Space Jungle* and *Trouble in the East* were accidentally reversed; the LP ends with *Space Jungle,* preceded by *Trouble in the East.*

The music on this LP comes from a concert held at New York University, a concert that proved to be a revealing and important reunion for several of the musicians. Bassist Charlie Haden had re-joined Ornette Coleman some months previously. Trumpeter Don Cherry re-joined for the occasion. Thus was re-assembled three-quarters of the quartet that Ornette first brought to New York in 1959, an ensemble whose music delighted, moved, excited, and sometimes outraged the New York jazz community, and also brought expressions of praise, curiosity, and puzzlement

219

for such *Ausländers* as Leonard Bernstein, Marc Blitzstein, and Virgil Thomson.

Joining Coleman, Cherry, and Haden that evening at the N.Y.U. Loeb Student Center were Denny Coleman, who was a mere toddler at the time of that first New York gig, and Dewey Redman, whose persuasive alliance of traditional and new ideas makes him an exceptional, complementary companion to Coleman.

Has Coleman's music changed in the past ten years? Of course it *has* changed, so the better question might be whether the changes in the music seem to be signs of growth. If one centers that question on Don Cherry, he will find trumpeting that has grown in sureness, in clarity, in invention, in expressiveness. I suppose that *confidence* is a key word in describing Don Cherry's growth. And so it is with Coleman's. There was an element of pleading in Ornette's early work—special pleading perhaps for the originality of his way of making jazz in the beginning. It seems to me that that emotional element is no longer there, perhaps because it no longer needs to be; his way of making jazz is now firmly established, a part of the tradition. Stylistically, there may be no difference between this and 1959 Coleman, except that there is more simultaneous improvising by the horns, as we shall see.

And how does this particular concert sound several months after? I reviewed the evening in *Down Beat* (in the issue of May 15, 1969, to be exact), so I have a fairly exact record of how I reacted after one fresh hearing in the concert hall. Now I can hear the music again, selected for LP, pursue it at leisure, repeat it, in some ways hear it better.

The record begins the way the evening did, with *Broken Shadows,* a harrowing dirge, which takes its place with Coleman's other outstanding dirges, *Lorraine, Peace, Lonely Woman, Sadness.* Notice the way the opening is laid out, with Redman at first providing an improvised obbligato to Coleman and Cherry, and then Cherry passionately doing the same for Coleman and Redman. Haden, meanwhile, almost *sings* beneath them. Coleman's solo is an exceptional example of his capacity for suggesting an evolving patter of emotions, and even tempos, without breaking his continuity, overall mood, or losing an attentive listener.

The brief theme itself of *Comme Il Faut* provides Charlie Haden with his resonant solo. He gives it a personal reading and then explores ideas that it suggests to him. Cherry's solo, with its fanfare-like opening phrases, shows a capacity comparable to Coleman's for setting up a free, almost ambiguous, tempo—or is it tempos?

Coleman's solo here was one of several during the evening which for me "picked up piece after piece and made it soar . . . His musical energy and grasp of tempo were wonderful. More important, of course, is his ability to sustain, develop, and vary an idea—this is the most orderly of players." He moves from desolation to affirmation to joy on *Comme Il Faut*, but none of these dominant emotions is without its undercurrent of irony or complexity. And the ending of the piece is like an anthem that surmounts its own anguish. (That French title, by the way, can be freely translated as "the right thing" or perhaps "what is needed.")

I decline to comment on the programmatic or ideological aspects of Charlie Haden's *Song for Che*. But Coleman's solo is, again, the kind of logical improvisation which repays the closest attention. And Haden again uses the theme itself as his point of departure for a singular solo. On this piece, on *Comme Il Faut* and on *Broken Shadows*, Haden evokes a remarkable range of sounds from his instrument. On that basis alone, this LP is an exceptional recital by this exceptional bass player. And that is an aspect of his work here which was much less audibly evident in the concert hall than it is on this LP, by the way.

Space Jungle is a collectively improvised, relatively lightweight, and perhaps light-hearted but far from frivolous piece. On it, Coleman plays his violin, Dewey Redman plays clarinet, and Cherry plays Indian flute, an instrument on which he gets a lovely sound.

I have saved comment on *Trouble in the East* for last because it was originally the last piece played—the concert's encore, in fact. The audience's response to it, or a part of that response, is audible here. It is a turbulent performance on the surface, but I would suggest that if one centers his listening on Dewey Redman's mournful and raucous phrases, the elements will fall into place. Hearing *Trouble in the East* again, I see no reason not to repeat my original response to it: "It was contrapuntally written and collectively improvised by all the horns, but it was like no other collective improvisation ever undertaken in this idiom or any other. It felt spontaneously ordered in all its aspects, and had the timeless joy and melancholy of the blues running through it. It had its feet planted on the earth and it spoke to the gods. It was one of the most exciting, beautiful, and satisfying musical performances I have ever heard." It is also, I would add here, a performance of almost perfect length. (1971)

≈

≈

≈

≈

Vintage Dolphy

GM 3005 D collects "live" Eric Dolphy concert performances from 1962 and 1963, three of them with his own
quartet, three of his participation in "third stream" works
by the album's producer, Gunther Schuller, and one
thirteen-minute concert "jam session." It seemed to me that
the occasion called for an effort to put Eric's work in
context, and compare his contributions with John Coltrane's and Ornette Coleman's.

The good die young, it is said. It is also said that the really gifted
artist who dies young gains a reputation that would have taken
longer had he lived.

There can be no question that Eric Dolphy, born in 1928, dead
of complications associated with diabetes in 1964, was a good
human being. Indeed, Charlie Mingus, who was not without his
cautions and suspicions about the motives of his fellow beings,
called Eric "a saint."

In my own experience, Eric Dolphy greeted life as he greeted
music, with an inquisitiveness, generosity, and enthusiasm that
was as infectious as it was natural. But his was not an enthusiasm
born of innocence or naiveté. Eric was alert, discriminating, and
selective, but he evaluated without being judgmental, and always
with modesty and grace.

Dolphy's reputation, however, has somehow not been given
quite the kind of posthumous rewards one would have expected.

Part of the problem, I think, had to do with the comparisons that were made about his work, comparisons with Ornette Coleman and with John Coltrane. It wasn't that the comparisons weren't welcome—and Eric worked with both men in important contexts. It is just that they weren't always very well made.

Since this album shows Eric in a number of settings, offers him such a range of challenges, and shows almost all the things he could do, all the approaches he knew how to take to improvising, it gives opportunity for some discussion of the things he did. But let it be said first that, matters of technique aside, any musical phrase here on any of his several instruments will show you that Eric Dolphy was a man born to make and communicate music.

Contrary to some misguided talk at the time, Eric Dolphy knew chords and chord changes and could improvise brilliantly according to their "rules" and conventions. In the present set, hear the jam session on *Donna Lee*. If Eric sounds "out" compared with most of the other players, he wasn't out of the chord changes. He just knew things to do with the extensions—correct things, if you will—that the others weren't likely to use, but that all the young players use today.

Charlie Mingus said something else important about Eric when he observed "he has absorbed Bird rhythmically." He had indeed absorbed Charlie Parker and I don't think that John Coltrane ever did that. The undercurrent in a Coltrane solo is still the Coleman Hawkins–Don Byas heavy/light accentuation that basically is as old as the earliest New Orleans jazz. And Coltrane did not get around to truly "free" improvising until the time of *Ascension*—until the time of his association with Eric. Previously, he had improvised on chord progressions, increasingly tight and challenging chord progressions on pieces like *Moment's Notice* and *Giant Steps*. Or he had improvised from a mode or an assigned series of notes, as on *Impressions* or *A Love Supreme*.

Then there is the question of Coltrane's prolixity: sometimes he seemed to need to run through all that he knew on almost every piece. ("Coltrane, you don't have to play *everything*," Miles Davis once said to him.) Virtuosity or not, Eric knew about the selectivity that is one key to art.

Ornette Coleman "taught me a direction," Eric said in 1960. I wish he had said "encouraged" rather than "taught," but I think the direction had to do with two things. First, Ornette's notes and phrases were more freely inflected, more vocally intoned than those of earlier jazzmen. For Eric, it was a matter of "getting the horn to . . . speak," as he once put it. (All of which led some cynics to declare that Ornette, and Eric too, couldn't play in tune!) The other encouragement had to do with playing "free," improvising not only without a chord progression but without any conscious use of a mode or scale.

On his own pieces, Ornette's improvisations do stray out of the basic key occasionally and in that sense can even be called momentarily atonal. But it happens that they can also be heard modally. That is an observation after-the-fact, however, and not Coleman's point of departure. To put it another way, to play modally isn't to play free, but to play free often turns out to be modal in practice.

What Ornette did through an intuitive leap, however, Eric accomplished step by step. And despite the likenesses, the results in each man's style are different. Take *Abstractions*. Gunther Schuller's piece is one of the real classics of the third stream, an atonal, serial work in mirror form—the closing portion, after the jazz player's middle cadenza, is an exact reversal of the opening. The work was premiered and recorded by Coleman, who sensed it, sized it up, and ran a parallel course to it. Dolphy goes inside *Abstractions* and his lines become, spontaneously, an integrated part of it. Both approaches are valid and musical, but I would call this performance a treasure, and almost reason enough in itself for the appearance of this album.

In his own Quartet set here, from the 1963 Carnegie Recital Hall concert, Dolphy features each of his instruments in turn. His selective, economical bass clarinet solo on *Half Note Triplets* shows him rid of any direct dependency on Charlie Parker's phrasing (his bass clarinet was the last of his horns to do so). And the intricate, undulating layers of sound, from his flute on Jaki

Byard's dedicatory *Ode to Charlie Parker* contrast markedly in sonority, texture, and approach. Eric's alto on *Iron Man* strikes me as one of the most amusing, ingenious examples of a jazz soloist's toying playfully with a single musical motive it has ever been my delight to hear.

Schuller's less familiar *Densities* again shows how Eric's "free" jazz improvising adapts itself perfectly to atonal composing. It also puts Dolphy and the other jazzmen virtually in charge, with the classical players even encouraged to join in their easy-going swing. And *Night Music* is *Nachtmusik* of a very American night-on-the town, complete with a passionate encounter the nature of which the listener is free to interpret for himself.

In a sense, I am sorry about the other people I have brought into this discussion but it all seemed needed to help set the record straight. At this point I should repeat the real reason for this LP: Eric Dolphy was a man born to make and communicate music, and any phrase from any of his instruments will tell you that immediately. (1986)

IV

REVIEWS AND OBSERVATIONS

≈
≈
≈
≈

Monk Unique

"The Unique Thelonious Monk" has received excellent press. Nat Hentoff in *Down Beat* gave it four and a half stars (damn all rating devices anyhow) because Monk remains "one of the insatiably, irrepressibly, and valuably individual jazzmen in our era." He "has an intense sense of drama (not melodrama) that can create a reflectively dissonant, almost hypnotic mood . . . and a sharply knifed penchant for shaping and reshaping a few key phrases into a hail of plunging aural mobiles." In *The Saturday Review,* Whitney Balliett called it "an essential record," saying, "Monk's style—loose, almost diffident dissonances, wry single-note lines, a laggard-like beat—is easily plumbed. Here he winds his way . . . keeping the melody always just below the surface and embellishing it more than reworking its chords. . . ."

One of the reasons I quote so much is that I have the feeling that I am getting to be a bore on the subject of Monk, whose current work I admire so much: everything he says he says musically—if he has no music to make he doesn't fill out a single bar with faked blowing or rambling. All is given in terms of a musical sensibility, or it isn't given at all (hear Miles Davis' *The Man I Love* on Prestige).

This is one of the most humorous jazz records ever made. The mutual agreement with which he makes him and you approach having some respectful fun with such warhorses as *Tea for Two* and *Honeysuckle Rose* is superb and is as far from mere ridicule as one could imagine. I will not attempt to describe how he does it: the effect is too subtle for the mechanics of the matter even to

229

hint at. The delicious *rubato* with which he will now and then approach a perfectly ordinary chord on one of the slower numbers, as if saying he just can't find the obvious, and then delight both of you as he hits it with the joke on yourselves at how obvious it really was—or surprise you both with a delightful dissonance— is alive with human commentary. He can even have fleeting moments of what sound like honest frivolity and we accept them because this is a man we are with and men can get frivolous.

Just You Just Me is one of his most carefully wrought sets of variations built on and around a melody: contrast Monk here with Oscar Pettiford. Pettiford's solos are really excellent but he is "blowing" on chords; Monk is building a set of variations, like Brahms, like Morton, with a large sense of musical form and with a constant sense of musical (not mechanical) expression. He is not, I would say, merely "embellishing" the melody. Fundamentally Monk is not an "entertainer," he does not "show" us anything. Nor is he really so important as an innovator (he was that, of course) as he is for one thing: Monk is an artist with an artist's deeply felt sense of life and an artist's drive for communicating the surprising and enlightening truth about it in his own way. And he has the artist's special capacity for involving us with him so that we seem to be working it all out together. Jazz has had precious few of his kind. (1956)

≈

≈

≈

≈
Collected Bird

The title of the collected *Ko-Ko* date on a new Savoy LP is simply "Charlie Parker" but the music represents of course the way it should be done, the way Savoy should have been doing it all along, the way *everyone* should do it from now on: a record date, all together, apparently complete (well almost, see below), takes and fragments in the order in which they were played.

John Mehegan's terse notes are excellent. He begins with a brief essay which is surely one of the most important written on Parker, Gillespie, and the whole movement. For example, ". . . using such a simple form as the blues, Parker was able to deal with the problems of line." His approach "evolved from the primal source of all music—time." "Dizzy and Parker approach . . . in basically different ways: Dizz through harmony, Parker through time." *The* point exactly, it seems to me. (And his putting it thus makes me rather dismayed at my attempt to get at rather the same point in a review here recently.) Furthermore, in his comments on the individual tracks, Mehegan has not only dealt with the knotty problems of the mysteriously shifting personnel of this date, but his straightforward comments on the music are quite welcome in the world of sometimes flabby, padded, equivocating, and just plain useless liner notes: "Miles lugubrious, unswinging, no ideas." "Moving, lyrical chorus by Parker . . . an equally moving piano solo . . . for some unknown, crazy reason cut at the fourteenth bar. Someone should have his head examined." On the other hand, such comments may frustrate a reviewer, leaving him little to say.

The discoveries here among the new tracks are the first take on *Thriving from a Riff,* including some excellent Gillespie; the "ballad" *Meandering;* the marked progress that Parker has made toward warming up by even the second take of the date; the way that bassist Curley Russell's strong beat makes up for some weak piano; and the very fascination of hearing the whole thing develop and evolve.

Some comments:

1) Why was Gillespie's name left out of the original personnel listing? Some more of Savoy's usual typos?

2) This date could not really be complete here, since the first twenty-four (?) bars of *Warming* are still missing. Are they gone for good? And if they're "unusable," why?

3) I have often felt Dizzy might be on piano on the original take of *Now's the Time:* someone seems to be cutting up Gillespie-like, trying to break Bird up (bar four of his first chorus, for example), and Dizzy has done this on records elsewhere (do you know that squeal on the record called *Slim's Jam,* for one?). Isn't the comping a bit simple for Bud Powell—even 1945 Powell?

4) The piano intros to the first two takes of *Thriving from a Riff* are certainly "chaotic rhythmically and harmonically," but the comping that follows is perfectly good. Could it be Bud kidding, "experimenting," or just being cantankerous? Why is there suddenly that piano solo first in the third take (previously issued) of *Thriving* and in none others? And although it is "Martian" harmonically, is it really amateurish—in fingering, say?

5) Mehegan says (and it has been said before) that Parker is alone on the closing "head" of the original take of *Thriving.* I still hear a faltering, cup-muted trumpet in and out of it, especially in the beginning.

6) Mehegan wonders why the first take of *Ko-Ko* was cut short—amusingly by Parker yelling, whistling, clapping, by the way. Wasn't it because if it had gone on someone would have had to pay Ray Noble some royalties? They do start playing the melody *Cherokee,* after all.

7) I wish Mehegan had had more to say critically about *Ko-Ko*

than calling it "incredible." He could have said a lot about how and why.

A lot has happened to the status of this session since some of it came out labeled simply as by "Re Bop Boys."

Finally, I have been looking at this cover off and on for some weeks now. It is so bad, so ugly, so absurd that I still find it hard to believe. (1957)

> I erred in hearing Bud Powell here, as John Mehegan had. The pianists were Argonne Thornton—later Sadik Hakim, and far less "Martian" by then—and, yes, Dizzy Gillespie, originally unidentified because of a contractual conflict. And it is he also on trumpet on the intro to *Ko-Ko,* where there is no pianist.

≈

≈

≈

≈ # Herbie Nichols
Introspect

"Love, Gloom, Cash, Love" by pianist Herbie Nichols is an exceptional recording—let it be clear that I feel that way about it. Since I find so much to admire in Nichols, in his approach to style, in his approach to the jazz tradition, in his approach to the piano, I regret not liking the record even more. He has dealt so well with so many problems (many of them often neglected by many young jazzmen), but there is one crucial problem that I do not feel he has dealt with yet.

We could call that problem *communication*, but since that word now brings up absurd connotations about "watering-down" and dishonesty, about forcing one's self with "wailing" mannerisms, and more important ones about communication *to whom*, I'll try to put my feelings about this record differently.

Nichols is original. He may remind us of Powell and Monk, and of Fats Waller and Teddy Wilson, but it is also obvious that he plays with a jazz style that is thoroughly Nichols. The things he can do with time and the fact that his rhythms and harmonies are interrelated, indeed inseparable, are exceptional. He is not at all interested in currently "hip" tempos, mannerisms, or finger dexterities, and on the piece he calls *S'Crazy Pad*, he shows he is not at all afraid of a steady "four" rhythm, of a modernized version of a simple '30s "riff tune" conception, of swing bass— and that he can bring such things off.

As a composer, he may work (as Monk often does) with basically simple and brief ideas. He has the capacity to turn and phrase them uniquely and to set them off with originality. And he can develop them compositionally.

He can do the same in improvising. It is possible that performances like the waltz *Love, Gloom, Cash, Love,* or *All The Way,* and the out-of-tempo *Infatuation Eyes* will be called "decorative" by some, but *Beyond Recall* and *Argumentative* are very well explored by *any* standards. And *Portrait of UCHA* manages to seem fully developed in rhythm, harmony, line, and at the same time, brief, complete, but quite uncluttered.

The problem of communication is one of feeling there is emotion in Nichols' playing, but it does not flow outwardly. These introspections (for several reasons, of a quality usually called "haunting") remain essentially introverted. For some players, such a problem does not exist: automatically his emotions go outwardly to others. I would imagine Nichols' problem is rather like one John Lewis had to deal with (or *perhaps* Teddy Wilson or Johnny Hodges or Lester Young), for Lewis does communicate emotionally, but it is as if he had to learn to project the *results* of his introspection to his listeners.

It is a special problem that only some of us are faced with, but I think Herbie Nichols may be one who is. (1957)

≈
≈
≈
≈

Silver Explorations

"Further Explorations" by the Horace Silver Quintet on Blue Note has a piece called *Melancholy,* and *Melancholy* is a piano trio performance, and it is slow. Its theme is an adept borrowing from Debussy. Silver's playing soon becomes a disjointed, double-timing series of interpolations of everything from bugle calls to gospel motifs, bop figures to archaic blues riffs. *Ill Wind* is given a scoring and a tempo that make it into something rather flip and does hardly anything with the implicit possibilities of its melody or mood.

The simplifications through which Horace Silver's solo style often has gone in the last year or so are still present. They involve less Bud Powell; they have lots of implicit ideas; they involve a relaxation—they are, I think, a preparation for a change. But the change has not come. The writing often attempts to make the group sound like a much larger one instead of taking advantage of what it is—a fairly common practice in the East nowadays.

So much for the shortcomings of the set. In the piece called *Outlaw* (maybe "Bandit" would describe the quality of this one better), Latin rhythms weave in and out of the performance in an effective way, a way which avoids both the absurdity of dropping them after the opening chorus or of maintaining them only as a kind of gimmick.

Safari is a very bop thing in the writing, in which Silver gets a bit too overbusy in his solo to take much rhythmic advantage of the fast tempo. The best piece of writing is, I think, a second countermelodic interlude in *Moon Rays.* It is really excellent, both "catchy" *and* sustaining, and, like an earlier success, *Hippy,* depends on the elaboration of fairly conventional and "mainstream" riff material into a longer rhythmic-melodic pattern.

That bit of writing, the successes involved, and the failures, give the key, I think, to the center of Silver's talent. Essentially, his conception is a strong modernization and elaboration of the kind of riff-blues-jump-group music of the 1930s and very early '40s. He is best here, as he was with the Jazz Messengers with Art Blakey, when he explores and elaborates such a conception as that. He can enlarge it, has fresh things to say within it, and it is a conception which reaffirms and even asserts some very important and basic things about jazz. When he tries for other things (as in *Melancholy*), he does not succeed—or has not yet succeeded—but the attempts are, of course, praiseworthy even so.

Tenor saxophonist Clifford Jordan is working around with Sonny Rollins' style, with a glance at John Coltrane on *Outlaw*.

The soloist on the recording is trumpeter Art Farmer. He is emphatically not a conventional Eastern hard cooker, but a trumpeter of experience, range, real originality within his medium, taste, and cohesion. At his best, he knows what he wants to say and from his opening phrase he says it with solos of unity and purpose—one cannot say that of many players. Except on *Pyramid*, he is generally at his best here—and certainly is on *Moon Rays* and on *Outlaw*.

The notes say something about the group becoming a "conveyor belt" for its kind of music. If the implication of that image is intended, it is pretty insulting and certainly untrue. (1958)

≈

≈

≈

≈
Three on Cannonball

I

It may take a long time for Julian Adderley to recover from his notices and his publicity. They have been unfair to his talent, his style, and his potential, it seems to me.

A great, undiscovered genius? Jazz has had perhaps six persons in its history whom one would call a genius. The new Bird? Charlie Parker authentically reinterpreted the jazz language. As far as we know, only one man did that before him, Louis Armstrong. And between them there were fourteen years, a *very* short time even for this liveliest art. I did not know until I read the liner notes on this LP—*"Portrait of Cannonball"* on Riverside—that there was a rumor that Adderley had worked out a modern style quite independently, not having heard Parker at all. Assimilation and mastery of form before Armstrong is represented by Jelly Roll Morton's work. And after Armstrong's work was absorbed, the master of form was Duke Ellington. And after Parker? I think Thelonious Monk. Not Adderley.

What Adderley is (or, at least, so far has been) is a blowing soloist, and, of course, like most blowing soloists from whatever style or period, not a revolutionary one.

This may not be his best record so far but it is well titled. It is the best portrait of him in the general terms of his style and his influences that I have heard, and the changes that it shows in his work since he first began recording bring out things I think have always been there.

If he has a *direct* debt to anyone, it is not to Parker. Excluding the "cool" school (whose debt is to Lester Young), he is probably the first altoist since Parker to break through, the first whose debt is *indirect* and one of general stylistic outlines. That in itself is an achievement and a sign. If he has a direct debt to anyone, it is to Benny Carter—and I was gratified to learn recently how highly Adderley esteems Carter.

That is certainly clear here. Also clear is less harshness and more discipline in the upper register, a greater dexterity, an increasing attention to intervals. But I find Adderley's work unsatisfying and it is up to me to try to explain why. At the end of his solos, I usually find myself asking just what he has said—in form, in melody and rhythm, and in content.

On *Minority*, his solo is based on cascading notes onto the constant reiteration of a single rhythmic motif. To indicate it, its equivalent in Morse code would be dash-dot-dot-dot. The same device is frequent in his solo on *A Little Taste*. *Straight Life* is a good mood piece, and the first part of his solo explores its mood. But he soon seems merely to be imposing phrases and runs into it. I cannot explain my feelings about his solo on *Blue Funk* without mumbling something about, "It doesn't seem to me to say too much."

Perhaps that is it. Adderley seems to toss off casually what he can play within the *technical* form of each piece but not within its emotional form or musical implications.

Pianist Bill Evans' solos here are always interesting; they are incomplete in a sense, it seems to me, not fully melodically or technically balanced, but they do explore some musical implications of the tune at hand and its harmony with originality, some order, and a pointed variety.

Adderley's do not seem to spring from the tunes or their chords but to be casually dropped into them and seem to be tossed off with little regard to formal or emotional continuity.

My reactions may be vaguely put, but that is the best I can do. Benny Carter's solos may not "wail" like Ray Charles' but each has a directly communicated content and each uses melodies that are appropriate and each is stated with purpose and sure awareness of the effect Benny Carter wants. He tells a story, as Roy Eldridge once put it. Adderley's best solo here is on *Nardis*. It has order, and it does tell a story. It is also relatively brief and at medium tempo—perhaps those facts mean something.

Trumpeter Blue Mitchell may suffer from having some of the same extravagant advance news spread about him as did Adderley. He seems here an able, adept post-Clifford Brown trumpeter with good tone, chops, and clean execution, an as yet somewhat undeveloped conception and direction, and therefore only the beginnings of an individuality and originality—but those things of course take more time and patience than will power to develop.

In passing, *Minority* (by Gigi Gryce) and *A Little Taste* (by Adderley) are both examples of a strange sort of tune that has cropped up again in the last few years. In line and rhythm they remind one of what the small chorus marches out and yells at the audience at the opening of an "intimate review." I say "again" because some stride pianists used to write that sort of piece. But why, again? (1958)

II

Cannonball Adderley is something of a popularizer, but a popularizer of a different sort. Adderley makes the jazz clubs. Further, his style is both more personal and more varied in its inception (besides predominant Parker, one hears Benny Carter, a bit of late John Coltrane, and recently a wholly unexpected snippet of Ornette Coleman), and he has a virtuosity that on occasion tosses out notes like handfuls of unicolored confetti. *"Jazz Workshop Revisited"* returns Adderley to "live recording" at a San Francisco club where a few years ago he did *This Here,* a rather posturingly executed gospel-style blues that became a hit. Adderley's current group is a sextet, still with his brother Nat (a Miles Davis-ish player) on cornet, and with Yusef Lateef (a sophisticated but becalmed Illinois Jacquet) on tenor saxophone and flute.

At present, the Adderley group's approach, that of a sophisticated blues band, is more varied and is often laced with big band effects. *Jive Samba* reflects the current fad for Bossa Nova for a relentless eleven minutes. Cannonball takes a well-paced solo on *Marney*, seems to mean what he plays on *Mellow Buno*, and makes a few knowingly engaging announcements to the audience between some of the numbers.

However, I should not leave Adderley without recommending his disciplined improvisations on *Autumn Leaves*, on Blue Note 1595 with a group that includes the real Miles Davis, for they are very good, and the record is probably Cannonball's best. (1963)

III

Cannonball Adderley was an associate of Miles Davis in some of the early "experimental" work. But his own inclinations usually keep him in the modern mainstream, and his great success as a leader has sometimes seemed to me as interesting socially as musically.

"The Cannonball Adderley Quintet In Person" is the latest of a series of albums his group has recorded before night-club audiences. It comes complete with applause, cheers, hoots, and announcements from Adderley—a former Florida schoolteacher—that feature a few "aints" and lots of down-home jive. The recital has "guest" appearances by Nancy Wilson, at this stage of her career enamored of Dinah Washington, and by Lou Rawls, a handsome, middle-brow blues singer. It also has instrumentals in which there are more blue notes per four-bar phrase than you might have believed possible. Indeed, to me the whole occasion has the air of a communal celebration in which a black middle-class determinedly seeks out its musical roots. One may welcome the quest, and hope it is a real one. One may also hope that Adderley's considerable talents will one day lead himself and his following to level on (let us say) that exceptional variation on *Autumn Leaves* which he recorded eleven years ago for Blue Note. (1969)

> In the later years of his too short career—he died in 1975— Adderley did return for inspiration to the Miles Davis *"Kind of Blue"* session in which he had participated, and undertake a modally oriented music for his groups.

≈

≈

≈

≈ Composers' Dilemmas

I

John Benson Brooks' point of departure for his *Alabama Concerto* is the series of "field" recordings made by Harold Courtlander and issued on Folkways as *"Negro Folk Music of Alabama."* He has used them in an extended "concerto" (actually it might be called a symphony) in which written themes, written solos, and improvised solos alternate.

First, let it be said that the musicians involved should get high praise, particularly Art Farmer and Barry Galbraith, and let it be said that this Cannonball Adderley is the Cannonball to be heard on Gil Evans' LP *"New Bottle, Old Wine"* which, I believe, is Cannonball coming of age as an individual, purposeful, story-telling soloist.

An undertaking like this one raises a lot of questions. The most obvious one is that of the form Brooks has chosen and its appropriateness. As the progress of the Modern Jazz Quartet from *Vendome* through the score for the movie *No Sun in Venice* clearly shows, the assimilation of a borrowed form to the point where it makes sense as jazz is not easy, and certainly not a result of the will to do so. And the more ambitious efforts of the past ten years are strewn with failures at similar tasks. But a relationship between jazz forms and classical suites and rondos has been obvious since at least 1895 and between jazz and both polyphonic forms and the theme-and-variations form since at least 1917. The question here is whether the symphony-concerto form is (or might become) an appropriate and fruitful one for jazz to borrow.

Some kind of answer comes from a comparison of most of the third movement and of the very successful second with the first and fourth sections. The second is by far the best. Brooks has used only two themes, used them well, and he chose two for which such juxtaposition has meaning (that's never an easy matter, of course, but a matter that, say, W. C. Handy usually handled excellently). Furthermore, this is the most openly improvisational section; that is, the most jazz-like to begin with, and the playing is very good. Beside it, the first and fourth sections are apt to seem an alternately pleasant and perhaps cluttered mélange of melodies, interspersed with brief variations that may get lost in a somewhat vague texture of the whole.

Another question is the way Brooks sometimes handles these themes. In no sense does he either hype them up (like the tasteless, banal Concert Hall "suite on folk themes" we are all too familiar with) or does he patronize them. But he does seem to have "cleaned them up" a bit. The "mistakes" of some unskilled performers can be a source of effectiveness and, as jazz has been showing since the beginning, such things can be meaningfully and boldly used by a more self-conscious artist. Furthermore, Brooks' very skillful, understated approach sometimes seems to imply more interest in the "charm" of such melodies than for their strength and life. The result is that, with quite opposite intentions, they may come off more as musical mood-setting than as music, more as a kind of first rate documentary film-writing (a thing rare enough, to be sure) than as music which grasps one's attention for itself.

But one glory of the self-conscious artist is that he must take chances on just matters. The irony is (and he knows it) that one seldom finds one's attention wandering when a Mahalia Jackson is singing. (1959)

II

The composer-arrangers who contributed to "*Cross Section Saxes,*" an LP led by alto saxophonist Hal McKusick, include Ernie Wilkins, George Russell, Jimmy Giuffre, and George

Handy, and foremost, this is their set. These men are in a peculiar position in jazz today, the position that the dramatist found himself in in the nineteenth century and that only the ballet, among the performing arts, has escaped. Just as the achievements of Henderson, Ellington, etc., were worked out originally with the specific talents of the members of organized groups in mind, so the best plays were created for continuing stock companies. Even when the dramatist later found himself cut off from such a source of inspiration, discipline, and tradition, he might write (as did the nineteenth-century concert composer) vehicles for certain virtuoso performers. One cannot be absolute about cause and effect, but one can say that when such possibilities of inspiration no longer exist for the writer or composer, his art (and even his craft) seems to suffer.

Nowadays, the jazz composer-arranger writes with little in mind but his own work and, when he is done, considers who might best interpret it. The same is true when (as was probably the case here) he is asked to write for a specific number of instruments. One of the chief virtues of Ellington's writing is the secret kind of balance it makes among soloist, group, and total composition. In this respect, these men discovered how the heritage and identity of jazz might be both preserved *and* extended; if they had not solved that delicate problem so well, jazz might well have been carried off in a strait-jacket of paper.

It seems to me that therein lies Giuffre's problem as a composer. He used to know the answer but perhaps his recent study and its consequent skills have forced him temporarily to work on other things. He has an individual talent (so individual that McKusick performing Giuffre the composer here almost sounds like Giuffre the player), but at the same time that he has developed it, he had produced a music which, as Dick Hadlock has rightly said, one is sometimes forced to judge by concert-compositional standards. The improvising jazzman is neither the heart of the matter (as in early Basie), a 50-50 partner (as in Henderson or earlier Giuffre), nor a subtly integrated essence (as in Morton or Ellington). Perhaps a subjective impressionism at the expense of emotional expressionism that one hears on Giuffre's treatment of *It Never Entered My Mind* here is a key to the problem.

The best works here are George Russell's. He is, at his best, a splendid combination of sophistication and depth, of awareness of his heritage as a jazzman, and range and variety of skills. These things come together excellently on *Stratosphunk* and the soloists, especially McKusick, respond to it. The only failure, it seems to me, is *The End of a Love Affair*. It is a superior torch song, but in what I would guess was an effort to avoid its hints of melodrama, Russell came a bit close to cuteness.

Ernie Wilkins largely confined himself to skillful sax-section voicings on his two tracks which, for the transcribing of Parker's *Now's the Time* solo turns an expressive *reality* into a merely pretty *object*, I'm afraid. George Handy's two scores are much the same; essentially conservative and capable sax-voicing and perhaps a relief from his flamboyant youth.

Pianist Bill Evans, in solo and support is so much something to hear throughout that I don't want to single out his *Stratosphunk* solo. Connie Kay, whether he is playing the one after-beat out of four on finger symbols (as assigned on Giuffre's *Yesterdays*) or accompanying the blues, shows a combination of disciplined musicianship and expressiveness that jazz has rarely seen the like of. But those remarks are to neglect Charlie Persip and Art Farmer among others, and one shouldn't. (1959)

≈
≈
≈
≈

The MJQ in Europe

"European Concert" is a two-record set by the Modern Jazz Quartet of performances taped in Sweden. The playing is on the whole so very nearly perfect that one almost wonders what this exceptional group of musicians can possibly find to do next. It is a kind of anniversary set in that the Quartet—John Lewis, piano and musical director; Milt Jackson, vibraphone; Percy Heath, bass; Connie Kay, drums—was formed nearly ten years ago at a recording session for which its four original members were gathered. They discovered that they enjoyed playing together very much and they decided to continue. They did so, intermittently at first and, finally, permanently. The remarkable fact is that they continue to play with the same life and commitment to improvisation that they had in the beginning, and with an enormous increase in expressive range and sensitive group interplay as well.

They are lucky, too, for on the surface everything the Quartet does *seems* cool and almost controlled, and anyone who wants to take their work as a sort of pleasant but lively background sound can apparently do so. But anyone who is a bit more receptive to the music will discover that under the surface there is a musical vitality and range that very few jazz groups have ever achieved.

Bluesology, in the present set, can probably stand for the depth, breadth, and delight of their achievement. The piece has been in their repertory since the beginning and it is written in the simplest of all jazz forms, the twelve-bar blues. It still inspires them to sublime melodic improvising—individually, collectively, and, in the spontaneous and captivating response between Jackson and Lewis, contrapuntally. Similarly, there is John Lewis's *Django*, a memorial to the French gypsy guitarist-turned-jazzman Django Reinhardt, and surely one of the major compositions of modern jazz. The Quartet has been playing it for more than six years—in fact, this is their third recording of *Django*—yet they continue to find something fresh in it, and they manage to convey its wide emotional range, from reverent solemnity to a redeeming joy, with deepening insight.

There are other delights: the superb Lewis piano solo on the Duke Ellington piece called *It Don't Mean a Thing;* he is momentarily suspended, abandoned by all accompaniment and left with only his own extended melodic lines to propel him, until, at a moment when the tension is almost unbearable, Heath and Kay quietly re-enter behind him. There is also the exploration, chiefly by Jackson, of the ballad *I Should Care,* and of Thelonious Monk's remarkable, brooding *'Round Midnight.*

One does have reservations: *Vendome* still seems to me rather forced and academic compared with the group's later efforts at jazz fugues, and, although I grant it is an exhilarating work-out, I still wonder if one can do justice to such a superior popular song as *I'll Remember April* at such a fast pace. However, in the light of what this set does achieve, I wonder if such reservations may not amount to mere carping. (1961)

≈

≈

≈

≈
Poetry from the Delta

The sixteen titles on *"Robert Johnson: King of the Delta Blues Singers"*—some of them previously unissued and some of them alternate takes—were done at several sessions in 1936–37, the only recording dates of self-accompanying Mississippi Delta blues singer Robert Johnson.

Johnson died not long after the last date and before he was twenty-one. Since then his reputation has been almost legendary. I think this commendable LP proves that it was deserved. He was a haunting singer, and he was a poet. I might also say that his work is a stark lesson to anyone who thinks that jazz and its progenitors are "fun" music or a kind of people's vaudeville. But one could say that about any good blues singer or any really good jazzman.

Johnson's work apparently is the direct and uncluttered product of the Mississippi Delta blues tradition, and it is also a revelation to those who believe that the authentic "country" blues is limited in emotion and tempo to the slow moodiness of, say, Bill Broonzy's later days. For there is a variety of tempo and rhythm and attitude here that is a credit to the tradition, and in the hoarse directness of Johnson's voice there is an immediacy that cuts directly through the twenty-five years since these tracks were made.

The best blues deal in their own way with basic human experience, with things that all men in all times and conditions try to come to terms with. If I did not believe that, I would not call them poetry.

"Me and the devil was walking side by side / I'm going to beat my woman until I get satisfied."

"I got stones in my pathway, and my road is dark as night."

"I got to keep moving, I got to keep moving. / Blues falling down like hail, blues falling down like hail. / I can't keep no money, hellhound on my trail / Hellhound on my trail, hellhound on my trail."

Those words are strong on paper, but when one hears Johnson sing them they are stronger still, and beautiful. His kind of emotional honesty takes bravery. And if jazz did not have such bravery in its background, it would surely not have survived.

Honor Robert Johnson. (1962)

≈

≈

≈

≈ # Double Concert

An evening divided between Sonny Rollins and John Lewis held a double promise. Rollins and his quartet were to play for the first half of the program. Lewis was to premiere his score for a new Italian film, *The Milano Story*. And there would also be a performance of Jim Hall's *Piece for Guitar and Strings*.

For Rollins, the promise was fulfilled brilliantly. From his opening choruses on *Three Little Words*, it was apparent that he was going to play with commanding authority and invention with a penetrating humor which included a healthy self-parody.

His masterwork of the evening was a cadenza on *Love Letters,* several out-of-tempo choruses of easy virtuosity in imagination and execution, and a kind of truly artistic bravura that jazz has not known since Louis Armstrong of the early 1930s.

The performance included some wild interpolations, several of which Rollins managed to fit in by a last-minute witty unexpected alteration of a note or two. To my ear, he did not once lose his way, although a couple of times he did lose Hall—and that is nearly impossible to do, for the guitarist has one of the quickest harmonic ears there is.

Rollins' final piece was a kind of extemporaneous orchestration in which he became brass, reed, and rhythm section, tenor soloist, and Latin percussionist all at once and with constant musical logic.

Hall's piece was carefully rehearsed and better played than on its recorded version. It is a work of skillful lyricism, but I wonder still if it has the depth of, say, Hall's lovely improvisation on *I Can't Get Started* earlier in the evening.

Lewis' five-part piece was a disappointment. It seemed naive in its scoring, in development of its ideas, and in abrupt transitions from jazz to quasi-Italian schmaltz and back again.

If the film is a farce comedy, the score may have a deliberately guileless quality in context. But a concert performance is another matter. In the past, Lewis' detractors have accused him of a kind of academicism. There was nothing very academic about this score. And much hasty commercialism has shown better craftsmanship. It is hard to believe that the man who wrote and scored *Odds Against Tomorrow* wrote this. It is almost impossible to believe that the same man also wrote *Three Little Feelings*. And it is no pleasure to say so. (1962)

≈
≈
≈
≈

Concert Treasures

By the mid-twenties jazz music was being recorded more or less regularly, and if those who heard the legendary figures of the past insist that the records by King Oliver or Bix Beiderbecke or Fletcher Henderson are a shadow of the reality, at least the records are there and in some quantity. A more recent legendary event, the appearance of Charlie Parker–Dizzy Gillespie quintets in the early forties, is now as much a part of the established jazz tradition as Oliver's Creole Band, but their music hardly got recorded at all.

In 1945, a small company, hastily formed as James C. Petrillo lifted a union ban on record making by AFM musicians, was willing to do six instrumentals of the then new music. One can hear the sometimes intricate unison lines, beautifully executed by Gillespie's trumpet and Parker's alto, breathing musically as one. And the solos are still excitingly personal after all the years of honorable assimilation by Parker-Gillespie followers, and not-so-honorable imitation by others.

Otherwise, to hear Parker-Gillespie on records, we have to depend on later re-creations. There is that searing 1947 Carnegie Hall concert, with hazily recorded rhythmic backing, but with Parker in dazzling performance, playing as if he were out to get Gillespie, and the trumpeter responding as if he were just not going to be got. There is also a 1950 studio date. Parker, particularly, was in excellent form and produced some of his best-recorded work; Thelonious Monk was on piano; and there is the strange choice of a drummer in Buddy Rich. Rich, powerhouse and technician, didn't have the rhythmic feel for this music.

Then, finally, a 1953 concert in Toronto did get recorded and now reappears on Fantasy, *"Jazz At Massey Hall."* If a reunion of Parker (pseudonymously "Charlie Chan") and Gillespie is not enough, also present are Bud Powell and Max Roach, *the* pianist and drummer of the idiom—a truly illustrious gathering not otherwise represented on records.

True, the music is from a concert, just as it happened and without benefit of studio retakes or corrections. But that also gives it a directness and immediacy that studio recordings don't have. The occasion caught Parker only about a year before a musical deterioration overtook him, and it caught Gillespie as his style was going through an effective retrenchment and simplification.

There is evidence on some numbers of a backstage bickering which carried over into the music, but nevertheless, the players make it musical—and they sometimes make it humorous as well, as when Parker and Gillespie banter with the unison parts on *Salt Peanuts.* Or when Parker, in the first solo on *All the Things You Are*, an otherwise graceful virtuoso exploration, jokingly runs off one of Gillespie's favorite interpolations before the trumpeter even gets his turn at the piece. Later on *Peanuts*, by the way, Roach has a nearly melodious drum solo. On *Wee*, Gillespie fluffs a few notes (if it matters) and the breakneck tempo nearly gets the better of Powell, who had not played publicly for several months before this appearance.

Then there is *Hot House.* The piece always inspired Parker to interesting things, and here he builds an intriguing structure, alternating a shimmering complexity of phrase with a subtle simplicity. And finally, *A Night in Tunisia*, with everyone in very good form—a succinct demonstration of the integrated trinity of imagination that these men possessed in rhythm, melody, and harmony.

Also largely taken from the same concert is *"The Bud Powell Trio."* There are good Powell records (chiefly on Blue Note,

Verve, and Roost), and there are poor ones, made at a time when Powell's rhythmic coordination was decidedly off. This LP is one of the go~d ones, and the best of it offers some of the best Powell we have. Several of the ballads on the LP are largely excursions in voicing and harmony, but pieces like *Cherokee, Embraceable You,* and *Jubilee* (actually *Hallelujah*) show Powell's fleet, agile melodic invention, and they also show (should there be any doubters left by now) his soundly personal assimilation of his elders, particularly Teddy Wilson. Accompanist Max Roach has a marvelous contribution on *Cherokee.* And bassist Charlie Mingus contributes so much that it is little wonder the rumor persists that he later re-recorded his part on these pieces.

The aforementioned *A Night in Tunisia* is the basis of *Tunisian Fantasy,* a part of another concert recording done at Carnegie Hall last year by Dizzy Gillespie, who led a large orchestra of brass and percussion assembled for the occasion. The *Fantasy* (which, incidentally, might have been better rehearsed in a couple of spots) is a set of variants on Gillespie's piece, one of them based on the main theme, one on the bridge, and one built around the interlude that introduces the soloists, etc.

It is the highest compliment to Gillespie's pianist Lalo Schiffrin, who wrote the *Fantasy,* to say that the work is as generally unpretentious as many comparable jazz pieces are pretentious, that it is almost constantly interesting, and that it fulfills one of its main functions beautifully—it inspires the trumpeter to play with joyful variety and with the compellingly graceful bravura that is Gillespie at his best. Schiffrin is Brazilian and he can authentically handle the kind of Latin percussion that the trumpeter has always found propelling.

The other selections on the LP are a mixed bag: a new version of Gillespie's *Manteca,* this time done largely as a bounding exercise for the percussionists and with a tongue-in-cheek that its title (meaning *lard*) might call for; *Kush,* featuring Schiffrin's episodic Latin piano; *This Is the Way,* with Gillespie's altoist Leo Wright; and *Ool Ya Koo,* with amiably theatrical scat singing by Gillespie and Joe Carroll—but never mind all that. (1962)

I should have known, heard, and reported that Charlie Mingus did indeed re-record and dub in his bass lines on the Parker–Gillespie concert performances, and pianist Billy Taylor did a bit of ghosting on the Bud Powell performances as well. The two LPs were more recently collected as *"The Greatest Jazz Concert Ever."*

≈

≈

≈

≈
Monk and Coltrane

"Thelonious Monk with John Coltrane" contains some alternate takes of pieces already issued and some entirely new material. To spell out the contents for a bit, *Functional* is a remarkable, unaccompanied piano solo. It is an alternate version to the one included on the LP *"Thelonious Himself"* and so different from the original that I think it should have been given a different title.

Off Minor and *Epistrophy* are alternate and briefer versions of performances from the septet date that produced *"Monk's Music."* The former has very good solos by Hawkins, Copeland, and Monk, the latter solos by Coltrane and Copeland.

Nutty, Ruby My Dear, and *Trinkle Tinkle* are by Monk, Coltrane, bassist Wilbur Ware, and drummer Shadow Wilson—the quartet that had an almost legendary stay at the Five Spot in New York during the summer of 1957, a prelude to Monk's rediscovery as a major jazzman and to his current popularity and surely one of the most important (and exhilarating) events in jazz in recent years.

These three selections were recorded and the tapes were labeled "for posterity" by producer Orrin Keepnews and set aside until contractual conflicts had been resolved, permitting their release now. They are strong experiences, and if they are not as good as the performances one heard those summer nights at the Five Spot, they are nevertheless exceptional jazz.

Each member of that quartet played with great enthusiasm and at the peak of his own abilities, and through Monk's music each man was discovering and expanding his potential almost nightly.

256

Monk and Coltrane had exceptional emotional rapport. Technically, on the other hand, they were superb contrasts. Coltrane's techniques are obvious, Monk's more subtle. At the same time that Coltrane, with his showers of notes and his "sheets of sound," seemed to want to shatter jazz rhythms into an evenly spaced and constant array of short notes, Monk seemed to want to break them up subtly and phrase with a new freedom. Monk is a melodist; his playing is linear and horizontal. Coltrane's approach is vertical. He is a kind of latter-day Coleman Hawkins.

But even Coltrane's earlier solo on *Epistrophy* shows that he found enormous harmonic stimulation in Monk's music—he seemed to know not only where Monk *was* but where he was headed as few players did. But again, as the quartet tracks show, and particularly *Ruby My Dear,* Coltrane also knew that Monk's melodies are very strong and important and that it isn't enough merely to run their changes. Over and over again here, Monk's materials discipline Coltrane and order his explorations in a way that no material has done since, it seems to me.

Ware is, like Monk, a melodist, and he also finds surprise twists even in the most traditional materials. Wilson, whose early work had the smooth evenness of a Jo Jones, responds to Monk's hints with enthusiastic and appropriate patterns.

Monk also got a remarkable variety of textures from this group—by playing with Coltrane, by playing polyphonically *against* Coltrane, by laying out and leaving Coltrane to Ware and Wilson, sometimes predominantly to one of them, sometimes to both equally.

Some details: On *Nutty,* after Coltrane has strayed further and further into elaborate harmonic implications of the piece, Monk enters for his solo with, as usual, a simple and eloquent reestablishment of the theme in paraphrase. He does the same on *Trinkle Tinkle,* with an even more subtle recasting of that intricate melody.

Ruby My Dear is a knowingly embellished version of a lovely piece. The end of Coltrane's opening solo has a particularly beautiful (and Monkish) effect of suspension, and Monk's decision to begin his solo with lightly implied double-timing was a near master-stroke of meaningful contrast.

The best quartet performance is *Trinkle Tinkle*. The one flaw is that the Monk's piece itself, unlike most of Monk's melodies, may be a bit pianistic in conception to be fully effective on saxophone. But the spontaneous interplay between Monk and Coltrane in *Trinkle Tinkle* is quite wonderful, as is Monk's intuitive logic in knowing just when to stop it and let Coltrane stroll along against Ware and Wilson. Ware's solo is good, and I'm afraid makes one long for those evenings when he would spin out several effortless choruses in each piece.

As I said, this solo *Functional* is quite different from the previous version. On the earlier releases, Monk manages to play variations on one of the simplest and most percussive of all blues phrases in a nine-minute *tour de force* of cohesive imaginative invention. Here we hear nearly 10 minutes of Monk playing the blues in a dramatic yet lyric curve of melody.

Other delights: the interplay of Ware behind Monk on *Off Minor*. Copeland's solo on the same piece; in his way he also knows the relationship of parts, of melody to harmony, in Monk's music.

Nostalgia can corrupt memory, of course, but even allowing for that, I don't think these quartet performances are quite up to the level one heard at the Five Spot from this group. However, *Trinkle Tinkle* very nearly is. The other two are fine performances. In its way, *Epistrophy* may be excellent, too. And *Functional* is a near masterpiece. (1961)

≈

≈

≈

≈ # Jazz Clubs Come and Go

During the summer a large New York jazz club, the Jazz Gallery, which had a touch-and-go career for a couple of years, finally closed its doors, this time apparently for good. Business at other jazz clubs is reportedly poor, and there are constant mutterings from the owners about "putting in some strippers."

Actually, the strippers might not help, for current business at all night clubs in New York City is evidently bad. It does not always go this way, however. Sometimes when the jazz clubs are packing them in, the uptown comics are playing to half-empty houses. And other times, even the most popular jazzmen can't make the overhead for a clubowner, while the latest French chanteuse or a comic plus ballroom dancers and a dog act can pack the house.

What does all this mean? Shall we give the usual answer and say that in the night-club business there is just no telling how things will go? Perhaps. But for the jazz clubs there may be a better answer. The history of such places—especially in New York but also in other big cities—has been directly tied to the evolution of the music. And most jazz clubs come and go as styles rise, become popular, and decline in their following.

For example, there is convincing evidence that the surest sign that there would be some business decline in clubs featuring modern jazz came about two years ago. By that time, an only slightly watered-down version of the modern idiom was becoming commonplace in the bars along 125th St. in New York City and in cocktail lounges and hotel watering-spots throughout the coun-

259

try. If something that sounds like modern jazz is being heard nearly everywhere, the music will probably soon begin to lose its special attractiveness for a segment of its following. This is not a matter of how things should be, of course, but of how they are.

There was a great deal of jazz in New York before there were any jazz clubs. And there continues to be good jazz of all styles played in many a bar and dance hall that has no reputation for specializing in the music.

Public awareness of night clubs specifically devoted to jazz music came with the repeal of prohibition, and the first jazz clubs in New York City were converted speakeasies, along 52nd Street between Fifth and Sixth avenues, and in Greenwich Village.

The Village spot was Nick's. The music was not advanced, but in those days it was generally very good, and it found a small audience. Eddie Condon's club is a current off-shoot of Nick's, and if the music in both places is not always as lively and interesting as it once was, it is more popular. Indeed, one or another sort of Dixieland has become a kind of solace music for the tired businessman who may well have attended Nick's during the '30s. Such a cultural lag, plus the nearly constant revivals that the Dixieland style experiences, keeps Nick's open, keeps Condon's open, and, until the wrecking crews moved in, kept Jimmy Ryans open as the only jazz club left on 52nd Street. Other now nearly legendary, 52nd Street clubs have long since gone. When they began, the Onyx, Famous Door, Kelly's Stable, and the rest had a real cultural, perhaps artistic, purpose. They presented small-group swing after it had developed among players who were refugees from the early big bands and before it had become popular. Some of the most advanced jazz of the mid-'30s was first heard along this street. And as the style became more accepted, these clubs flourished—with Coleman Hawkins, Roy Eldridge, Billie Holiday, Charlie Shavers, Pete Brown, Art Tatum, and others.

Then, when modern jazz began to develop in the early '40s, it was soon heard along 52nd Street. But in presenting it the clubs were at first simply following their policy of booking the most interesting and talked-about younger players, players they could afford to hire.

Meanwhile, as swing became the established jazz style, a group of slightly more pretentious and more expensive clubs had sprung up, popularizing it further and bringing it to a slightly more affluent audience. After its downtown start with such music, the Café Society was even able to move uptown with Teddy Wilson, Albert Ammons, Pete Johnson, et al. And with such popularization, there came borderline artists like Hazel Scott.

Soon, just about every patron who was going to discover small group swing music had done so. And elsewhere the surface devices of the style became commonplace. The first clubs to go under were the expensive ones like Café Society Uptown.

Then 52nd Street saw that modern jazz was not just a certain group of young players but a whole new school of music, and the clubs tried to make the transition in full. One narrow basement spot even jammed Dizzy Gillespie's 1947 big band onto the small bandstand.

It was too late perhaps; the street's work was done, and the music was new. The clubs tried strippers, and a few tired locations were still holding out with the unclad women and the blue lights when the wrecking crews moved in a few years ago to tear down the area and make way for office buildings.

Gradually, modern jazz found refuge in a new group of clubs, just as swing had done before it. They were the Royal Roost, Bop City, and Birdland. Only the last endured, probably because it has consistently booked the popularizers of the style and its early successes—George Shearing, for one—and even people like Perez Prado and Big Jay McNeely as they became popular.

For several years, Birdland was the only modern-jazz club in New York City. One of the first signs that, at long last, modern jazz was about to receive a wider public popularity and acceptability was the mid-'50s appearance, first, of the original Basin Street and then of several new downtown jazz clubs. The Café Bohemia. Then the Five Spot on the East Side, followed by the

Half Note on the West. And most recently, a switch from folk back to jazz at the Village Vanguard.

The Bohemia had a short career with jazz but, for a while, a highly successful one. Its success announced a larger audience for modern jazz.

But as leaders like Art Blakey and Miles Davis began to get their new audience, their prices inevitably rose. At first, the Bohemia tried to keep up by raising its own prices. But finally, the club dropped jazz. Meanwhile, there were the Five Spot and the Half Note, which, to establish themselves, booked good but less expensive players.

With the close of the Bohemia, there was the Village Vanguard to take up some of the slack with groups like Davis', the Modern Jazz Quartet, and Bill Evans.

The Vanguard has had one of the most interesting histories of all New York City night clubs. In the late '30s, it provided a haven for the then-established swing idiom, fulfilling something of the same function as the two Café Society clubs. In 1940 Roy Eldridge was there, demonstrating that by that time, even an advanced swing player, such as he, was finding a larger following, and it was possible to make him the top of the bill at the Vanguard.

By the time modern jazz was developing, however, the Vanguard was presenting cabaret acts—some of the best cabaret acts. For examples, Judy Holliday and Betty Comden and Adolph Green did some of their first work at the Vanguard.

It was probably inevitable that once modern jazz had become more acceptable, Vanguard manager Max Gordon, who likes jazz and wants to present it, could book it in as the main attraction, and he did, beginning a few years ago.

There are other cultural-lag clubs besides Condon's and Nick's, of course. There are clubs like the Embers (slightly more expensive, slightly more ornate) and a more rowdy version of the same approach, the Metropole. The general fare, however, is a somewhat watered-down swing, most often featuring trumpeters.

The lag has begun to catch up, by the way. Our tired business-men no longer get a shock from Charlie Shavers, or even from Jonah Jones in one of his more advanced, Eldridgelike forays. Apparently, it all sounds pretty much the same to him now; 1938 has become just as acceptable as Dixieland.

By and large, then, clubs rise and fall as jazz evolves, in direct relationship to changes in the music, the gradual spread of taste for those changes, and the clubs' adaptability to those changes. Some exist to harbor new styles, some to present those styles as they become more popular, others to offer jazz as middlebrow nostalgia. If a club is flexible enough, it can find new purposes for itself, or modify its old ones, and endure.

In the short run, such a view may not be very encouraging or helpful to a young musician worrying about next week's gig. Or to a clubowner worrying about last month's bills. In the long run, it may be helpful to a musician planning a career, or to an alert clubowner looking to his future.

The implication here is that the work of some existing jazz clubs in New York City may be almost done now and that this is the reason business is not good. If there is some advice that might profitably and properly be given to the owner of a smaller and less expensive club, it might be: don't put in the strippers and don't hire the safe, bland groups unless you absolutely have to. Try to hang on. In the long run, you may be better off if you identify yourself at least partly with the most advanced playing around. Put in a good group playing an established style that really *plays*, and complement it with a newer group. You may soon find yourself with the next young jazz audience in attendance. And to stay in business, that is the audience you will have to get. You may be sure that whoever gets that audience will be running the next successful jazz club in New York. (1962)

≈
≈
≈
≈

The Ellington Era

I

The three-LP set from Columbia, *"The Ellington Era, 1927–1940,"* is the first volume of a promised series of two, the second to be ready in about a year and to cover the same period. It is also the first extensive retrospective that this major artist has had on records in the United States.

Duke Ellington made his first recordings in 1924, and on the surface they make him seem a jazz musician on the wrong track, even in danger of derailment—or perhaps no jazz musician at all. They are stiff and jerky rhythmically, and they abound with the superficial jazziness, the *do-wacka-do* and *voe-de-oh-doe,* of the period. But under the surface, Ellington showed in *Rainy Nights* that he had gone to the right source to learn what was then known about orchestrated jazz, to Don Redman and specifically to his score for Fletcher Henderson called *Naughty Man.* And we note that on *Choo Choo* Duke Ellington had produced an interestingly structured piece of his own. He also had several promising instrumentalists, particularly trumpeter Bubber Miley. It was Miley, as the passionate soloist and the introducer of strong, indigenous themes, who seems to have affirmed for Ellington his calling as a jazz musician.

The Columbia set begins with the first important Ellington-Miley collaboration, *East St. Louis Toodle-Oo* (pronounced, by the way, *toadlow*). It is still an impressive performance, but Miley's anguished wa-wa horn dominates it, and Miley also dominates the second important joint work, *Black and Tan Fantasy*. Ellington's orchestral effects and secondary themes seem weak and perhaps affected by comparison. But paradoxically their very sophistication held the most promise for the leader's development. And before he was through, Ellington proved that his own ideas could be assimilated and transmuted so as to become not only appropriate to the idiom of instrumental blues and jazz, but authentically extend its range.

Ellington became the great composer-orchestrator of jazz, the great leader of a large ensemble, the master of form in jazz and the great synthesizer of all its elements. But to achieve those things, he had to take the idiom that Miley represented, take what he had learned from Redman and Henderson, take his own innate urbanity, and start all over again, with a completely new approach to big-band jazz.

Redman and Henderson had converted the dance band with its reed, brass, and rhythm sections into a jazz band by using jazz effects and themes, and employing improvised solos by jazz musicians. The turning point for Ellington came when he was hired by a new night club—an uptown spot offering sometimes lurid stage shows and what was then called "jungle music" mostly for "slumming" white patrons, a place called the Cotton Club. He found himself, then, having also to do the work of a show band or a pit band, and because he faced that fact squarely, he rediscovered orchestral jazz in the most brilliant and durable style of all.

He became a superb jazz orchestrator—he was already destined to become an exceptional writer of themes—and he learned his craft, like any good popular artist, from anything and everything that crossed his path. He learned from his own accomplished post-ragtime, "stride" piano. The style is orchestral; it imitates a band. If we compare, say, the 1928 piano version of *Black Beauty* with his orchestration, we can hear him virtually assigning the piece, finger by finger, off the keyboard to his horns and reeds. He also learned from the "light classics," Broadway scoring, radio studio orchestras. And he learned from his own orchestra, individually and collectively.

* * *

The orchestra is, as has been said, Ellington's real instrument, and he has worked with it as the great playwrights have worked with their companies of actors, as the great choreographers have worked with their own troupes of dancers, as the great European composers have worked for specific instrumentalists or singers, each learning from the other. Ellington's became a truly collaborative art among leader, soloist, and group. It is a tribute to him that the careers of his sidemen have sometimes been less illustrious after they have left him. All the great Ellington works depend on a subtle relationship between soloist and group, between what is written (or perhaps merely memorized) and what is improvised, between the individual part and the total effect. A great Ellington performance is, therefore, not a series of sometimes brilliant episodes, but a whole, greater than the sum of its parts. He learned how to discipline improvisation and how to extend orchestration—to the enhancement of both.

Ellington did take early lessons in scoring from his keyboard style, but he soon was to rid his writing of specifically pianistic aspects and wrote more directly for the resources of the horns themselves. He also was to free his work of a dependence on ragtime and its rather static and abrupt rhythm and phrasing. For example *Rockin' in Rhythm,* an early success still in the Ellington books, has the pulse of ragtime piano shaping its movement. New, more flexible and mobile ideas of rhythm and phrasing were Louis Armstrong's crucial and pervasive contribution to the music, of course, and one can hear an Armstrong-inspired propulsion already beginning to burst through in the 1930 performance of *Old Man Blues,* specifically in Cootie Williams' marvelously agile trumpet solo.

Two years later came a rhythmic turning point in *It Don't Mean a Thing,* with its prophetic subtitle, *If It Ain't Got That Swing.* The piece was obviously conceived as an instrumental although it was first recorded with a vocal by Ivie Anderson, taking over (it seems clear) part of the passage first designed for Johnny Hodges' alto. Thus, *It Don't Mean a Thing* is an orchestral and not a pianistic piece, and it is written with the new swing phrasing throughout.

Sometimes busy ragtime phrasing does reappear, particularly in *Tiger Rag* variants like *Slippery Horn*, *Bragging in Brass*, or *The Flaming Sword*. These are usually brilliantly executed show pieces, but they are always in some sense melodic and rhythmic museum pieces as well. But by 1937 and *Harmony in Harlem*, it is clear that a collective and flexible swing was becoming almost second nature for the Ellington orchestra. One's only reservation, and it is a tentative one, is drummer Sonny Greer, whose playing fits excellently with the older or the regressive style.

Excellent orchestration is also almost second nature, and there are swirling colors on *Merry-Go-Round* and brooding sonorities on *The Saddest Tale* that might in themselves attest to Ellington's pre-eminence.

What is still imperfect is a just employment of the leader's melodic sophistication, particularly in the blues idiom. Thus, *Bundle of Blues*, in 1933, brilliantly juxtaposes Cootie Williams' resilient growls and blues-feeling against responses from the orchestra. But Ellington offers a secondary theme that is perhaps a little too chic, a little too sentimental. Similarly, *Echoes of Harlem*, with an Ellington interlude for saxes that takes on very different life in Williams' earthy trumpet paraphrases later in the performance.

A truly balanced assimilation of Ellington's suaveness first occurs on *Blue Light*, I think, done in late 1938. To achieve it, he cut back to a very small group and two soloists, with his piano introducing, organizing, commenting, and offering a contribution and summary of its own at the end. Barney Bigard's liquid clarinet theme is so fragile it seems to be embellishments on a single low note. Then Lawrence Brown's trombone with a robust and beautiful second melody. Then Ellington. *Blue Light* is a continuously developing whole, nothing extrinsic, all parts in balance. Following it, *Slap Happy* by the full orchestra and from the same record date, or *Portrait of the Lion* from a month later, are similarly cohesive and lack only first-rate melodic material to rank with the very best Ellington. Thus, Ellington was prepared for the great works that followed, beginning in 1940: *Blue Serge, Ko-Ko, Concerto for Cootie, Sepia Panorama*. And for the shining satellites that gather around their brilliance: *Harlem Air Shaft, Rumpus in Richmond, In a Mellowtone, Across the Track Blues, Jack the Bear, Main Stem*, and the rest.

I have said little here about Ellington the popular composer of melodies like *Mood Indigo* or *I Let a Song Go Out of My Heart*, but both are worth comment in our context. *Mood Indigo* brilliantly cuts across the compartmentalized sections (trumpets, trombones, saxophones, rhythm) of the swing band, being touchingly scored for trumpet, trombone, and clarinet—a succinct example of how Ellington reinterpreted the resources of the jazz orchestra. *I Let a Song Go Out of My Heart*, on the other hand, is one of several examples of an Ellington theme that was conceived instrumentally and had to be revised, and revised downward, when it was turned into a popular song.

Nor have I said anything about Ellington's extended works. The two-part *Diminuendo and Crescendo in Blue* from 1937 is included in the Columbia set (and like several other selections presented annoyingly out of order, being placed after some 1938 selections, which are themselves out of order). It is a very interesting piece, but has lately been converted into an up-tempo crowd-pleaser for tenor saxophonist Paul Gonzalves.

Nor have I said enough about the individual soloists except in passing. I have not mentioned Joe "Tricky Sam" Nanton's guttural trombone counterpart to Miley's and Williams' growl trumpet; nor Rex Stewart's enticing discoveries about his cornet; nor baritone saxophonist Harry Carney, without whose sound and drive Ellington would not be Ellington.

I have proposed 1938 to 1942 as the peak years for Ellington. But I have also spoken of Ellington as a major artist, one of the few men in jazz history truly deserving of that title. And an artist's accomplishments spread themselves before and beyond their peak. So one looks to almost any period of his career and finds high achievements. And Ellington is above all a supreme *popular* artist. If mambos are now in demand, he may play some mambos; if limbos are popular, he may do limbos; if a program of popular dance band ballads interests him, he will do one. And he will do them all with integrity and sometimes with brilliance. He can meet an audience on its own level and, more often than not, transport it up to his.

Charlie Parker's genius had its roots in such popular music as Ellington's, but his audience was inevitably smaller and it took diluting popularizers to spread his ideas. Thelonious Monk took fifteen years to find any audience at all. Ornette Coleman's audience is so far largely confined to the poets, painters, and musicians who (like Coleman himself) will be called on to answer for American prestige, not now but fifteen years from now.

Ellington's audience still has at its core couples who danced to his *Sophisticated Lady* on their honeymoons. And he may in that sense be the last great popular artist that jazz will ever have. (1963)

II

"The Ellington Era, 1927–1940," Volume Two is, like its prede cessor, Volume One, a collection of three LPs, drawn in this case from forty-four old 78 r.p.m. titles. To say that it is not quite so good a collection overall as the earlier one is perhaps not to say very much. In Duke Ellington we are dealing with one of our greatest musicians, and his relative failures may interest us as much as the successes of lesser men.

I shall not attempt exhaustive comments on the new volume, for it seems to me that in 1966 it would be more appropriate to try to put in perspective this man's whole recorded career to date rather than dwell in detail over a part of it. Let what follows, therefore, stand as some appreciative jottings by one listener on some of the music at hand.

The album necessarily begins less auspiciously than the previous one, for that set already gave us versions of *East St. Louis Toodle-oo*, *Black and Tan Fantasy*, and *The Mooch*, the early collaborations with trumpeter Bubber Miley that had so much to do with the affirmation of Ellington's talent and direction as an orchestrator and leader. But here the first titles do show Ellington trying out his soloists (and the second piece, *Take It Easy*, indicates what good ones he had by 1928); or they show him trying out various textures and effects and discovering an ensemble character for his orchestra; or they show him, on *Move Over*, cautiously experimenting with unusual structures; or they find him significantly testing several personal moods withing the basic blues form. However, the first LP in the album ends with the expanded, 1932 version of *Creole Love Call*, an appropriate juxtaposition of themes from Miley and Rudy Jackson, and this version of *Creole Love Call* is the first great reassessment and reorchestration of the early pieces, in part because of the appropriate modesty of Ellington's own contributions in scoring.

And here is Ellington in his 1932 version of *Rose Room* providing his soloists with encouraging background figures strictly to the chordal contours of the piece. Another arranger at the time might have plowed through with riffs on a harmonic makeshift, and hoped for the best.

Ellington's own *Showboat Shuffle*, from three years later, is a gem of momentum, in theme, in variations (written and improvised), in orchestration, and in technical execution.

The 1935 *Reminiscing in Tempo*, originally issued on four ten-inch 78s, is almost unique among Ellington's extended works. It is not an alliance of several themes like the earlier long works, nor is it a suite, like most of the later ones. *Reminiscing in Tempo* is a sustained exploration of one main motive and some complementary ones. There are solo moments, but Ellington's real vehicle in the piece is the orchestra, its resources and textures. *Reminiscing in Tempo* is the sort of instructive piece of American music that might be in the repertory of every "stage" band in our high schools and colleges. (Ah, but will it ever replace the Stan Kenton *kitsch* which so many of our band instructors inflict on their charges? Those who accept the press-agentry about Kenton's "innovations" and "artistry," cannot know Ellington's work.)

Azure, neglected perhaps because it is so simple, is one of Ellington's most affecting slow, introspective mood pieces. It has a release that is perhaps a bit weak, but its main strain is superbly scored. And its melody is neither vocal in character—as, say, *In a Sentimental Mood*—nor sentimental—as *Lost in Meditation*. A ritual sentimentality can be the curse of sophistication, and an urbane sophistication is the cornerstone of Ellington's genius in its successes and its failures alike.

So, I have used *genius*, a word that is easy to use, but a quality not so easy to demonstrate, and impossible to "prove." If I were to pick an apparently casual, unassuming piece here for such a demonstration, I think it would be the cryptically titled *Old King Dooji* from 1938. On this work Ellington provided a continuously varied theme and presented it with written and improvised variations. Most of the jazz composers around him at the time would have broken such material into snippets, orchestrated it much more simply, spread it out, and made several pieces out of it, depending for their effects on the force of repetition of two-bar riffs. Yet Ellington's logical little work is neither disparate nor overloaded.

In a sense I am carping to say so, but it seems to me that there are better ways to present Ellington's career than the one Columbia is using. It would be more enlightening to have his music documented year by year, and record date by record date, than to keep going over the same thirteen years with each album. Probably some listeners will feel that Columbia is simply putting together all the Ellington material it happens to have on hand in good 78 copies as each set comes due. I doubt it, and it may be that the company feels the procedure it is using makes the material more marketable. (For all I know, it does.)

In any case, it is not time to stop. Still pending are the 1937–38 versions of *East St. Louis* and *Black and Tan*, two more instances in Ellington's career where a return to former glories, and using different soloists, brought about superior versions. There is the 1939 recording of that marvelously titled piece, *Doin' the Voom Voom*. Compared with the original version of ten years earlier, it is a revelation of the technical evolution of jazz ensemble playing, particularly in the rhythm sections, and of Ellington's evolving ideas of sonority. It is also succinct evidence of the master's influence. For over the years *Doin' the Voom Voom* was raided, literally two bars at a time, by swing-band arrangers as source material for their "originals."

And just in case Columbia should run out of studio-made records, there is, say, the sound track to Ellington's 1935, all-musical movie short, comprising the important suite, *Symphony in Black,* the rights to which should not be difficult to clear for LP. No, it is not time to stop. (1966)

≈

≈

≈

≈ # Four Pianists:
Four Minority Views

I. Oscar Peterson

Popular art, we are told, finds its chief effect in an emotional immediacy. On that basis there can be no doubt of the effectiveness of Oscar Peterson as a popular artist. And it does not take much reflection in tranquility to discern Peterson's virtues. They are engagingly obvious; perhaps too obvious to need talking about. At least they are obvious enough so that his admirers are usually surprised to discover that there are those who have reservations about his playing.

There are two inevitable words in any talk about Oscar Peterson: *technique* and *swing*. Perhaps neither is the *mot juste*. There can be no question about the finger dexterity of Peterson's piano, certainly; he can handle the shortest notes and the fastest tempos. There are recorded versions of *Indiana* and *Elevation* (to take two from dozens of possible examples) that are very fast and on which Peterson offers a plenitude of notes with a rhythmic exactness and sureness that only a few jazz pianists could equal.

But technique is as technique does. If a reference to musical technique also implies musical expressiveness, then it might be better to say that what Peterson has is facility. Quite often his dexterity seems to be a detriment. He cannot resist, it seems, obvious triplets, scales, and arpeggio runs as they occur to him, and time and again he will interrupt the perfectly respectable musical structure he has been building to run off such pianistic platitudes.

Nor, it seems, can Peterson resist a jazz cliché. For example, he even interrupts the theme statement of so delicately rendered a line as Clifford Brown's *Joy Spring* (an almost perfectly titled piece, by the way) with a hoary and inappropriate riff. One might almost say that Peterson's melodic vocabulary is a stockpile of clichés, that he seems to know every stock riff and lick in the history of jazz. Further, his improvisations frequently just string them together. One has the feeling that Peterson would eventually work every one of them into every piece he plays regardless of tempo, mood, or any other consideration; it would simply be a matter of his going on long enough to get them all in.

Possibly the biggest cliché in Peterson's style is his constant preoccupation with the blue notes. Miles Davis has said that he sounds as if he had to *learn* to play the blues. He certainly sounds as if he were out to prove he had learned to, for on nearly every piece he plays *at* the blues. And for Peterson, these plaintively expressive musical intervals will often lose their effect, sometimes within less than two choruses, since he uses them so constantly and indiscreetly.

There could probably be no more succinct contrast to such cliché-mongering than the presence of bassist Ray Brown in Peterson's group. Brown's virtues are many—his sound, his excellent and sympathetic swing, his joyous and natural commitment to the act of playing. His solos (take the recent ones on *Kadota's Blues* and *Tricrotism*, or his more celebrated variations on *How High the Moon*) do contain some stock effects, and they prove that there is nothing innately wrong with stock effects. Brown uses them as parts of a personally developed musical context; he grasps the meaning of these traditional and durable ideas, and as he uses them we inevitably see them in a different light and glimpse the sound basis for their durability. All of which is quite a different matter from glibly piling up such phrases, one on another.

The question of Peterson's swing is perhaps similar. If there were some mechanical means for measuring swing, Peterson might get a score of 100%. And there can be no question that he is a rhythmically engaging player, Peterson seems to know everything there is to know about swing—except perhaps its essence, its musical meaning. For, as he bounces along, Oscar Peterson never seems to have the creative momentum in his lines that is perhaps the real *raison d'être* for swing.

I have spoken of his fast tempos, and I should also compliment his slow ones, for Peterson has a range in tempos that few jazzmen can duplicate. He seems to be able to play, unembarrassed, with the same bounce and cleanliness, fairly slow, medium, and fast.

Peterson is obviously indebted to the Nat Cole of the forties (when Cole was a jazz pianist) and to Art Tatum. Some may feel that Peterson's facility and sophistication allow him to fill out ideas that Cole merely suggested. But Nat Cole had a sense of melodic order and, though one might question his taste in melodic ideas, often his constructions had a relatively sustained design. By comparison Peterson seems to think only from one two-bar riff to the next.

At slow tempos Peterson does use a directly Tatumesque manner—a recent performance of *Ill Wind* is an example. Whatever one's final opinion of Tatum, there is a wonderful sense of pianistic adventure and an arresting harmonic imagination in his playing. Peterson's pastiche seems to me mechanical. His heavier touch seems inappropriate to such a style, and his monotony in dynamics is dramatized in such moods.

With such a heritage, Peterson would seem to belong to the thirties and, for all his harmonic sophistication, indeed he does. His rhythmic sense, his manner of phrasing is the clue to that, of course, and with his facility a kind of rococo version of 1930s jazz piano is probably inevitable. For all his dexterity, his phrasing is so deeply rooted in the earlier period that when he occasionally reaches for a Parkeresque double-timing (as on the aforementioned *Joy Spring*, for example) he seems a bit strained and uncomfortable. He has recorded with almost every major player from the thirties and on occasion he has shown commendable sympathy for their work. One thinks particularly of his accompaniments to Roy Eldridge, say: he begins with the sparsest and simplest textures which gradually build, and buoy up the trumpeter, inspiring him to a third, perhaps a fourth improvised variation. On the other hand, on the LP called *"Soulville"* he glibly accompanies Ben Webster, and spells him in solo, with an almost constant rattling of blue notes and tired riffs—under the circumstances the level of sustained inspiration Webster shows on that LP seems to me a marvel of marvels.

I began by repeating the dictum about the immediacy of popular art. (But is not Beethoven emotionally immediate?) Surely anyone who has watched early Chaplin will question that criterion, for obviously the best popular art refutes it. So also will anyone who has heard Armstrong or Ellington, Parker or Monk. Jazz long ago showed that its best players could provide a more durable aesthetic experience, and that its best recorded works are not transient but survive the moment and even span the years. (1963)

II. Martial Solal

One of the best jazz pianists in the world plays in France and, as far as I know, to this writing has not been in the United States. He is Martial Solal. He was born in Algiers and began playing jazz in 1940. After the second World War, he inevitably gravitated to Paris. As I imply, it is not enough to say that Solal is exceptional for a European jazzman: it could be that Solal will develop an importance which, like Django Reinhardt's, is greater than considerations of geography or even of instrument.

Not that I would particularly like to demonstrate any of this by those of his recordings which have so far been released over here. One LP presented him when his style was still largely unformed, and the most recent offers a Solal doing an incongruous Erroll Garner pastiche (but there is discreetly assimilated Garner in his best playing) and also performing some more or less experimental, unaccompanied pieces—pieces of a sort which do not seem to suit his fundamentally conservative approach. However, we have also had released here his delightful variations on Bemsha Swing in a scoring of the piece by André Hodeir. And we have heard his wonderfully sympathetic joint recordings with Sidney Bechet. These included a couple of rare moments by Solal, particularly in the way he humorously abstracted the melodic line of *All the Things You Are* and rephrased and almost constantly reharmonized the single-note motif on *It Don't Mean a Thing*.

Solal's best playing invites one to deal with basics, and deal with them in a rather awed way: what a completely *natural* musician this man is! To pay him the highest compliment, he seems as natural a musician as was Bechet. The foreign jazzman's usual problem seems not even to occur to him: not only can Solal swing, he swings with a vitality that is personal, and a sureness which allows him rhythmic variety and variation of a sort that many American jazzmen of his generation have not even attempted. He has fine pianistic technique, but it reveals itself so soundly and so musically that one may be almost unaware of his proficiencies. He puts nearly every idea to a directly musical use, and time and again one notices Solal quietly employing effects which might easily be turned into blatant grandstanding by a less discreet and dedicated player.

Above all, Solal answers the basic criterion: he invents interesting, fresh, and personal music.

Solal apparently feels that a serious jazz player should provide most of his own repertory, one appropriate to the larger considerations of his style. I wonder if many of his pieces (at least the few that I have heard) would be more than "interesting" in the hands of another player, or, let us say, in the abstract. But they become increasingly suited to Solal's own work. Most important, they allow him performances which seek to be a continuum; that is, in which a theme-statement at the beginning and its reiteration at the end do not seem so isolated as they have for so long in jazz. In this I think Solal (like Charlie Mingus and, on occasion, Cecil Taylor) has faced one of the most pressing problems of form. For it no longer seems sensible in modern jazz for the exposition of a theme merely to set a tempo and a chord structure for improvising, and then disappear completely.

Perhaps this sort of thing is easiest to see in the way that Solal handles familiar thematic material of another man. As he performs Duke Jordan's *Jordu,* his opening exposition is rather free, allowing for rhythmic variation, melodic paraphrases, interesting changes of register, and fleeting embellishments. As the performance unfolds, one realizes that these alterations are rather specific hints of the personal way that Solal will later improvise on the material. Further, many of his variations are thematic or at least make use of fragments of the theme-melody. And about half-way through the performance, he reiterates the theme rather directly as if to re-establish the order of things. Solal uses these organizing thematic signposts with the same naturalness that Thelonious Monk does. They also allow him striking forays into the implication of a piece without inviting disorder. Most fascinating of all is a kind of improvising in which Solal alludes to the structure of the theme almost phrase by phrase and rest by rest. But he echoes this structure, not with paraphrases of the theme but with *new* melodies which fit its patterns of phrasing.

The performance of *Jordu* that I have been discussing is on an LP called *"Jazz à Gaveau"* which was recorded at a public concert by Solal's trio (Guy Pedersen, bass; Daniel Humair, drums) and which I shall briefly review. The masterpiece of the occasion was *Aigu-Marine,* a contemplative but never precious improvisation, beautifully rendered, and with a striking technical discipline. It is probably the best example of the continuous flow of theme-into-variations in the recital, although *Dermaplastic* also seems very good in this respect. Both *Gavotte à Gaveau* and *Nos Smoking* (yes, a bilingual pun) alternate two separate tempos with complete naturalness (again, one thinks of Mingus) and on the fast portions of the latter, Solal performs with a really delicate ease. On the former, staccato fragments that at first seem isolated soon reveal themselves as part of a careful, yet still spontaneous, structure (here one thinks of Charlie Parker and Ornette Coleman as well as Monk).

I seem to be indulging in a panegyric. I do not mean that. I will take one exception—perhaps it is subjective—that Solal's wit is perhaps too prevalent. Thus, a piece like *Averty, C'est Moi* is in blues form but that seems merely a convenience or convention—

he is obviously neither a blues man in the traditional sense, nor does he discover the contemplative mood that players like Benny Carter or Earl Hines have found in the idiom. But perhaps it is more of—what shall we call it?—understated, puckish Solalian lyricism. (1963)

III. George Shearing

A few years ago, pianist George Shearing said that "Lennie [Tristano] could never be happy compromising, as I am doing." Shearing's frankness and lack of delusion are admirable to be sure. What he was and is doing is popularizing modern jazz to a widespread success.

I am not absolutely sure that musical popularizers are a reviewer's business. They do introduce large numbers of people to a musical style—at least so I am told. But for every listener who moves on, hundreds of others stay with the popularizer; one of the originators of modern jazz, Dizzy Gillespie, had a good audience before Shearing arrived, but Shearing has a larger audience than Gillespie has or probably ever will have. In any case, popularizers always appear and are always going to appear.

However, there are popularizers and popularizers. One of Benny Goodman's functions was to spread a music that Fletcher Henderson had evolved several years before and do the same for some of Count Basie's pieces as well. Goodman contributed more than merely that, to be sure, but his treatment of Henderson's style involved no particular compromise or dilution.

I suppose that if popularizers become a constant preoccupation, a reviewer will be wasting a great deal of time. And at worst he may end up making them the objects of a kind of snobbish abuse. On the other hand, a reviewer probably should discuss them from time to time to describe what he feels they are up to and to say how much compromise and dilution he hears in their work.

I begin with Shearing because Capitol has recently issued a kind of summary album of his career, "The Best of George Shearing." As a pianist, Shearing is able and fluent, although as a jazzman he has occasional problems with phrasing and swing. More important, he is capable of a lot more inventiveness than he usually offers. And it seems to me that his basic compromise is to play as if he were not really emotionally involved with what he is doing, even when he allows himself to do something musical.

His group's approach comes partly from its instrumentation (piano, vibraphone, guitar, plus bass and drums), and the formula usually involves an opening theme-statement by the three melody instruments. The tone is terribly chic and usually employs some rather gimmicky and mechanical rhythmic displacements. Then we get a chorus from Shearing of single-note treble lines, followed by another chorus of locked-hands block chording. Finally, a repeat of the first chorus.

The selections in the new album are usually laid out in that manner, although a few supplement it with a string section, or some "Latin" percussion, or the applause of a "live" audience.

To be more specific, *Lullaby of Birdland,* which has some rather abruptly chunky work by the rhythm section, involves no solos except some bass breaks, and *You Stepped Out of a Dream,* with a conga drummer added, involves no solos at all. *September in the Rain* has an opening chorus with some trite embellishments from the pianist, moves on to a good modernish piano variation played rather tepidly, then to some mechanical block-chording. On *You Don't Know What Love Means,* Shearing offers a tinkly, obvious, cocktail-style variation. The quintet turns Lester Young's movingly ironic blues, *Jumpin' with Symphony Sid,* into a lightweight ditty, and Shearing plays four frothy choruses that nevertheless are very well organized. On *You Stepped Out of a Dream,* Shearing delivers an unexpected solo in a Teddy Wilson style; on *East of the Sun* he does capable Oscar Peterson. *Roses in Picardy* has piano notes and runs, but no real ideas. So does *September Song,* along with some writing for strings that is so trite as to be funny. *Early Autumn* has a good enough half-chorus played, once again, with tinkling shallowness. A version of *Honeysuckle Rose* is done in a sort of quasi-earthy style, with lots of blue notes and a boogie-woogie bass figure.

There is one exceptional performance: an extended reading of

Little White Lies, with real group swing, very good drumming, good solos by guitar and vibes, and Shearing showing the basic debt of his modern style: somewhat simplified Bud Powell. (1964)

IV. Ahmad Jamal

Pianist Ahmad Jamal is a success: he has several best-selling LP's, a supper-club following (which otherwise displays little interest in jazz), and several direct imitators. He has also received the deeper compliment of having admittedly affected the work of an important jazzman. His success should surprise no one, and his effect on Miles Davis should prove (if proof were needed) that good art can be influenced by bad.

Clearly, Davis responds to some of Jamal's interesting and very contemporary harmonic voicings and the very light, and impeccably accurate rhythmic pulse of Jamal's trio, particularly in the support he got from his bassist, the late Israel Crosby, and from his drummer, Vernell Fournier. Further, Jamal has the same interest in openness of melody, space, and fleeting silence that Davis does. But for the trumpeter these qualities can be aspects of haunting lyric economy. For Jamal they seem a kind of crowd-titillating stunt work. Indeed, in a recital like *"Ahmad Jamal at the Blackhawk,"* recorded in a San Francisco night club, it appears that Jamal's real instrument is not the piano at all but his audience. On some numbers, he will virtually sit things out for a chorus, with only some carefully worked out rhapsodic harmonies by his left hand or coy tinklings by his right. After that, a few bombastic block chords by both hands, delivered *forte,* will absolutely lay them in the aisles. And unless you have heard Ahmad Jamal blatantly telegraph the climax of a piece, or beg applause en route with an obvious arpeggio run which he drops insinuatingly on the crowd after he has been coasting along on the graceful momentum of Crosby and Fournier, then you have missed a nearly definitive musical bombast. The set in question includes slow and medium standards—Jamal this time seems to favor Richard Rodgers and Jimmy Van Heusen especially—and a blues by Jamal which is performed with a kind of slick sophistication one would have thought impossible within that basic jazz form. (1963)

> There is an aspect of Ahmad Jamal's music which I did not discuss above and certainly should have; the matter of his left-hand chord voicings. Jamal used the same "rootless," "open" voicings heard in Bill Evans' work. Technical note: if I voice my chords omitting the root notes, a given chord can have any of several identities, can lead more easily to a greater variety of succeeding chords, and can accommodate a greater variety of notes and turns in a melody line. Violinist Joe Kennedy Jr., a boyhood friend raised like Jamal in the Pittsburgh area, says that he heard Jamal using such voicings in youthful jam sessions in the mid-1940s, voicings he had learned in his "classical" piano training.
>
> All of which of course raises the question of who played them first in jazz, and who played them most influentially. But whoever undertakes to pin down that matter of jazz history should of course keep in mind that rootless chords were commonplace in Stravinsky and Bartók in the early part of the century. (1990)

≈
≈
≈
≈
Celebrating
a Centennial

Ebony, the monthly of rather *Life*-like style and tone, is the most durable of the several successful magazines of the Chicago Negro publishing house, Johnson Publications. Last fall, there was a special issue of *Ebony* on the occasion of the 100th anniversary of the Emancipation Proclamation.

There were accounts of Negro-American history, Negro women, the future of civil-rights leadership, the Negro press, Negroes in entertainment, Negroes in painting, Negroes in business. Undoubtedly many congratulations gathered around the issue. But perhaps now that initial responses have settled down, one may take a second look.

It is perhaps not my position to say so (it may not be my position to say any of this), but I confess that Negro American life as reflected in this special issue of *Ebony* has about as little to do with the life of most Negro Americans as I have observed it— observed it in Virginia, in Los Angeles, in Philadelphia, and in New York—as I can imagine. Less to do with the grinding realities of Negro American life than, let us say, an issue of *Life* magazine has to do with the realities of American life in general, which is little enough.

Be that as it may, the rejoinder would surely be that this is a "showpiece" issue. And certainly in a publication devoted to Negro achievement, Frederick Douglass belongs, W. E. B. DuBois belongs, Mary McLeod Bethune belongs—so do all the others who are there and who are justly celebrated and famous. And so, for all I know, do the apparently affluent Negro bankers, businessmen, and lawyers pictured in the book belong, along with the chicly turned-out social worker on page 89, the conventionally busy housewife on page 90, plus Harry Belafonte, Sidney Poitier, and Sammy Davis, Jr.

But I have ransacked this issue in vain for a single mention of the name Louis Armstrong. (Was it there, hidden away? Did I miss it?) For a single mention of Billie Holiday. For a mention of Charlie Parker. Or Lester Young, Count Basie, Thelonious Monk, Miles Davis. . . .

I do find a photograph of a statue of W. C. Handy, as it stands in a park in Memphis. And I do find Duke Ellington, as "Jazz Composer and Band Leader," on page 229, among "America's 100 Most Influential Negroes." Of jazz or jazzmen, that and nothing more.

What in the world impresses *Ebony?* An enormous cultural contribution like jazz, a music that has been called America's contribution to the musical arts? Apparently not. And W. C. Handy's statue, plus the catch phrase "the father of the blues," is surely not much recognition for the blues, an original musical-poetic form of which an important American literary critic, Stanley Edgar Hyman, is willing to say with justice, "Yet they are true art . . . and they are or should be our pride." They are not *Ebony's* pride apparently. Could the blues be *Ebony's* ignorance? Surely not. What then? *Ebony's* shame?

And if the opinions of American, British, and Continental critics do not convince *Ebony,* what will?

Would *Ebony* like to know, then, that there is hardly a trumpet player in a U.S. symphony orchestra who has not been affected by Louis Armstrong's style—that as a result of his work almost every player now uses a slight vibrato that European brass men do not have (and, ironically, that the younger jazz players do not have either)? Or that contemporary classical composers write very differently for trumpet than their predecessors did because of the way Armstrong, and the jazzmen who followed him have rediscovered the wider resources of the instrument?

In other words, if the superb artistry of this man does not impress *Ebony*, would the prestige of classical music impress? If not classical music, then would *Ebony* be impressed with how much watered-down Dizzy Gillespie one hears gushing from one's television set?

In short, if *Ebony* is not impressed with Negro jazz musicians, would *Ebony*'s standard allow it to be impressed with the fact that, one way or another, jazz has affected almost all European and American music, top to bottom?

I have said that this issue of *Ebony* had little to do, in my opinion, with the realities of Negro American life. And I have indicated that I harbor the suspicion that the editorship ignores some of those realities because it is not really proud of them.

Well, I think that the white man should feel shame over many aspects of Negro American life, for his part in having brought them about, and his continuing part in keeping them as they are. But I also know that none of us is going to get anywhere until we admit to the realities of Negro life.

I further know that jazz is a reality of Negro life in America, and that all of us should be enormously proud of it. (1964)

> The foregoing may seem to be something of a period piece, a relic of a time when such a thing did happen, surviving into a time when such a thing would not happen. Perhaps it is not altogether that, however. Although *Ebony* would not now ignore such important accomplishments of African-American culture as it did in 1964, other black institutions may still ignore them, or at least not exactly celebrate them. It is now possible to obtain a Ph.D. in musicology specializing in jazz, and degrees have been awarded to young men and women who did their dissertations on Duke Ellington, Lester Young, Coleman Hawkins, and other great figures and movenents in the music. But few of them have been awarded to young black men and women, and none, as far as I know, has been awarded by the music departments of predominantly black institutions.

≈

≈

≈

≈
Concert with
High Moments

The occasion was a concert at the Loeb Student Center of New York University by the Ornette Coleman Quintet with Coleman on alto and violin; Don Cherry on trumpet, cornet, and an Indian flute; Dewey Redman on tenor, Charlie Haden on bass; and Ornette's son Denardo Coleman on drums. The occasion was also something of a reunion. Cherry and Haden were in the first group that Ornette Coleman brought to the old Five Spot in New York in the late fall of 1959 (was it really *that* long ago?). But the program featured seven new compositions by Coleman, and one by Charlie Haden.

Beginning with the first piece, *Broken Shadows*, with Coleman and Redman in dirge tempo and Cherry playing an obbligato, it was evident that I was going to have a problem throughout the evening. When I first heard Denny Coleman on a record a couple of years ago, I was happy to take at face value the attitude that, whereas there was obviously much he didn't know about drums, he played what he played with a promising naturalness, good spirit and personal feeling. Those things are not enough, to be sure, but they are the right beginning.

Something has gone awry. Young Coleman was loud at this concert (he was also amplified—more on that in a moment), and he was, it seemed to me, insensitive in his loudness. He was careless in what he played behind the soloists. For example, he missed Don Cherry's dynamics and tempo alterations of *Who Do*

286

You Work For? and he didn't hear the quality of Haden's solos. In this music one mustn't miss such things. Swing is becoming a problem. Tempo is becoming a problem. The time has come, I think, when Denny Coleman's technical shortcomings are beginning to stand in the way of what he wants to express and causing him to push. I'd suggest that the moment has arrived for a teacher—and, no, nobody asked me.

Charlie Haden. Well, Charlie Haden was also wired into the huge rock-type amplifier at the back of the stage. The result was to buzz and blur one of the most precise and buoyant bass sounds I know of. During the second half of the program, Haden removed the small mike from inside his bass strings and put it on a low stand on the floor. It helped—some.

Cherry is a better, more confident trumpeter than he was nine years ago; he has ideas and approaches of his own in this music now. And Redman's relative conservatism seems to me a very good contrast in the group.

Beginning with the second number, *The Anthem,* Coleman picked up piece after piece and made it soar. And for the record, I will also mention his solo on *Comme Il Faut* which was exceptional. His musical energy and grasp of tempo were wonderful. More important, of course, is his ability to sustain, develop, and vary an idea—this is the most orderly of players. But Coleman does, on occasion, keep an idea going somewhat past the point of inspiration and deep interest, and into the point of simple ingenuity.

Also for the record, I will mention *Space Jungle,* a relatively lightweight piece for which each man brought out the alternate instruments listed above, because Cherry's Indian flute gave a lovely sound.

Still, I did feel the program lacked variety. There was a sameness about several of the pieces, a sameness of approach perhaps, for concert listening. Maybe the evening should have been shorter by a piece or two.

As I sat in the hall thinking about all of the above, and wondering if there was any way I could sum up my varied and sometimes dissatisfied impressions of the evening, came the last piece, *Trouble in the East*. It was contrapuntally written and collectively improvised by all the horns, but it was like no other collective improvisation ever undertaken in this idiom, or any other. It felt spontaneously ordered in all its aspects, and had the timeless joy and melancholy of the blues running through it. It had its feet planted on the earth and it spoke of the gods. It was one of the most exciting, beautiful, and satisfying musical performances I have ever heard.

Yes, it got recorded. (1969)

≈

≈

≈

≈ # Spoofs in a Set of Two

In 1965, I contributed two columns of parodies to *Down Beat*. I think they're worth a second look these many years later, if only as period pieces.

I

The Beatles aren't likely to be reviewed in this magazine, and after contemplating what a distinct loss this will be to many readers, I have decided to offer impressions of how the next Beatles LP—whatever it contains and whenever it appears— *might* be received elsewhere by certain commentators:

GENE LEES (in *HiFi/Stereo Review*): I did not realize what a fine composer Paul McCartney was until I heard his pieces, *And He Loves Her, And She Loves Him,* and *Does She Love You?,* performed for me by a group consisting of Stan Getz, Bill Evans, Cal Tjader, and the Oscar Peterson Trio (Ray and Ed sat in with the other guys besides playing with Oscar as usual). Now I know that McCartney is the greatest writer of popular melodies since Gershwin, an honor I have previously bestowed on Henry Mancini and Antonio Carlos Jobim. What McCartney's tunes deserve is recordings by singers like Vic Damone and Chris Connor, whose work does not reflect the angry nihilism of so much of today's jazz, who do not receive the arid support of foundation grants and hence are not put out of touch with their audiences, and who are generally acknowledged by people in the business to be tireless perfectionists with matchless voices. This will come about unless the business boys of the record industry have all lost their minds, as I said they had last month. When I think about all this, it makes me want to punch them right in the ears.

NAT HENTOFF (in *The Reporter*): While admiring the penchant for meatily satiric rebelliousness encountered in these four young men from Liverpool, I increasingly deplore the fatuous, egregiously minimal American ability to accept this basically rhythm-and-blues music as seminally performed by such arcane, burning blues men as Howlin' Mudbelly and such bracingly acid younger bards as Bobby Dilly. The album cover is a tonsorial gas.

WHITNEY BALLIETT (in *The New Yorker*): The Beatles, a rumple-headed British rock-and-roll quartet whose members look as self-contained as four, neat bowls of sour cream in mid-February, clang, bang, blat, bleat, and bellow their way through a program of twelve mewling blues and ballads with a let's-put-on-some-agony air. The group's vocalist, a moon-faced, callow-voiced youth named Paul McCartney, sings as if he half expected a shrewish mother to scold him for paying too much attention to the girls; when the other three join him in chorus, he seems as relieved as a timid ball-carrier whose perilous, unpending broken-field run is suddenly abetted by a team of blocking backs. The Beatles' drummer, who desports the racy name of Ringo Starr, has all the verve of a rusty automaton, except for an exemplary split-second on *What If She Does Love You?* when one of his cymbal strokes shimmers with a sshhZZzz that faintly echoes the nonpareil style of Sidney Catlett.

JOHN S. WILSON (in the Sunday *New York Times*): The youthful, shaggy-top Beatles, strident progenitors of the so-called Mersey Sound and the ones who pungently started it all, are still the best of the English export rock and rollers. Perhaps that is because their roots lie among American blues men. Their early hit was Chuck Berry's winning, irreverent *Roll Over, Beethoven,* and they were once known as the British Everley Brothers. The group has a propulsively rocking beat, and lead man Paul McCartney sings with cleanly mellow melodiousness on *She Couldn't*

Love You Less. However, several long-winded numbers are extended to the point of tedium on this disc.

ERIC LARRABEE (in *Harper's*): Fortunately for future aesthetics, no one can be quite certain at the time what will turn out to have been consequential. To our young people, the Beatles quartet is important now, but to our jazz and popular-music critics they are not. Jazz has been remarkable from its beginnings for its variety if only because of the diversity of elements that contributed to it. There seems no reason to argue that the Beatles, although they are not jazzmen, are unworthy, for, labels aside, they are a part of what our music in the over-all subsumes. And that music is now international chiefly because so many people in other countries can perform it. The Beatles come from the Liverpool (England) docks, and their musical leader, Paul McCartney, professes to having been musically nourished on American stylists Bill Haley, Frankie Laine, and Elvis Presley. According to the liner notes half the numbers in their remarkably energetic new album are traditional blues, the other half being bluesy ballads. But it's a long way from the Mississippi Delta. (1965)

II

You may have noticed that, with the rising popularity of coffee-house "folk" singers, certain of the more prolific jazz journalists have turned their attention to the idiom. Whatever their comments may reveal about our folkniks, they seem to reveal, well, something or other about our jazz writers.

Here are several quite imaginary reviews of various Bob Dylan LPs of the last few years from publications that followers of this magazine might not otherwise see. Alert readers will notice that there are apparently two writers using very similar names.

RALPH J. GLEASON, *San Francisco Chronicle*, 1965: Recognition of the fact that Bob Dylan is the greatest spokesman for freedom since Thomas Paine and the most penetrating social commentator on American life since Lenny Bruce is essential to an understanding of the current mores of our young people.

Dylan's iconoclastic view of the American priorities can be heard on his new LP, called *Freedom Now for Murph the Surf*. And as expressed in his poignant *Shucks, They Persecute with Money, Ma,* they may turn out to give them a hit single. Call Dylan a passing fad and you're sadly wrong.

GEORGE FRAZIER in the Phoenix, Ariz., *Globe:* Who is this sloppy, snotnose upstart of a whinesinger, with his filthy jeans, his tangled doormat of hair, and his ugly ideas of what makes up a nice song? You don't, if you're a growing boy, speak to your elders this way—you really don't. Where was he when Lee Wiley and Mabel Mercer told the truth about it all and only Zolotow and Ferguson and I knew? Not yet in his cradle, I dare say. I tell you true, if Bix could come back, he'd show them.

LeRoi Jones in *Kulchur:* The kid's numbers seem to lie outside the Black Arts . . . which is that they have nothing whatever in common with the beautiful insane things of Saroah Thaunders or the outbursts of Aylbert Aller, which do so much to make our stopover in the U.S. bearable, or the new blues of Fisha Wawique . . . have you heard her *Lovers and Mothers?* It'll turn you over. . . . But listen to his *Mao's Got the Bomb, Mom!* . . . Where it *is!* Whether he knows it or not, he's on the good side. But don't expect a capricious jazz clubowner or decadent artifact white critic to know it, no matter what they *say!!*

TOM SCANLAN in *Army Times:* Now, believe it or not, the sharp operators along Tin Pan Alley have turned over the blues and the folk idiom to the children for even more nonmusical noisemaking. Unless they bring back the swing era, and quick, when musicians were really concerned with entertaining and communicating with their audiences, good music in this country is through.

RALPH GLEASON in *FM/Stereo Guide,* 1962: Bobby Dylan the highly touted, passing fad of a "folk" artist, has unruly hair, wears disheveled clothes, and looks like he could use a good meal. He sounds like a square fugitive from a 1947 rally for the Progressive Party, right down to his garn-teed hick accent. He's in favor of the Human Race and worried about the Bomb, and I sympathize, but what I want of songs is that they be beautiful, not mournful.

PETE WELDING in *Blues Unlimited Brochure #23¹/₂:* White and in his 20s, Minnesota's lanky Bob Dylan, a singer and self-accompanying guitarist and harmonica player, and a consistently favored recording artist, seems an unlikely blues bard. But he is currently universally recognized as one of the most earthy, intense, surging, memorable, impacted, restless, direct, forceful, powerful, furious, and viable of our young, deep-dish folk singers, and a perfect antidote to the sterile, banal, insipid, puerile, monotonous, grotesque, self-parodying performers that some of our formerly great urban rhythm-and-blues men have become. (1965)

≈

≈

≈

≈
Some Kind of
Advance Guard

The title *"Sun Ra and His Arkestra—Sun Song"* is perhaps a portentous, or at least curious, billing for a jazz LP, particularly when one is reminded that it was originally recorded (and obscurely released) over ten years ago. Titles of selections, such as *Call for All Demons, Transition, Future, New Horizons,* affirm the impression. But the style and content of the music are anything but advanced, even for ten years ago; they are indeed quite conservative and suggest that Sun Ra is somewhat miscast as a leader in the avant garde. For me, the music is not only conservative, it is professional—and, that being granted, frequently glib, not to say frequently shallow and rather dull.

Something of the same impression continues in the two volumes of *"The Heliocentric Worlds of Sun Ra,"* which offer somewhat more recent manifestations of the pianist-composer's work. Again, the titles refer vaguely to affairs of space and things cosmic (*Outer Nothingness, Other Worlds, Nebulae*), but this time a great deal of the music is self-consciously "weird," with lots of eerie tympani, echoing bells, and low-pitched sounds from bass clarinet and bass trombone.

On other numbers, such effects are larded around soloists who exhibit their fondness for some of the better-known players of the new jazz. The result is rather like encountering Ornette Cole-

294

man's cousin, wandering around in next week's reruns of the *Science Fiction Theater.*

Indeed, I suspect that if Sun Ra were to cool it on the cosmos and the fourth dimension, and to turn his hand to studio and sound-track work, his talent, his considerable skill, and his professionalism would flourish. (1968)

≈

≈

≈

≈
Recognition, Prestige, and Respect: They're Academic Questions

We have a favorite pastime in jazz—we musicians, reviewers, historians, journalists, fans. When we get together in almost any combination, the conversation will sooner or later turn to laments that jazz is not understood, does not have the respect, the prestige, the support that the music has rightfully earned and that our symphonies and our opera companies have. We have gone on to complain that established classical critics, most music educators, and others of influence not only don't know the music and don't listen to it, but are ignorant of its very nature and of the concerns and intentions of its musicians.

A great deal of what is said on such occasions may seem like self-indulgence if not downright self-pity. But that being acknowledged, it is true that jazz does lack prestige and the kind of support that goes with it, and that it could well use the kind of support that, let us say, Franz Schubert's music has in the United States.

However, let's look more closely at a typical example of such support. In Washington, we have an underwritten, partly tax-supported arts complex, the Kennedy Center. New York's Lincoln Center preceded it. And large arts centers now dot our major cities while smaller ones can be found in cities of populations of perhaps 300,000 citizens.

Musically speaking, why are these centers there? Are they all there, as one might assume, because Bach, Haydn, Verdi, and the rest were great composers? And because the musical culture and tradition they represent is one that America has legitimately adopted and sees as part of its own heritage? Such a conclusion seems sound enough, but perhaps it jumps a step. The Lincoln and Kennedy and Los Angeles Arts centers are not there because Handel, Brahms, and Puccini were great composers. They are there because everyone knows that they were great composers. Even citizens who will never be seen at our arts centers and will never buy a Beethoven recording know it. And they know it because the work on that musical tradition and its great composers has been done.

One can take Music Appreciation A-1 in any third-rate college, taught by the worst dolt on the music faculty, and learn something substantial about Bach, Mozart, and Chopin because the work of critical selection, musical analysis, biography, music history, and the availability of the scores of these composers have been done. And until we do that kind of work in jazz, until we do the selection, analysis, biography, and music history, we will not have the recognition, prestige, and support we claim to want and need. Ellington may very well be *the* major figure in twentieth-century American music, but unless Americans do the requisite scholarly work and critical work on him, he will surely be forgotten.

To repeat myself for a moment, the Kennedy Center is not there because Schumann wrote some excellent music, but because everyone knows Schumann wrote some excellent music. Remember, that for over a century Bach was not considered a great composer simply because no one had done the work on him: the work of biography, analysis, praise, and publication. When he became a great composer in everyone's thinking, his music did not change. It simply got played and heard and talked about.

One may contend of course that tastes change and that taste changed in Bach's favor. And of course changing taste is always a part of the risk in any received cultural activity. Bach may again fall out of favor to some extent. Tchaikovsky, for example, is nowadays falling back into favor among musical highbrows. However, with the work of criticism, publication, study, and performance of Bach's music going on since the late nineteenth century, we may be sure that Bach will never again be thought of as he once was: historically interesting for certain techniques which his music perfected but which were old-fashioned. Bach's fashion may falter; his real reputation will not.

Let me put all of this by analogy. Shakespeare is still a living dramatist in the English-speaking world, his works still affecting millions of people directly and indirectly, and the meaning of his plays still affecting the sensibilities of Western civilization—even for people who have never read him or seen him performed, and never will. But in order for that to be so, a lot of linguistic study and textual analysis; a lot of editing, and footnoting and publishing; a lot of biography, social and dramatic history, literary criticism; a lot of teaching at all levels have gone on and continue to go on. All that, as a source not only of the plays' survival in the classroom, but of their continuing public performance, recognition, and respect.

The story does not stop there. Almost any young dramatist who has anything valid to offer the theater automatically gains a certain prestige because of Shakespeare's high accomplishments. If he works in theater, if he works in the tradition that produced Shakespeare, he works in a respected tradition, even if he is the most rebellious *avant-garde* figure not writing in that tradition.

And to remove the analogy, any young jazz musician who has something to offer should gain public prestige simply by working in the tradition of Morton, Armstrong, Ellington, Parker, and Monk.

Jazz musicians, and most of their followers, are not used to thinking of their music in such terms—or at any rate, they are barely beginning to. And I am not suggesting we try to turn any musicians who are not so inclined into scholars or critics. But if we want the understanding and prestige and longevity we claim to want from the world at large, all of us ought to understand the function of such scholarly and educational activities, and encourage them. Futhermore, the musicians among us might want to remember that it was a major composer, Felix Mendelssohn, who probably had the most to do with Bach's belated acceptance into the pantheon of great European masters.

Jazz musicians have traditionally had to seek out their audiences for themselves in the popular arena. They do not, like Handel and Brahms, have a large portion of that audience awarded to them by an established and prestigious cultural continuity. A continuity that is maintained in large part by thousands of courses in music appreciation and the hundreds of courses on the symphony.

However, as I am implying, it is not only the audiences who will profit from a widespread knowledge of the music's history. There is a more personal stability and sense of purpose that such a knowledge awards the individual performers. A second viola player in a Midwest American symphony knows what musical values he represents and where he belongs in a long tradition of high accomplishment. Traditionally, most jazz musicians have not had that sense of themselves. We should be able to offer a tenor saxophonist, lucky enough to have a weekend gig, knowledge of his history and a sense of his mission, so that he may say to himself, perhaps faced with a noisy and inattentive audience, that, although he may not be Coleman Hawkins or Lester Young or Sonny Rollins, he does belong with them in a music which they helped to forge so adventurously. If we can do that, I think we will have served both him and the music well.

I think I know as well as anyone that one takes great risks in submitting any artistic pursuit to the demands of scholarship, and that there are hazards in taking any aesthetic activity into the classroom. Anyone who has had Shakespeare ruined by a teacher more concerned with the state of Shakespearian scholarship than with the human insight of the plays, anyone who has had Mozart's music trivialized by a mechanical or insensitive presentation, anyone who has witnessed the history of architecture reduced to an exercise in Marxian-Leninist social theory will know how terrible the risks can be. But they are risks that have to be taken.

From such a point of view, what does jazz need? The list is

enormous. Although there have been a few commendable biographies of jazz musicians, there have not been nearly enough. I will cite only Coleman Hawkins and Art Tatum as two major figures with no biographies to set the knowledgeable mind to work on a list of its own.

Scores? The works of Duke Ellington, whether they can be gleaned from surviving written materials or must be notated off recordings, should be published in complete authoritative editions. But Ellington's works would merely be a beginning. Every American music library should have its Don Redman and Fletcher Henderson collections; its Sy Oliver, Edgar Sampson, and Jimmy Mundy volumes; its Gil Evans—but the list (again) is a long one.

I need only mention, surely, that the critical history of the music undertaken by Gunther Schuller still stands virtually alone.

And what if we had a detailed study of Ellington's harmonic language, and of Billy Strayhorn's? At a practical level, we might save future American composers and orchestrators a decade of work out of their careers. At an artistic level, well, think of the possibilities.

Furthermore, we are still plagued with basic classroom texts on jazz history that are inadequate. One of them is by now fairly notorious for constant inaccuracies in its musical examples and analyses, and for its almost page-by-page mistakes of fact. Almost all of them give away the ages of their authors in that they clearly give greater emphasis and praise to the period of the writer's own adolescent awakenings to the music.

Walter Allen's monumental bio-discographies of King Oliver and Fletcher Henderson should not only be a source of pride for us all but should be the models for dozens of such studies, and I assume I do not need to name artists' names here to affirm the need. Meanwhile, all of us would do well to know about and welcome discographical work on Eric Dolphy; and we should know Lewis Porter's study of Lester Young, Thomas Owens' microfilmed but still unpublished study of Charlie Parker's style, Jerry Valburn's compilation of Ellington's non-studio recordings,

Arnold Laubich's Art Tatum discography. Even those of us who may never use or read such studies should know of such activities because their very existence benefits us all, musicians and audiences, as well as teachers, journalists, and historians. The seriousness of such work is a major source of the serious attention and prestige we need.

Actually, jazz musicians in their own ways have taken similar approaches to history and tradition. A prominent bass player, while recently expressing puzzlement and even condescension towards the scholarly writing and analysis that is now beginning in jazz, admitted in almost the same breath that he had learned his own craft by notating Jimmy Blanton's bass parts and learning them. And Ray Brown's. And by seeing how he could meet the great challenge of Mingus, by sheading with Charlie's records. He was even grateful, he added, to a record-collector friend who showed him how Walter Page's strong lead in the Basie rhythm section rewrote the history of the instrument ("wrong" notes or not), and how Johnny Lindsey's strong 1920s sound was not the simple bass "slapping" of the period.

I am not proposing (I trust) the sort of musicological research, music history, and biography, evaluation, and analysis that have as their real purpose only the production of still more musicology. I have in mind some very practical matters. For one, it is simply wrong—morally and artistically wrong, if you will—that concert after concert by our student jazz orchestras go by without a single jazz classic on the program. At best, we may get a *Moonlight Serenade* in a chorus-and-a-half for the old folks, or we get someone's arrangement of a familiar Ellington tune (re-orchestrating Ellington makes about as much sense as re-orchestrating Ravel or Stravinsky, and for the very same reason).

I think that any student trained in jazz performance should know what Ferd Morton, Don Redman, Fletcher Henderson, (above all) Duke Ellington, and Thelonious Monk, and the other major composer-orchestrators have contributed to the music. He should know intimately what Louis Armstrong, Lester Young, and Charlie Parker stood for as improvisers (i.e., as spontaneous linear composers), and he should know these things not only by hearing them on recordings but by performing them. And performing them, not only as an honorable musical past from which he can learn, but as a body of living musical art which is regularly brought before audiences. A music which has no past worthy of serious attention probably has little present, and may have no future at all. And the past should be the concern of all of us ultimately for the sake of the music's audiences, present and future.

We might even envision a time when a student clarinetist, graduating from a jazz performance program, will be required to improvise respectably well in the styles of Sidney Bechet, Jimmy Noone, Omer Simeon, Benny Goodman, and Barney Bigard. Or a tenor saxophonist give a chorus or two after Coleman Hawkins, Lester Young, Dexter Gordon, Sonny Rollins, John Coltrane, ending (surely) with choruses in an approach of his own.

In short, we all need to show that we are absolutely serious about this music as a contribution to world culture. And that means that we must treat it in the same way that man has always treated a past which he wants preserved and respected for the sake of the present and the future. (1990)

Index